BUSINESS AND LEGAL FORMS

FOR

INTERIOR DESIGNERS

BUSINESS AND LEGAL FORMS

FOR

INTERIOR DESIGNERS

TAD CRAWFORD
EVA DOMAN BRUCK

ALLWORTH PRESS, NEW YORK

11   10   09   08   07   8   7   6   5   4

Published by Allworth Press, an imprint of Allworth Communications, Inc.,
10 East 23rd Street, New York, NY 10010.

Cover design by Derek Bacchus
Book design/typography by SR Desktop Services, Ridge, NY

Library of Congress Catalog-in-Publication Data
Crawford, Tad, 1946—
    Business and legal forms for interior designers / Tad Crawford, Eva Doman Bruck.
    p.   cm.
    Includes bibliographical references and index.

    ISBN-10: 1-58115-097-0
    ISBN-13: 978-1-58115-097-1

    1. Interior decoration—Practice—United States—Management. 2. Business—Forms.
I. Bruck, Eva Doman. II. Title.
NK2116.C66   2001
729'.068—dc21   2001003495

This book is designed to provide accurate and authoritative information with respect to the subject matter covered. It is sold with the understanding that the publisher is not engaged in rendering legal, accounting, or other professional services. If legal advice or other expert assistance is required, the services of a competent attorney or professional person should be sought. While every attempt is made to provide accurate information, the author and publisher cannot be held accountable for any errors or omissions.

Contents

A System for Success

The knowledge and use of good business practices is an essential step toward success for any professional or company, including the interior designer and the design firm. The forms contained in this book deal with the most important business transactions that a designer or design firm is likely to undertake. At the back of the book is a CD-ROM that will allow the designer to customize and easily revise the forms. The fact that the forms are designed for use, and favor the designer if negotiations are necessary, give them a unique value.

Interior design projects differ with respect to the scope of work, level of complexity, and individual client's personal vision. As necessary as it is to be flexible and adapt to different conditions, it is as important to the interior designer to have standard ways of processing the work flow and an organized system for keeping track of project details. The purpose of *Business and Legal Forms for Interior Designers* is, in part, to provide information, systems, and forms that are useful to the organization and smooth functioning of the business side of the interior design studio. It is possible to adopt the entire system, or as is often recommended, to alter its parts to fit the particular needs of the individual firm. Each of these forms can be used alone or integrated in a comprehensive system of organization. The forms are designed to serve the purposes of the independent business owner or partner, an employee of an interior design firm, or an interior design department of either an architectural firm or an organization with an in-house property management division.

The Order of the Forms

The order of the forms is based upon the general chronology of events that occur in the course of doing business in the interior design profession (with forms for the more sophisticated contracts coming last). In some areas, however,

forms dealing with specific activities may be grouped together. To start, the jobs index is the point of origin because it provides each assignment with a job number. Following the opening of a job number, a job sheet is begun where all project details are captured, including ongoing time and costs.

As soon as the prospective client asks for an estimate or a bid, and invites the designer to attend meetings and visit the site, and/or submits accurate documents that reveal enough information about the proposed assignment, it is possible to formulate a project plan and budget. The difference between an estimate (an approximate calculation) and a bid (a specific proposal) is that the numbers in a bid are binding (as long as specifications and schedules are not changed by the client). In the estimating format, this particular form can be used as a worksheet to calculate estimated costs and time; in the summary format, it can also be submitted as part of the official estimate. With the addition of two columns, it can also serve as a status and variance report. With the budget and schedule in place, the interior designer is ready to write a comprehensive proposal with the proposal form, as well as a comprehensive production schedule. Time sheets are used to record staff time expended on both billable and nonbillable activities.

The creative log is the place to record all the materials gathered in the planning and research phase of the assignment. These can include client's swatches and magazine pictures, research documents, samples, photographs, and catalogues. For existing sites, the initial survey form is used to document the condition of the site, including measurements, photos, documents, and other material evidence of the site's physical state. In the case of new construction, the interior designer will need to have an accurate set of architectural and construction drawings, including plans, sections and elevations, ceiling plans, and other relevant documents. The project drawings log is the index for tracking all plans and other interior design drawings generated by the interior designer for each project. To keep track of specs, bids, and agreements with a variety of contractors, the contractor log form is a handy tool. Similarly, the purchase log is the one-stop record of specs, bids, and agreements, including samples, swatches, photos, and details drawings needed to keep a handle on all purchases. To simplify the process of soliciting vendors' bids and/or estimates, making sure to use the same specs with competing vendors, use the estimate request form. The estimate log can then be used to keep track of the competing estimates and/or bids coming from vendors. Once decisions are finalized as to which vendors to use, as well as what purchases to make, the purchase order is used, either by itself or with a formal contract, to place orders for the selected goods and services.

Any time it is necessary to send documents, samples, and any other goods, a transmittal form is used to identify the sender, the addressee, and the items being transported, whether by hand, mail, courier, or facsimile. To keep a handle on the various items in transit at any one time, especially when using more than one form of shipping, use the traffic log form. Very often, furniture, carpeting, drapery, appliances, and other hardware are available before the site is ready to accept them. The inventory log is the place to keep track of everything in storage.

A very useful form is the status report for the client. It is an easy way to communicate an assignment's progress in regular intervals, as well as to highlight issues that need to be addressed. An extremely important form is the work change order. Using it can mean the difference between losing money and making a profit on a project. It is the safeguard against capricious and indecisive clients. The billing index provides the interior design studio with invoice numbers as well as a handy guide for reviewing the status of payments due. A comprehensive billing form is included in this section, as well as a statement form and a collection letter. The receipts log is used to organize the myriad purchase receipts incurred by a project. The payables index provides a way of tracking all incoming bills as well as a system for having these bills reviewed and identified as billable or not. The credit reference form is used to ensure that an unknown client has a satisfactory history of bill payment. Even the most successful interior design firms continue to market themselves, no matter how busy they are with current work. The marketing checklist is used to track the ongoing effort of making sure that there is a constant flow of prospective new projects.

The forms then shift to focus more on the relationships of the firm with the world beyond the firm, especially contractual relationships. The complexities of the contract between the design firm and a client are considered with respect to both residential and commercial projects, and a contract summary form is included for use within the firm. The very important client approval form is given as an adjunct to the designer-client agreement. Contracts with fabricators, photographers, sales agents, lecture sponsors, and merchandising companies follow. A nondisclosure form for submitting ideas is included. There is a contract for use with an independent contractor, an employment application, an employment agreement, a restrictive covenant for employees, and a project employee agreement. The book concludes with a copyright application and a trademark application.

Handling Contracts

A contract is an agreement that creates legally enforceable obligations between two or more parties. In making a contract, each party gives something of value to the other party. This is called the exchange of consideration. Consideration can take many forms, including the giving of money, or a consultation, or the promise to consult, or pay for a consultation in the future. An in-depth study of contracts and interior design appears in the chapter titled, "Basic Contract Law for Interior Designers," by Laura Mankin.

All contracts, whether the designer's or someone else's, can be changed. Before using the contracts in this book, the designer should review them with his or her attorney. This gives the designer the opportunity to learn whether local or state laws may make it worthwhile to modify any of the provisions. For example, would it be wise to include a provision for arbitration of disputes or are the local courts speedy and inexpensive to use so no arbitration provision is necessary?

The contracts must be filled out, which means that the blanks must be completed. Beyond this, however, the designer can always delete or add provisions on any contract. Deletions or additions to a contract are usually initialed in the margin by both parties. It is also a good practice to have each party initial each page of the contract except the page on which the parties sign.

The designer must ascertain that the person signing the contract has authority to do so. If the designer is dealing with a company, the company's name should be included as well as the name of the individual authorized to sign the contract and the title of that individual (or, if it isn't clear who will sign or that person has no title, the words "Authorized Signatory" can be used instead of a title).

If the designer won't meet with the other party to sign the contract, it would be wise to have that party sign the forms first. After the designer gets back the two copies of the forms, they can be signed and one copy returned to the other party. As discussed in more detail under letter contracts, this has the advantage of not leaving it up to the other party to decide whether to sign and thus make a binding contract.

If additional provisions that won't fit on the contract forms should be added, simply include a provision stating, "This contract is subject to the provisions of the rider attached hereto and made a part hereof." The rider is simply another piece of paper which would be headed "Rider to the contract between _____ and _____ dated the ___ day of _____, 20___." The additional provisions are put on this sheet and both parties sign it.

Negotiation

Understanding the business concepts behind the forms is as important as using them. By knowing why a certain provision has been included and what it accomplishes, the designer is able to negotiate when faced with someone else's contract. The designer knows what is and is not desirable.

Contracts require negotiation. The forms in this book are favorable to the designer. When they are presented to a client, fabricator, or contractor, changes may very well be requested. The explanation in this book of how to use each form should help the designer evaluate changes that either party may want to make. The explanation should also help the designer understand what changes would be desirable in forms presented to the designer.

Keep in mind that negotiation need not be adversarial. Certainly, the designer and the other party may disagree on some points, but the basic transaction is something that both want. This larger framework of agreement must be kept in mind at all times when negotiating. Of course, the designer must also know which points are nonnegotiable and be prepared to walk away from a deal if satisfaction cannot be had on these points.

When both parties have something valuable to offer each other, it should be possible for each side to come away from the negotiation with a winning feeling. This win-win negotiation requires each side to make certain that the basic needs of both parties are met so that the result is fair. The designer can't negotiate for the other side, but a wise negotiation strategy must allow the other side to meet its vital needs within the larger context that also allows the designer to obtain what he or she must have.

It is a necessity to evaluate negotiating goals and strategies before conducting any negotiations. The designer should write down what he or she must have and what can be conceded or modified. The designer should try to imagine how the shape of the contract will affect the future business relationship with the other party. Will it probably lead to success for both sides and more business or will it fail to achieve what one side or the other desires?

When negotiating, the designer should keep written notes close at hand as to goals and strategies. Notes should be kept on the negotiations too, since many conversations may be necessary before final agreement is reached. At certain points the designer should compare where the negotiations have gone with the original goals. This will help the designer to evaluate whether he or she is conducting the negotiations according to plan.

Most negotiations are done over the telephone. This makes the telephone a tool to be used wisely in negotiations. The designer should decide when he or she wants to speak with the other party. Before calling, the designer should review the notes and be familiar with the points to be negotiated. If the designer wants the other party to call, the file should be kept close at hand so there is no question as to where the negotiations stand when the call comes. If the designer is unprepared to negotiate when the other side calls, the only wise course is to call back. Negotiation demands the fullest attention and complete readiness on the part of the designer.

Oral Contracts

Despite all the forms in this book being written, it is worth addressing the question of oral contracts. There are certain contracts which must be written, such as a contract for services which will take more than one year to perform or, in many cases, a contract for the sale of goods worth more than $500. So, without delving into the full complexity of this subject, certain contracts can be oral. If the designer is faced with a party who has breached an oral contract, an attorney should certainly be consulted for advice. The designer should not give up simply because the contract was oral.

However, while some oral contracts are valid, a written contract is always best. Even people with the most scrupulous intentions do not always remember exactly what was said or whether a particular point was covered. Disputes, and litigation, are far more likely when a contract is oral rather than written. That is another reason to make the use of written forms, like those in this book, an integral part of the business practices of any designer whose work may someday have value.

Letter Contracts

If the designer feels sending a well-drafted form will be daunting to the other party, it is always possible to adopt the more informal approach of a letter that is signed by both parties. In this case, the contracts in this book will serve as valuable checklists for the content and negotiation of the letter contract. The last paragraph of the letter would say, "If the foregoing meets with your approval, please sign both copies of this letter beneath the words AGREED TO to make this a binding contract between us." At the bottom of the letter would be the words AGREED TO with the name of the other party so he or she can sign. Again, if the other party is a company, the company name would be placed beneath the words AGREED TO as well as the name of the individual who will sign and that individual's title. This would appear as follows:

AGREED TO:
XYZ Corporation

By: _____
        Alice Hall, Vice President

Two copies of this letter are sent to the other party who is instructed to sign both copies and return one copy to the designer for his or her files. To be cautious, the designer can send the letters unsigned and ask the other party to sign and return both copies at which time the designer will sign and return one copy to the other party. This gives the other party an opportunity to review the final draft, but avoids a situation in which the other party might choose to delay signing and the designer would not be able to offer a similar contract to another party because the first contract might still be signed.

If the designer should ever sign a contract which the other party does not sign and return, it should be remembered that any offer to enter into a contract can always be revoked up until the time that the contract is actually entered into. The designer can protect his or her position by being the one who is last to sign, by insisting that both parties meet to sign, or by stating in the letter a deadline by which the other party must sign.

Standard Provisions

The contracts in this book contain a number of standard provisions, called "boilerplate" by lawyers. These provisions are important, although they will not seem as exciting as the provisions that relate more directly to the designer and the design process. Since these provisions can be used in almost every contract and appear in a number of the contracts in this book, an explanation of each of the provisions is given here.

Amendment. Any amendment of this Agreement must be in writing and signed by both parties.

This guarantees that any changes the parties want will be made in writing. It avoids the possibility of one party relying on oral changes to the agreement. Courts, by the way, will rarely change a written contract based on testimony that there was an oral amendment of the contract.

Arbitration. All disputes arising under this Agreement shall be submitted to binding arbitration before _____ in the following location _____ and shall be settled in accordance with the rules of the American Arbitration Association. Judgment upon the arbitration award may be entered in any court having jurisdiction thereof. Notwithstanding the foregoing, either party may refuse to arbitrate when the dispute is for a sum of less than $_____.

Arbitration can offer a quicker and less expensive way to settle disputes than litigation. However, the designer would be wise to consult a local attorney and make sure this is prudent in the jurisdiction where the lawsuit would likely take place. The arbitrator could be the American Arbitration Association or some other person or group that both parties trust. The designer would also want the arbitration to take place where he or she is located. If small claims court is easy to use in the jurisdiction where the designer would have to sue, it might be best to have the right not to arbitrate if the disputed amount is small enough to be brought into the small claims court. In this case, the designer would put the maximum amount that can be sued for in small claims court in the space at the end of the paragraph.

Assignment. This Agreement shall not be assigned by either party hereto, provided that the Designer shall have the right to assign monies due to the Designer hereunder.

By not allowing the assignment of a contract, both parties remain more certain with whom they are dealing. Of course, a company may be purchased by new owners. If the designer only wanted to do business with the people who owned the company when the contract was entered into, change of ownership might be stated as a ground for termination in the contract. On the other hand, money is impersonal and there is no reason why the designer should not be able to assign the right to receive money.

Bankruptcy or Insolvency. If the Client shall become insolvent or if a petition in bankruptcy is filed against the Client or a Receiver or Trustee is appointed for any of the Client's assets or property, or if a lien or attachment is obtained against any of the Client's assets, this Agreement shall immediately terminate and the Client shall return to the Designer all of the Designer's work which is in the Client's possession and grant, convey, and transfer all rights in the work back to the Designer.

This provision seeks to lessen the impact on the designer of a client's bankruptcy. Such a provision could appear in a contract with corporate clients, merchandisers of products licensed by the designer, fabricators, or other suppliers. However, the bankruptcy law may impede the provision's effectiveness.

Complete Understanding. This Agreement constitutes the entire and complete understanding between the parties hereto, and no obligation, undertaking, warranty, representation, or covenant of any kind or nature has been made by either party to the other to induce the making of this Agreement, except as is expressly set forth herein.

This provision is intended to prevent either party from later claiming that any promises or obligations exist except those shown in the written contract. A shorter way to say this is, "This Agreement constitutes the entire understanding between the parties hereto."

Cumulative Rights. All rights, remedies, obligations, undertakings, warranties, representations, and covenants contained herein shall be cumulative and none of them shall be in limitation of any other right, remedy, obligation, undertaking, warranty, representation, or covenant of either party.

This means that a benefit or obligation under one provision will not be made less because of a different benefit or obligation under another provision of the contract.

Death or Disability. In the event of the Designer's death or an incapacity of the Designer making completion of the work impossible, this Agreement shall terminate.

A provision of this kind leaves a great deal to be determined. Will payments already made be kept by the designer or the designer's estate? And who will own the plans in whatever stage of completion has been reached? These issues are best resolved when the contract is negotiated.

Force Majeure. If either party hereto is unable to perform any of its obligations hereunder by reason of fire or other casualty, strike, act or order of a public authority, act of God, or other cause beyond the control of such party, then such party shall be excused from such performance during the pendency of such cause. In the event such inability to perform shall continue longer than ____ days, either party may terminate this Agreement by giving written notice to the other party.

This provision covers events beyond the control of the parties, such as a tidal wave or a war. Certainly the time to perform the contract should be extended in such an event. There may be an issue as to how long an extension will be allowed. Also, if work has commenced and some payments have been made, the contract should cover what happens in the event of termination. For example, must payments be returned?

Governing Law. This Agreement shall be governed by the laws of the State of _____.

Usually the designer would want the laws of his or her own state to govern the agreement.

Liquidated Damages. In the event of the failure of XYZ Corporation to deliver by the due date, the agreed upon damages shall be $____ for each day after the due date until delivery takes place, provided the amount of damages shall not exceed $____.

Liquidated damages are an attempt to anticipate in the contract what damages will be caused by a breach of the contract. Such liquidated damages must be reasonable. If they are not, they will be considered a penalty and unenforceable.

Modification. This Agreement cannot be changed, modified, or discharged, in whole or in part, except by an instrument in writing, signed by the party against whom enforcment of any change, modification, or discharge is sought.

This requires that a change in the contract must at least be written and signed by the party against whom the change will be enforced. This provision should be compared to that for amendments which requires any modification to be in writing and signed by both parties. At the least, however, this provision explicitly avoids a claim that an oral modification has been made of a written contract. Courts will almost invariably give greater weight to a written document than to testimony about oral agreements.

Notices and Changes of Address. All notices shall be sent to the Designer at the following address: _____ and to the Purchaser at the following address: _____. Each party shall be given written notification of any change of address prior to the date of said change.

Contracts often require the giving of notice. This provision facilitates giving notice by providing correct addresses and requiring notification of any change of address.

Successors and Assigns. This Agreement shall be binding upon and inure to the benefit of the parties hereto and their respective heirs, executors, administrators, successors, and assigns.

This makes the contract binding on anyone who takes the place of one of the parties, whether due to death or simply an assignment of the contract. With commissioned works, death or disability of the designer can raise complex questions about completion and ownership of the art. The issues must be resolved in the contract. Note the standard provision on assignment in fact does not allow assignment, but that provision could always be modified in the original contract or by a later written, signed amendment to the contract.

Time. Time is of the essence.

This requires each party to perform exactly to whatever time commitments they have made or be in breach of the contract. It is not a wise provision for the designer to agree to, since being a few days late in performance could cause the loss of all benefits under the contract.

Waivers. No waiver by either party of any of the terms or conditions of this Agreement shall be deemed or construed to be a waiver of such term or condition for the future, or of any subsequent breach thereof.

This means that if one party waives a right under the contract, that party has not waived the right forever and can demand that the other party perform at the next opportunity. So the designer who allowed a client not to pay on time would still have the right to demand payment. And if the client breached the contract in some other way, such as not returning original art, the fact the designer allowed this once would not prevent the designer from suing for such a breach in the future.

Warranty and Indemnity. The Designer hereby warrants that he or she is the sole creator of the Work and owns all rights granted under this Agreement. The Designer agrees to indemnify and hold harmless the Client from any and all claims, demands, payments, expenses, legal fees, or other costs based on an actual breach of the foregoing warranties.

This provision protects one party against damaging actions that may have been taken by the other party. Often, one party will warrant that something is true and then indemnify and hold the other party harmless in the event that it is not true. For example, a designer selling a design may be asked to warrant that the design is not plagiarized. Or the designer may ask a subcontractor to warrant this to the designer. If in fact, the design has been plagiarized, this would breach the warranty. The party breaching the warranty would be obligated to protect the other party who has been injured by the warranty not being true.

Using the Checklists

Having reviewed the basics of dealing with the business and legal forms, it is time to move on to the forms themselves and the checklists that will make the forms most useful.

These checklists focus on the key points to be observed when using the forms. On the organizational forms, the boxes can be checked when the different aspects of the use of the form have been considered. For the contracts, the checklists cover all the points that may be negotiated, whether or not they are in the contract. When, in fact, a point is covered in the contract already, the appropriate paragraph is indicated in the checklist. These checklists are especially valuable to use when reviewing a contract offered to the designer by someone else.

For the contracts, if the designer is providing the form, the boxes can be checked to be certain all the important points are covered. If the designer is reviewing someone else's form, checking the boxes will show which points they have covered and which points may have to be altered or added. By using the paragraph numbers in the checklist, the other party's provision can be quickly compared with a provision that would favor the designer. Each checklist for a contract concludes with the suggestion that the standard provisions be reviewed to see if any should be added to what the form provides. Of course, the designer does not have to include every point on the checklist in a contract, but being aware of these points will be helpful.

Basic Contract Law for Interior Designers

by Laura Mankin

It is important for an interior designer to be familiar with the concepts of contract law that govern the designer's transactions during the ordinary course of business. A contract is a legally enforceable promise, or a set of promises, made by parties to a specific agreement. "Legally enforceable" means that a party seeking the enforcement of a promise may do so in a court of law. The court will recognize the duties owed by each party and grant remedies in the event that one of the parties fails to perform a specified contractual obligation.

When entering into what one hopes will be an amicable working relationship, it is difficult to look into the future and anticipate a dispute. However, as this chapter will illustrate, in order to be protected in a commercial transaction, it is in the designer's best interest to finalize the agreement in a written contract before proceeding. The purpose of reducing an oral agreement to writing is to help clarify the contracting parties' expectations and intentions, and to serve as a vehicle for enforcement of certain promises should a dispute arise between the parties. With careful planning and proper preparation, many of the potential pitfalls of contracting can be avoided by following the recommendations laid out in this chapter.

Creating a Valid Contract

In order to be considered legally enforceable, a contract must comply with four basic requirements: (1) the parties must have the legal capacity to contract, (2) there must be a mutual assent to the agreement, (3) there must be consideration, and (4) the execution of the contract must

Laura Mankin is an attorney specializing in intellectual property and entertainment law. She is a graduate of Columbia Law School.

not further an illegal purpose or contravene public policy by including harshly unfair clauses disadvantaging the weaker party. These requirements merit closer examination, as a court will generally not enforce an agreement that lacks any one of these elements.

CAPACITY

In order to have the requisite "capacity" to enter into an agreement, an individual must be over the age of eighteen (twenty-one in some jurisdictions). A minor who enters into an agreement and then changes his mind may not be forced to comply with the terms of the contract. With the exception of certain contracts (usually those contracts that deal with necessities such as food and clothing) individuals under the age of eighteen are able to void any agreement they enter into, leaving the other party without legal recourse. Agreements entered into by minors are not necessarily void, but rather voidable at the discretion of the underage party. Although dealing, and therefore contracting, with individuals under the age of eighteen is not common for a designer, it is an important bit of contract law to keep in mind.

The contracting parties must also have the mental capacity to enter into an agreement. Individuals who have been declared incompetent by judicial proceeding do not possess the requisite capacity to enter into binding agreements. Under specified circumstances, intoxicated persons are considered legally incompetent, as they are unable to understand the nature of the agreement they have entered. Generally, agreements *involving mentally infirmity* are void, meaning neither party may seek enforcement. If a party to the contract fails to meet any one of the capacity requirements, it may serve as a defense for the nonperforming party in a breach of contract suit.

When contracting with a corporation, it is important to keep in mind that the agents representing the corporation only have contracting capacity to the extent that it is legally conferred by the corporation's board of directors. Only those agents (including employees) vested with the explicit power to enter into contracts on behalf of the corporation have the ability to bind the corporation to an agreement. Make sure that the signatory to the interior design contract has the authority to commit the corporation into such an agreement, as a contract entered into by an individual who has exceeded the powers conferred by the corporation may be held to have no legal effect.

Some states require an interior designer to be licensed. In such states, contracts entered into by unlicensed designers can be considered void. Make sure that any designer with whom you will be dealing is properly licensed in order to avoid any unnecessary problems.

MUTUAL ASSENT

"Mutual assent" is often said to be a "meeting of the minds" over the significant terms of an agreement, and can be generally understood to mean valid *offer and acceptance*. When two parties wish to enter into an agreement with each other, no matter how small the obligation to be taken on, a negotiation of terms between the parties generally proceeds any finalization of the agreement. A contract results when one of the parties to the negotiation makes a sufficiently definite promise to do, or to refrain from doing, something (offer) and the other party accepts this offer (acceptance).

The Offer

In making an offer which is capable of being validly accepted by the other party, the offer must: (1) indicate a clear intent to make a contract, (2) be sufficiently definite so that a court can determine the actual intent of the parties, and (3) be communicated to the other party.

In order to be considered an offer, the statement must, on its face, express a concrete undertaking or a promise to the other party. This promise, in its definiteness, must be distinguishable from mere negotiations. Therefore, an advertisement, general price quotations, or statements of general intent are not considered offers, but rather invitations to make offers.

A designer may offer a particular prospective client some specific service at a specified or estimated price, and if the other three necessary contractual elements are met (capacity, legality, and consideration), the offer would be ripe for acceptance. In this case, the client's acceptance of such an offer would bind the designer to its terms.

In considering whether or not an offer is in fact valid, and therefore creates the opportunity for a valid acceptance, several "essential" elements are necessary. The subject matter of the contract and the intended offeree must be made clear, the price or estimated price must be included, the nature of the work to be performed must be described in sufficient detail, and the payment arrangement and performance schedule must be set. The presence or absence of any one of these elements will be critical in a court's determination as to the validity of an offer.

A definitive undertaking, promise, or commitment to the offeree will usually indicate that a valid offer has been made. A designer's estimate, or language such as, "I quote" or "I estimate that the project would cost" are not likely to be considered valid offers. More definitive language is generally necessary, such as "I quote . . . for your immediate acceptance." Advertisements are sometimes a source of confusion.

Although advertisements may appear to be offers to the general public, they are merely invitations for offers. Because they are generally not directed toward a particular individual, advertisements, catalogs, circular letters, and the like containing price quotations are usually insufficiently definite to be considered valid offers capable of being accepted.

The offer must state the essential terms of the proposed contract in order to be considered a legally enforceable contract, but it is also in the best interest of the designer to be as specific as possible when putting the offer and the contract in writing. A particular case, *Gold* v. *Charlotte Finn, Inc., et al.*, (644 N.Y.S. 2d 771), illustrates this point. As a result of the specificity of terms in the written agreement between the parties in this case, the court allowed the designer to retain a "nonrefundable" $5,000 design fee for plans that were submitted to the client but never executed. The court held that the designer was entitled to retain the fee because the written agreement clearly stated that the fee was to be triggered upon the submission of design scheme plans, regardless of whether or not they were ever used. This case is discussed in greater detail later on in the chapter. The more specific and definite the contract terms are, the less likely surprises are to arise during the contractual relationship and the more likely the terms will be enforced by a court.

Duration of the Offer

The power to accept a valid offer ends when the offer is terminated (by expiration, revocation, or rejection). Direct communication with the other contracting party is generally the most common way in which an offer is terminated. For example, a designer offers to redesign an owner's living room for $5,000, and the owner says that he would like to consider the offer. The designer, prior to any further communication, informs the owner that the designer will not do the job for any less than $6,000, and the prior $5,000 offer has thereby been revoked. Unless the designer has specified the time period for which the offer will be "open" or "on the table" or some consideration has been given by the other party in return for the offer, the offer will be considered open for a "reasonable amount of time," and if no such time period is specified, the designer can revoke his or her offer at any time prior to acceptance. There are specific situations in which an offeror may intentionally limit the right to revoke the offer. For example, suppose a designer offers a special rate to a prospective client, and says that this rate will be available for the next thirty days. The offer will be open for acceptance by the client for the specified thirty days. If the client fails to accept within the stated time period, a contract has not been formed.

There are two instances in which a contract may be considered "irrevocable" for a period of time. In an option contract, when the offeror has received some consideration from the offeree in return for a promise not to revoke the offer, the offer may not be revoked during the agreed-upon time period. Secondly, when a merchant makes a written, signed offer, which promises to keep the offer open for a specified length of time, the offer is "firm" during that period.

The Acceptance

An acceptance is an unequivocal and absolute acceptance of each term of the offer. The accepting party may signify acceptance by agreeing to such terms verbally, in writing, or by beginning performance. For example, a designer, after looking at a client's bedroom, makes an offer to create new design plans for $2,000. The client may accept such an offer by sending a check, which is then received and subsequently cashed by the designer. Obviously, some gray area exists, and many times a particular situation is open to interpretation as to whether or not there was an actual offer or acceptance, which is why reducing such an agreement to writing is beneficial for both parties.

As with the offer, the acceptance must also meet certain standards. The acceptance must be clear, unqualified, and in the manner required by the offer. If a client sends a designer an offer to pay $100,000 for the redesign and refurnishing of three rooms in the house, and the designer refuses to do the work for less than $125,000, this is a *counteroffer*. A counteroffer serves as a constructive rejection of the original offer, and, after it is made, the offeree (who made the counteroffer) may not revive the original offer. If, however, the designer wishes to preserve the original offer while at the same time exploring the possibility of a larger fee, it is possible to communicate that the offer is not expressly rejected, but the designer would like to discuss the possibility of modifying the terms. If the request is consistent with the idea that the designer is still keeping the original proposal under consideration, such an attempt to negotiate will generally not be construed as a termination.

An agreement may later be proven to lack mutual assent. Circumstances, such as mistake, duress, misrepresentation, and undue influence, which would negate mutual assent and render the contract invalid, will be examined in greater detail later in this chapter.

CONSIDERATION

A promise must not be one-sided—each side must be prepared to give something of legal value to the other, and there must be a bargained-for exchange. For example, a designer and a homeowner enter into an agreement in which the designer will prepare designs for and execute the redecoration of a living room in return for a specified amount to be paid by the client. Each side has given legal consideration—

the designer will render services to the client, and the client in exchange will pay the designer. Consideration need not be exchanged at the same moment; a mere promise to pay or to render services is sufficient to constitute consideration.

In general, business contracts in a commercial setting are assumed to be a bargained-for exchange as a result of the commercial nature of the agreement. The commercial value of the consideration being exchanged will generally not be questioned by the court. If a designer offers services for an extremely reduced rate, the money provided by the client would still constitute consideration and satisfy this contractual requirement to create a legally binding agreement.

Sometimes a contract may appear to be supported by consideration, but is actually lacking the legal requirement to create a binding agreement. These contracts, although not very common in the area of interior design, do merit a brief discussion. In general, these types of agreements can be grouped into five categories: illusory promises, moral obligations, past consideration, preexisting duty, and illegal consideration. An *illusory promise* exists if either of the parties entering into the contract can choose not to perform their contractual obligations. For example, a client promises to pay a designer $5,000 for design plans for a remodeled living room and the designer promises to deliver the plans unless the designer decides to go on vacation instead. In this example, the designer has the option not to perform the duties and, therefore, the contract is voidable. Contracts based on promises that are made out of a *moral obligation* are not considered to be supported by legal consideration, and they are therefore unenforceable. Contracts that are based on *past consideration* lack sufficient legal consideration to be enforceable. For example, a designer helps a client, who is also a friend, choose furniture for a new living room. If, after the completion of the project, the client/friend promises to pay the designer for this help, the promise is not enforceable, as the work was done without the expectation of compensation. If a party is already under a *preexisting duty* to do something, re-promising to perform an action or do something he or she is already under an obligation to do is not legally sufficient consideration, and the contract is unenforceable. The issue of preexisting duty most commonly arises when one of the parties seeks to change the terms of the contract after there has already been an offer and an acceptance of the contract terms. Changes made to a contract after performance has already commenced are unenforceable (unless they are supported by additional consideration), because the parties have a preexisting duty to perform their contractual obligations according to the original terms of the agreement.

LEGALITY

A court will refuse to enforce a contract that seeks to further an *illegal purpose* or one that contravenes public policy by including harshly unfair clauses to the disadvantage of the weaker party. Any contract which requires a designer to provide plans or execute arrangements that do not conform to building or public safety requirements will not be enforced.

In order to insure that all agreements that are entered into will be considered enforceable in the event of a dispute between the parties, the designer should review the agreement with the four elements in mind: Capacity, Mutual Assent, Consideration, and Legality.

Contracts and Quasi Contracts

A contract may be a straightforward *express* agreement in which all promises are communicated through language, either oral or written. For example, a designer promises to remodel a client's kitchen; in exchange, the client promises to pay the designer $5,000. In the absence of such express language, a contract may be *implied* by the parties' conduct which indicates they assented to be bound, e.g., a client watches a designer remodel the client's kitchen, knowing that the designer mistakenly thinks that they have agreed that the designer will be paid for this work. The client will be obligated to pay the designer based on the implied contract between them.

Lastly, the court recognizes a group of agreements called *quasi contracts,* which are not actually contracts at all. A quasi contract is a legal obligation created by the court in order to prevent one party from unjustly benefiting at the expense of another. The court will order the enriched party to pay the other party the value of the service received. In Tennessee, a contractor brought an action against homeowners for materials and labor furnished in construction of a bathroom that was added onto a house. In this case, the contractor, Paschall's, Inc., did not contract with the homeowners, Mr. and Mrs. Dozier, but with their daughter, Mrs. Mary Best, and grandson, Mr. Ronald Cheney. Materials and labor for the completion of the project were furnished by Paschall's at the request of Mrs. Best and Mr. Cheney, who resided within the house in dispute. The contracting parties, Best and Cheney, subsequently became insolvent, and the contractor sought to recover a personal judgment against the homeowner, as the bathroom addition added value to the home. Since there was no intention on the part of the homeowners to enter into the contract, the contractor looked to quasi contract as an avenue for relief. The court held that "Quasi contracts are not based upon intention of parties but are obligations created by law," and "where a materialman or subcontractor furnishes labor or materials which benefit the property of a person with whom there is no privity of contract, an action on quantum meruit (or quasi contract) may lie against the landowner to recover the reasonable value of said labor and materials so furnished." (*Paschall's Inc.* v. *J.P. Dozier*, 407 S.W.2d 150)

This form of remedy may also apply to an interior designer in the following situation: A designer contracts with a client to remodel the client's kitchen. The designer becomes ill and is unable to continue after completing half of the job. The designer cannot sue on the contract, but may recover the benefit conferred on the client under a theory of quasi contract. As such, it is important for a designer to be aware of this avenue for enforcement and fee collection.

Why Should the Contract Be in Writing?

Although the law requires only certain contracts to be in writing, some agreements, by law, *must* be evidenced by a writing signed by the party against whom enforcement is sought. In any case, it is certainly in the best interest of the designer to reduce *all* agreements to a written instrument. The Statute of Frauds, which is rooted in seventeenth-century English law but remains a living part of modern American law via individually adopted state statutes, spells out the circumstances under which a contract, in order to be enforceable, must be in writing.

There are essentially five situations in which the Statute of Frauds may affect a designer entering into a contract. A contract must be in writing if: (1) an executor or administrator promises personally to pay estate debts, (2) the contractual obligations of the parties contain promises that by their terms cannot be performed within one year, (3) one person promises to pay the debt of another, (4) the contract involves an interest in land, and (5) the contract covers the sale of goods priced at $500 or more.

Promises made by an executor or administrator to become personally responsible for the debts of the estate must be in writing to be legal-

ly enforceable. Suppose a client, for whom the designer has completed work, dies and leaves behind an insolvent estate. If the executor or administrator makes a personal promise to pay the designer's fees for the project, the designer may then proceed against the executor or administrator as he or she would have been able to proceed in collection against the client—but only if this assumption of payment by the executor or administrator is evidenced in writing.

It is important to note that any contract that by its terms cannot be performed within one year must be evidenced in writing. This means that the contract cannot be completed within one year of the date of the agreement, not the date on which performance is begun. Contracts that fall into this category generally have restrictive time lines that run over one year. For example, a designer contracts with a client to aid in the decoration of a newly built home. The agreement is dated August 1, 2002. The construction schedule for the home does not schedule the completion of the home until December 1, 2003. The designer cannot even begin performance until the home is fully constructed, and certainly cannot complete performance of the contract within a year of the date of the agreement.

Promises to pay the debt of another must be in writing in order to be enforceable. If a client of the designer should become insolvent and a third party undertakes the payment responsibilities of the client, this undertaking must be evidenced in a writing in order for the designer to collect from the third party.

A promise creating an interest in real property must be in writing. Of course, such interest includes contracts for the sale of real property, but also includes leases for more than one year, easements of more than one year, mortgages, and most other security liens. During the ordinary course of business, the designer will generally not be involved in such a contract, but it is an important rule of law to be aware of: Any transaction involving such an interest in real property must be in writing to be enforceable.

Probably the most significant application of the Statute of Frauds for the designer to keep in mind is the requirement that a promise for the sale of goods of $500 or more is not enforceable unless evidenced by a signed writing. This is particularly important when a designer is responsible for purchasing materials, furniture, fixtures, and other design elements and then reselling them to the client at a marked-up price. It is important for there to be written agreements at either end of this transaction (both with the merchant and the client) to make these undertakings (both the sale to the designer and the purchase from the designer) enforceable by the designer.

There is an important exception to this requirement: specially manufactured goods. If a manufacturer creates goods whose value is in excess of $500, are specially manufactured at the request of the designer, and are unsuitable for sale to other buyers in the manufacturer's business, the designer may be required to purchase the ordered goods, even in the absence of a written agreement.

It is essential that an interior designer keep in mind these situations that require written instruments when making agreements with both clients and merchants. Although only these specific situations require writings by law, it is in the designer's best interest to reduce all agreements to a written form to avoid any possible confusion or dispute.

ORAL CONTRACTS

An agreement made orally may be valid, but reliance on such agreements is not advisable. Evidence of mutual assent is necessary for any contract to be valid, including oral contracts. The burden of proving the existence of mutual assent falls on the party seeking enforcement of the contract. Additionally, it must be demon-strated that the terms of the contract are sufficiently definite to be enforceable. The burden may prove problematic for a designer who has entered into an oral agreement with a client to render services, and is therefore unable to rely on a written instrument to substantiate the designer's claims.

This problem is illustrated by a dispute that arose between an interior designer (Mr. Castelli) and two homeowners (Lynn and George Lien) for whom he had rendered services. (*Castelli Designs* v. *Lynn Lien and George Lien*, 910 S.W.2d 420). The designer helped the client make the decision to purchase the home and provided a renovation budget. The parties, however, did not "sign a written contract for his services." The couple knew that they were over budget, Lynn had even commented to one of her acquaintances at a party during the renovation that her "wallpaper cost more than some people make in one year" and that her husband "was going to kill her because she was over budget." As the costs of the materials continued to mount, Mr. Castelli reminded her that she was selecting very expensive materials to which she replied that she did not want her husband's "neurosurgeon friends from Nashville [to] come and see us live in a shack."

The fees for the project were enormously larger than the Liens claimed to have agreed to. After refusing to pay amounts due on statements presented to them by Mr. Castelli, the homeowners dismissed him as the designer. The designer then filed suit against the Liens for the outstanding portion of the interior design fee. The parties differed significantly on several of the material terms of the contract. The court found that the parties' differing versions of the contract indicated that the parties lacked the requisite mutual assent necessary to all contracts in that, "they did not have a meeting of the minds concerning the essential terms of their agreement." In finding this, the court was unable to hold that a valid contract existed, rather, "the evidence does not establish a contract whose terms are sufficiently definite to be enforced. We are unable to discern any clearly defined, mutually agreed upon terms relating to the scope of the work, the cost, and the time for performance. All that remains without these terms is an agreement to pay whatever the designer charged and that sort of agreement is simply too general to be enforced." Castelli's failure to reduce the terms of the agreement to writing with sufficiently definite terms barred contract theory as an avenue for recovery against the Liens. The court, with the help of expert opinion testimony by other interior designers, was left to make an independent determination of the value of Castelli's interior design services, costing him a considerable amount of money.

As it is commonly designers who end up suing clients for payment for services rendered, it is extremely important for a designer to use a written contract with clients. This will minimize the potential for uncertainty and confusion between the parties and for any court settling a dispute between them.

Some contracts may be enforceable simply because they meet the formation requirements discussed above. Others, however, as discussed above in the context of the Statute of Frauds, must be memorialized in writing in order to be recognized by the court.

WRITTEN CONTRACTS

As the discussion of oral contracts indicates, it is in the best interest of the designer working with clients and other contractors to spell out the specific terms of their relationship and expectations in a written instrument. Terms such as project scope, project description, time frame for completion, and fee rate and formula should be as specific as possible.

Specificity of Terms

The requirement for certainty in contracts serves several needs: to determine whether parties intended to contract at all, to determine when a breach has occurred, and to formulate an appropriate remedy. (*Aviation Contractor Employees, Inc., v. U.S.*, 945 F.2d 1568.) The more specific a contract is in outlining the terms of the agreement, the more likely a court will be able to enforce these terms in full. The benefit of such an agreement is illustrated in a New York case, *Gold v. Charlotte Finn, Inc., et al.* This case demonstrates the importance of contract specificity of terms. In this case, an interior designer was engaged by the client to produce a plan for the redecoration of the client's master bedroom and bath. The parties executed a written agreement which called for a non-refundable "design retainer fee" of $5,000 plus a $25,000 deposit for material to be ordered by the designer. It was specified that the $5,000 fee was triggered when the firm prepared a design scheme and submitted it to the client for approval. After the design scheme was submitted by the designer to the client, but before any of the work was actually commenced, a dispute arose between the parties. The client then sought the refund of $30,000.

The court held that since the "parties' written agreement made clear that the $5,000 forwarded by the client to the designer was to be a non-refundable minimum fee upon the submission of the design scheme, the designer was entitled to retain the $5,000, whether or not the client eventually decided to proceed." (*Gold v. Charlotte Finn Inc., et al.*, 644 N.Y.S.2d 771.) As this case illustrates, it is in the designer's best interest to have all portions of the agreement reflected by specific terms.

Design Fee Formula

One of the most important terms to include in the contract is the method of calculation used in determining the designer's fee. A contract that adequately spells out the terms for such payment will likely be enforced by a court as it is written. A dispute arose between a client (Mr. and Mrs. Kahle) and a builder (John McDonough) who had entered into a contract to build a house on a lot purchased by the client. John McDonough was asked by Mr. and Mrs. Kahle to prepare a construction budget and McDonough agreed to "figure up a rough estimate." McDonough figured out an estimate, and upon presenting it to the Kahles, emphasized that it was inexact because many of the project's specifications had not yet been finalized. McDonough explained the type of contract he used for his clients and said that he could not use a fixed price contract, which would require him to build the house for a set amount, unless the plans were further along than the preliminary drawings provided by the Kahles. The alternative was a cost-plus-fixed-fee contract, which gave the client the opportunity to make changes and be closely involved in the construction process. After considerable negotiation, the parties entered into a cost-plus-fixed-fee agreement. McDonough met with and discussed every stage of the project with the Kahles. When a dispute arose between McDonough and the Kahles, the court held that, "McDonough adequately met his obligation to keep them informed of the costs. The appellants chose the cost-plus-fixed-fee contract for its inherent flexibility. It is designed for clients who plan to make numerous changes, and be involved on a daily basis throughout construction with input, comments, and changes." As a result of the builder's care in informing his clients and reducing the terms of the agreement to writing, the builder was awarded all costs and fees due from the client. (*H. Scott Kahle* v. *John McDonough Builders, Inc.*, 85 Md.App. 14)

This case underscores the importance of a written agreement spelling out the terms of the

design fee. Such a situation can easily be applied to an interior designer's work. Fees for interior design projects are generally computed in two different ways. First, the designer may charge his clients the retail price of the items used in the project plus a design fee, (since the designer purchases the items at much less than retail, this markup is substantial), or the designer may use a smaller markup on the items used in the project and then charge a larger design fee. It is important to state which of these formulas is to be used and clearly define the computational method.

If a client would like to be involved in the everyday selection of fabrics, colors, furniture pieces, and decorative objects, he may be a suitable candidate for the first fee formula, in which there is a larger cost placed on each individual item but a smaller fee charged for the designer's services. A client who wishes to be less involved in the interior design process, and therefore places a greater premium on the designer's services, may wish to pay a larger design fee and smaller markup on each item. Whichever method the client and designer agree upon, it is necessary to reflect this understanding in the contract and for the designer to keep the client informed of costs and progression of the project.

Contract Interpretation

One of the principal goals of contract law is to protect the reasonable expectations of contracting parties and to provide parties with a clear idea of how the agreement they have entered into will be interpreted in the event of a dispute. Contract interpretation is the way in which a court decides which party's interpretation shall prevail in the event that there is a discrepancy in understanding the contractual language.

Should a dispute bring the client and the designer to court, there are several standard rules of contract interpretation which a court will use to construe the terms of the agreement. It is important for a designer to be aware of these rules and their significance, as almost any disputed contract will be interpreted under them.

Parol Evidence

Generally, a contract is held as the final expression of the parties' intentions, and any other expression, written or oral, made prior to the writing, as well as any oral expressions contemporaneous with the writing, are inadmissible to alter the terms of the writing. This rule, however, only bars the introduction of evidence that seeks to alter, contradict, or add to a final version of a written agreement. Other forms of evidence, which do not seek to contravene the writing, are admissible to aid in the interpretation of the contract. Evidence that proves that there was a defect in the formation (i.e., the agreement was made under fraud, mistake, duress, or illegal circumstances) is admissible in disputing the enforcement of such an agreement. Parol, or extrinsic evidence, may also be offered if there is a dispute as to the meaning of a term in the written agreement. Lastly, this type of evidence may be admitted to support a claim of lack of consideration. For example, a client claims that $2,000 has been given as full and complete consideration, and now the designer owes the client performance. The designer may introduce outside evidence to show that the sum has never been paid, and therefore no obligation to perform exists.

The side bar, "Standard Rules of Interpretation," gives a general list of rules for standard contract interpretation. This is a good list to use when reviewing a final agreement for any terms that might be open to multiple interpretations.

Standard Rules of Interpretation
❏ Courts shall refuse to consider parol evidence (any expression, written or oral, made prior to the writing, as well as any oral statement made contemporaneously with the writing that, if admitted into evidence, would contradict the terms of the written agreement).

❏ Courts shall not infer terms that are different from those in the parties' contract.

❏ All the writings that are part of a contract shall be interpreted as a unit.

❏ Words shall be interpreted consistently throughout the contract.

❏ Words shall be construed according to their "ordinary" meaning unless it is clearly shown that they were meant to be used in a technical sense, in which case the technical meaning will be applied.

❏ Courts will attempt to construe a contract as a whole, and specific clauses will be subordinated to the contract's general intent.

❏ When there are inconsistencies, handwritten insertions take precedence over typewritten insertions; typewritten insertions take precedence over terms in the printed form.

❏ When there are differences among drawings, more recent drawings take precedence over older drawings. More detailed drawings take precedence over less detailed drawings. Large-scale drawings take precedence over small-scale drawings made at the same time. Specifications usually prevail over drawings.

❏ Words ("seventeen thousand dollars") take precedence over disparate figures ("$1,700").

❏ Some contracts contain statements that establish the order of precedence among documents. When there is no pre-established order, inconsistencies must be resolved by reading the contract as a whole.

❏ Ambiguities in a contract are construed against the party who prepared the contract, absent evidence of the intention of the parties.

❏ Courts will generally consider the custom and usage in the particular business and the particular locale where the contract is either executed or performed.

❏ Obvious clerical errors shall not affect the proper interpretation of a contract.

❏ Words that have been erased or crossed out shall be ignored.

Performance and Breach of Contract

Entering into a contract makes all parties to the agreement responsible for performing their contractual obligations. The extent to which these obligations are met as they become due will determine whether there has been a breach of the contract. When one of the contracting parties has an absolute duty to perform and subsequently fails to do so, such action or inaction will result in a breach of the contract. The extent to which the breaching and nonbreaching parties have performed to that point will affect the significance or the materiality of the breach. The concept of absolute promises is applicable to the types of agreements most commonly entered into in the field of interior design. A client makes a promise to pay a designer for services to be rendered at a particular time. The promise and the duty are absolute; failure of either party to perform will result in a breach of the agreement.

Partial Performance/Substantial Performance

If a designer has fulfilled only part of a contractually obligated performance, there is generally no right to payment from the client under traditional contract law. As discussed earlier in the chapter, if a designer has "substantially performed," usually meaning completed more than half of the contractual obligation, he may pursue a noncontractual remedy to avoid the unjust enrichment of the client. Under this theory, the designer, unless acting in bad faith, will most likely be able to recover payment for the portion of work completed.

Dispute over workmanship is often a focal point in disagreements over whether a designer has adequately performed or not. This was the central point of contention in a dispute involving a homeowner, interior designer, and a contractor in Tennessee. *Custom Built Homes* v. *G.S. Hinsen Company, Inc.* arose out of a dispute over the workmanship of residential renovations. An interior designer, G.S. Hinsen Company, Inc.—who was hired by the owner, Dan Clark—hired a contractor, Custom Built Homes, to perform the work. However, because the owner was dissatisfied with the renovations, the designer withheld final payment to the contractor.

Custom Built Homes had been hired by G.S. Hinsen in accordance with an agreement between G.S. Hinsen and Dan Clark. During the course of the construction, Custom Built Homes periodically submitted requests for progress payments to G.S. Hinsen, and G.S. Hinsen made corresponding payments to Custom Built Homes for the work performed. Before the project was substantially completed, the client informed G.S. Hinsen of his dissatisfaction with portions of the work. Custom Built Homes performed remedial work on portions of the house with which the client was unhappy, but disputed the remaining complaints about the quality of its work. Although G.S. Hinsen had been paid in full by the client, the firm withheld payment on Custom Built Homes's final bill in an attempt to induce Custom Built Homes to satisfy the client's demands for remedial work.

The court held that G.S. Hinsen had the burden of proving Custom Built Homes's breach of contract and that the essential elements of any *breach of contract* include, "(1) the existence of an enforceable contract, (2) nonperformance amounting to a breach of the contract, (3) damages caused by the breach of contract." Because Dan Clark had paid G.S. Hinsen in full for the contracted project, the court found that G.S. Hinsen had failed to prove that it had been actually damaged by Custom Built Homes's purported breach of contract, "The faulty workmanship, if it occurred, damaged Mr. Clark's home. Since Mr. Clark has already paid the full agreed-upon price for the renovations, G.S. Hinsen has received the full benefit of his bargain with Mr. Clark and has not been injured."

The interior design firm was unable to withhold payment from the contractor based solely on the complaint from the client. If G.S. Hinsen was required by Dan Clark to correct the defective work at his own expense, the firm could then look to Custom Built Homes for damages. As no such demand was made by Dan Clark, no claim for damages could be made by G.S. Hinsen against Custom Built Homes.

This case illustrates the duties of performance owed by individual parties to a contract and from whom a remedy may be sought in the event of a breach. This case also illustrates the importance of clearly spelling out performance obligations and standards in the written agreement, so that proving a breach will be an easier task.

Defenses to Breach of Contract/ Events That Excuse Performance

There are a variety of defenses that can be offered in response to a lawsuit for breach of contract. In addition, certain events may excuse the performance of obligations owed pursuant to the contract.

Defenses to Formation

If a party is able to evidence absence of mutual assent or absence of consideration, the contract will be rendered unenforceable. An absence of mutual assent may arise due to the following excuses: mistake, duress, misrepresentation, or undue influence. If a defendant is able to prove any one of these excuses, performance will not be directed by the court.

In order for performance to be excused on the grounds of a mistake, the court must determine whether only the party seeking relief was mistaken (called a unilateral mistake), or all parties to the contract were mistaken as to a fundamental element of the contract (a mutual mistake). Courts have generally held that performance is not excused in the case of a unilateral mistake, unless the mistake was (1) as to a basic assumption on which the contract was made, (2) the mistake will have a material effect on the purpose of the contract, and (a) the party seeking relief does not "bear the risk" of the mistake (the risk is allocated to him by agreement of the parties, or (b) he is aware, at the time the contract is made, that he has only limited knowledge with respect to the facts to which the mistake relates but treats this limited knowledge as sufficient, or (c) the risk is allocated to him by the court on the ground that it is reasonable in the circumstances to do so) and the effect of the mistake is such that enforcement of the contract would be unconscionable, or (d) the other party had reason to know of the mistake or his fault caused the mistake. (Restatement of the Law, Second, Contracts, § 153)

A common example used to illustrate a unilateral mistake is particularly appropriate for this chapter. Suppose an architect is taking bids for interior design work on an upcoming project. The architect receives six bids all around the $30,000 mark and a seventh for $20,000 (due to an unknown or unnoticed computational error by the designer). The architect accepts the $20,000 bid from the designer and incorporates it into a budget, which is then accepted by the client. The designer then notices the computational error and attempts to revise the bid. Unless the designer is able to show that enforcement of the contract would be "unconscionable" *and* that the architect has not relied on the bid, a court will require the designer to perform the work for the quoted amount.

However, if the mistake is mutual, which means made by both parties, performance will most likely be excused by a court. For example, an interior designer contracts with a client to procure certain chairs from an antique dealer thought by both the designer and client to be authentic early nineteenth-century woodwork. If it is discovered that the chairs are not authentic, the designer is no longer obligated to deliver nineteenth-century antique chairs under the contract. Both parties were mistaken as to the chairs, and therefore performance for both parties is excused.

Duress, misrepresentation, and undue influence generally involve illegal pressure to enter the contract or some form of fraud. The party seeking avoidance of the contract must show that there was a representation made by the other party that was intentionally not in accordance with the facts, or that he was unfairly coerced into entering into the contract.

As indicated earlier in this chapter, these are the general concerns a designer should keep in mind when reviewing the circumstances of the offer and acceptance leading to the contract formation. It is important for the designer to be aware of the circumstances surrounding the contract and the intentions of the other party.

Other Defenses: Impossibility, Impracticability, and Frustration of Purpose

In general, any party to a contract is liable for a breach of that agreement, even if, for example, the performance of the promises the designer made in the contract have now become significantly more difficult to perform, through no fault of the parties. The difficulty may arise from an unanticipated change in circumstance that quite often makes performance more burdensome and expensive. Contract law encourages predictable results by having parties place their expectations and obligations to writing. In doing so, contract law has traditionally limited performance exceptions to instances in which performance becomes impossible due to a circumstance that arises after the contract is executed. Impossibility was originally limited to three situations: (1) death of a party necessary for performance, (2) government intervention, and (3) destruction of the subject of the contract. In the event that a party has partially performed prior to the occurrence of the "impossible" circumstance, that party may sue under a theory of quasi contract, as discussed previously, for any services rendered or payments already made. For example, if a client contracted with an interior designer to remodel a living room, but the house was subsequently destroyed in a fire, both the designer and the owner would be discharged from their respective contractual obligations. Due to the changed circumstances, the designer's performance has become impossible. Suppose, however, that the client had already made a partial payment to the designer. The designer will probably be required to return the payment to the client since performance is impossible.

Over time, this strict rule limiting excused performances to such extreme situations led to particularly harsh results, and the courts developed a second category of excused performance—impracticability. In order for a contract to be considered impracticable, three elements must be present: (1) the party seeking discharge of the contract must evidence extreme and unreasonable difficulty and/or expense in fulfilling the contractual obligations, (2) the impracticable circumstance must be one which was not foreseeable, and (3) the party seeking relief from the contract must not have agreed to assume the risk of the event which is now put forth as a reason to be excused from performing. However, in some circumstances, where one party has been excused from performance and the other has already conferred some type of benefit, the latter party may seek restitution. For example, suppose a designer furnished funds for new carpets which were installed in the client's home. The house was subsequently burned down in a fire. The client would not be required to rebuild the house in order to fulfill the contract, the designer would most likely be entitled to restitution for the expenses incurred in procuring the carpets.

Sometimes unexpected changes in the cost of performing contractual duties threaten to cost the designer money, but do not rise to the level of impossibility or impracticability. Under these circumstances, unless this situation has been specifically provided for in the contract, the designer would be forced to render performance as required by the contract and incur the additional expense. By including a "changed circumstances clause" in the contract, a designer can avoid such a result. This type of a clause provides for the renegotiation of the designer's fee if there is an unexpected material change in the circumstances surrounding the contract.

Absence of mutual assent is more likely to occur in the course of a designer's business, but the absence of consideration as an excuse for performance is worthy of mention. An agreement which lacks consideration, (something of legal value must be given, and there must be a bargained-for exchange) is not actually a contract at all. For example, a gratuitous promise, such as "I will redesign your kitchen for free because you have done so many nice things for me," is generally unenforceable in a court.

Should the designer have a change of mind, the recipient of the promise would be unable to force the designer to perform.

Remedies/Damages

When damages are sought against a party breaching a contract, the court will usually use a monetary calculation to determine the amount the nonperforming party must give the injured party in order to put the injured party in the position they would have occupied had the contract not been breached. Generally, out-of-pocket costs (including any expense incurred in finding replacement goods or services) and loss of profits are factored into this equation.

Although these "expectation damages" are generally sufficient in most breach situations, in some instances they are insufficient or inappropriate. For example, if lost profits are not easily determined, utilizing this expectation damage calculation would be inappropriate. In this case, where no loss of profit can be proven, the court will try to restore the status quo (put the plaintiff in the same position as if the plaintiff never entered the contract) by awarding "reliance" damages.

In some cases, the contract itself will provide a schedule of damages for nonperformance, which may take the form of a fixed sum or a formula for calculating the damages. When effectively drafted, only these damages will be available to the parties in the event of a breach. Liquidated, or stipulated damages, which represent the parties' own intentions, will be enforced by the court unless there is a showing that based upon the facts known to the parties at the time the contract was made, the damage provision is fair and reasonable.

Punitive damages, which are designed to punish the breaching party, are not available unless, "the conduct constituting the breach is also a tort for which punitive damages are recoverable." (Restatement (Second) of Contracts §

355.) This generally requires a showing of fraud, malice, or oppression. Factors that will determine the amount of punitive damages granted include: plaintiff's cost of litigation, the financial condition of the defendant, and the grossness of the conduct of the defendant.

Equitable Remedies

Some agreements, due to the fact that they lack one of the essential elements in contract formation discussed earlier, do not constitute an enforceable contract. Assume the parties, however, have acted as though they have entered into a binding agreement. Where is an injured party to look for relief when damaged by the other party's nonperformance? Courts of equity, available only to those parties guilty of no wrongdoing themselves, exist to award damages when no contract exists. For example, a designer and a client discuss the remodeling of the client's living room. The client mistakenly believes that there is a contract and sends the designer a check for $5,000. Under the theory of restitution (under which the injured party receives the profit of the other party, rather than its own expectation damages), the client will be able to recover the $5,000. The theory of restitution is based on the idea that the "breaching" party should not be "unjustly enriched" at the expense of the injured party.

Bieber-Guillory v. *Aswell*, a case involving an interior designer who brought a suit against a homeowner for amounts due as a result of an agreement to remodel the family home, illustrates how a court may decide on damages. In this case, no agreement was ever reached between the interior designer and the homeowner with respect to her fees or prices for merchandise (which were not disclosed until the homeowner received the designer's bill). No terms were ever negotiated, and no agreement was ever executed between the parties. As there was not a written contract, the court decided to award damages to the interior designer on the basis of unjust enrichment (meaning the homeowner should pay for the value of services and goods received). The court held that there were five elements required to prove unjust enrichment: "(1) an enrichment of the defendant; (2) an impoverishment of the plaintiff; (3) causation between the enrichment and the impoverishment; (4) an absence of justification or cause for either the enrichment or the impoverishment; and (5) no other remedy available at law." The court found all of these elements to be present in this case, and the designer was awarded the exact calculation of the worth of the services. In order to avoid such an unpredictable result, all of the expectations of the parties and the terms of the agreement should be spelled out, in advance, in a written contract.

A second case illustrating the concept of unjust enrichment involved material and labor furnished by a contractor at the request of the son and daughter of the homeowners. In this case, *Paschall's Inc.* v. *J.P. Dozier*, (407 S.W.2d 150), the contractor contended that the materials and labor were furnished with full knowledge and consent of the homeowners, who then refused to pay for the material and services. The court held that because the homeowner was aware of the improvements being made to the house, and that the bathroom enhanced the value of the house, the contractor was entitled to the value of his services under a theory of unjust enrichment.

Although a dispute between the designer and the client is not the situation one would like to envision upon entering into a working relationship, considering and applying prevention tactics can save countless hours and dollars in the long run. By creating contracts that clearly express the intentions of the parties, future disputes are less likely.

Mechanic's Lien

One of the most effective ways in which a designer can protect himself in the event of a client's breach of contract is to immediately file a mechanic's lien for the value of work performed and materials furnished during the course of the project. A "mechanic's lien," created by state statute, is defined by *Black's Law Dictionary* as a lien "securing priority of payment of the price or value of the work performed and materials furnished in erecting or repairing a building or other structure, and as such attaches to the land as well as buildings or improvements erected thereon." Statutes enacted in all fifty states as well as in the District of Columbia provide some type of "mechanic's lien" provision, under which a designer may be able to seek recovery. However, the mechanic's lien statutes as well as the judicial analysis of those statutes is not consistent from state to state, therefore, individual state statutes should be consulted for state-specific details.

Most mechanic's lien statutes were enacted primarily for the benefit of construction professionals (i.e., builders and general contractors). However, some states, such as Florida, specifically name interior designers in listing the groups that may file mechanic's liens.

Fla Stat. Ch. 713.03(1) provides:

(1) Any person who performs services as architect, landscape architect, interior designer, engineer, or surveyor and mapper, subject to compliance with and the limitations imposed by this part, has a lien on the real property improved for any money that is owing to him or her for his or her services used in connection with improving the real property or for his or her services in supervising any portion of the work of improving the real property, rendered in accordance with his or her contract and with the direct contract.

(2) Any architect, landscape architect, interior designer, engineer, or surveyor and mapper who has a direct contract and who in the practice of his or her profession shall perform services, by himself or herself or others, in connection with a specific parcel of real property and subject to said compliances and limitations, shall have a lien upon such real property for the money owing to him or her for his or her professional services, regardless of whether such real property is actually improved.

Some states, such as New York, provide those who are not in direct privity with the owner (for example, a designer who contracts through a general contractor rather than directly with the owner) a separate form of relief. The New York statute allows a designer to file a mechanic's lien for uncompensated services and/or materials, but the recovery is limited to the total price agreed upon by the general contractor. Other states, such as Pennsylvania, permit a designer to file a lien directly against the owner, regardless of the price the general contractor agreed to.

Most states require that the improvements, work done, and/or materials provided must have been done so with the express or implied consent, or, in some cases, the written consent of the owner. Additionally, many statutes require that the designer substantially perform under the contract and that a mechanic's lien be filed within a certain amount of time after the work is ceased and/or completed.

Two cases, which were litigated in Maryland, illustrate the important role a mechanic's lien can play in securing the rights of someone who has rendered services and then is not paid. In both cases the court was called upon to determine whether or not a mechanic's lien could be awarded in excess of the party's agreed-upon cost for the project. In the first case, *Jones.* v. *J.H. Hiser Constr. Co.*, (60 Md. App. 671) the court found that the builder's failure to keep the client apprised of the ongoing and escalating construction costs barred his right to a mechanic's lien in excess of the originally agreed-upon amount. Whereas in *Kahle* v. *McDonough Builders, Inc.*, (85 Md. App. 141) the court found that because a builder had conferred with the client before purchases, kept in close communication with the client, and generally discussed various changes, selections, and extras requested by the client on a routine basis, the builder was able to recover nearly the full amount of his cost-plus-fixed-fee via a mechanic's lien, despite the fact that this amount was in excess of the amount originally agreed upon by the parties.

As the cases discussed above illustrate, a mechanic's lien can be an effective way for a designer to protect against nonpayment for services and/or materials. It must be emphasized, however, that these statutes vary from state-to-state and an individual state's statute should always be consulted prior to reliance.

Statute of Limitations

Generally, state statutes limit the amount of time in which a party has to commence an action (i.e., bringing suit against another party). The statute of limitations on a particular claim begins to "run" from the time plaintiff's right to sue is complete. Failure to commence an action within the applicable period of time may permit the defendant to raise the statute of limitations as a bar to the plaintiff's suit. For example, in New York the statute of limitations for actions based on express or implied contractual obligations is generally six years. If a designer wishes to sue an owner for breach of contract, he must do so within six years of the owner's breach or the claim may be barred.

Generally, the remedy sought by the plaintiff will determine the applicable statute of limitations. Going back to the earlier example of the New York plaintiff, if, for example, the plaintiff has been awarded a sum as a result of an arbitration proceeding, under New York law, the plaintiff only has one year within which to commence an action to compel the defendant to pay the award.

Mitigation of Damages

Once a contract has been breached, the non-breaching party is under a duty to "mitigate damages." This means that once notice is received of the breach, the nonbreaching party may not continue to incur further expenses or costs and must make reasonable efforts to lessen the damages incurred as a result of the other party's breach. Generally, in the context of construction contracts, the duty to mitigate damages generally means not continuing work after the owner's breach. For example, a designer has been contracted to work on the decoration of a living room, and the parties have agreed that payments will be paid within thirty days of owner's receipt of an invoice from the designer. If the owner fails to pay an invoice within the requisite time established in the contract, and after notice from the designer, the owner still fails to cure the breach, the designer must stop working on the redecoration. Because the designer has notice of the owner's breach, she is under a duty to stop work (and therefore lower her own damages) on the project. The same is true for goods purchased by the designer on behalf of the owner. If, after the designer has procured the goods, the owner, in breach of the contract, refuses to accept them, the designer is under a duty to try to resell the goods in a commercially reasonable manner.

In some cases, mitigation of damages includes accepting alternative contractual opportunities. For example, a designer enters into a contract to provide consulting services for the remodeling of a kitchen. Two weeks after entering into the contract, the owner decides to go with another designer and terminates the original agreement. If the designer is able to procure a project similar in kind and compensation, she is under a duty to accept the project. If the designer does not accept the second project, and sues the original owner for damages, the damages will most likely be reduced by the amount the designer could have earned by accepting and completing the second project.

Failure to mitigate generally bars the non-breaching party from recovering those damages that may have been otherwise avoided. Finally, it should also be noted that a nonbreaching party who satisfies the duty to mitigate can usually recover the expenses of mitigation.

Arbitration Provisions

Upon entering into an agreement, contracting parties may choose to include an arbitration provision in the contract, both voluntarily submitting any dispute to an independent third party for resolution. Most states have enacted some form of state arbitration legislation, based on either the Uniform Arbitration Act (UAA) or the Federal Arbitration Act. Whether based on the UAA or the Federal Arbitration Act, most statutes establish similar rules for parties who have consented to arbitration. Generally, these rules:

❏ Make agreements to submit future disputes to arbitration irrevocable;

❏ Give the parties seeking arbitration the power to obtain a court order compelling the other party to arbitrate;

❏ Require courts to stop any litigation when there is a valid agreement to arbitrate pending arbitration;

❏ Authorize courts to appoint arbitrators and fill vacancies when one party will not designate the arbitrator or when an arbitrator has withdrawn or is unable to serve;

❏ Limit the court's power to review findings of fact and application of the law by the arbitrator; and

❏ Set the specific procedural defects that could invalidate arbitral awards and give time limits for challenges. (Steven M. Siegfried, *Introduction to Construction Law,* The American Law Institute, 1986.)

In the 1960s, a uniform set of arbitration rules for members of the construction industry, the Construction Industry Arbitration Rules, were developed. These rules are administered by the American Arbitration Association (AAA). These arbitration rules give members of the construction industry in all fifty states a standard uniform set of arbitration rules. Approximately twenty-five industry organizations, including the American Society of Interior Designers, constitute the National Construction Dispute Resolution Committee (NCDRC) which sponsors the arbitration procedure specially designed for the construction industry. The full text of the Construction Industry Dispute Resolution Procedures (In information on the Construction Industry Arbitration Rules and the AAA can be found at *www.adr.org.*

As discussed above, arbitration involves voluntary submission, and as such, a party cannot be compelled to arbitrate an issue unless she has specifically consented to do so. As a result, contracting parties who wish to invoke arbitration as the form of dispute resolution generally stipulate this in the original contract. Depending upon the issues the parties wish to be resolved by arbitration, they may contractually prescribe which issues are to be arbitrable in the event of a dispute. A "broad form" arbitration clause, like the one recommended by the AAA, submits the parties to arbitration in the event of nearly any dispute:

"Any controversy or claim arising out of or relating to this contract, or the breach thereof, shall be settled by arbitration administered by the American Arbitration Association under its Construction Industry Arbitration Rules, and judgment on the award rendered by the arbitrator(s) may be entered in any court having jurisdiction thereof." (From the AAA Web site)

Arbitration is generally less structured in terms of procedural rules and rules on evidence than a judicial litigation, and an arbitrator, who is selected by the parties, generally has more discretion in fashioning a remedy. In addition, since the arbitrator is not a judge, but rather someone with industry-related experience, the dispute can be heard by an individual with a deeper understanding of the issues. It is also worth noting that arbitration decisions are final, unless arbitrary, fraudulent, or capricious. Unless otherwise limited or expanded by federal or state statute, attacks on arbitration awards are generally limited to:

❏ Fraud in the making of an arbitration agreement;

❏ Misconduct by the parties or the arbitrator (the award was procured by corruption, fraud, or undue means);

❏ Partiality or lack of power by the arbitrator (the arbitrator was guilty of misconduct in refusing to postpone the hearing upon sufficient cause shown, or in refusing to hear evidence pertinent and material to the controversy, or of any other misbehavior by which the rights of any party have been prejudiced); or

❏ A violation of public policy.

Although in many cases arbitration is a less expensive and quicker method of dispute resolution, there are still some who prefer the traditional judicial system to the private arbitration proceeding. This preference is usually based on the fact that the arbitrator's decision is not appealable (except as discussed above), attorney's fees are not recoverable, and arbitration is not always less expensive than litigation. In determining whether or not to include an arbitration clause in an agreement, the designer should consider all of the factors discussed in this section as well as refer to the individual state's arbitration statute, to determine whether or not an arbitration clause would be advantageous to the designer.

Jobs Index

The Jobs Index is the source of all project numbers. The purpose of the project number is to identify all the components of an assignment. Job numbers are used on job sheets, time sheets, purchase orders, invoices (incoming and outgoing), transmittals, and all other project records. It is the link to all project-related costs and material.

As soon as a prospective client introduces an assignment, it is useful to open a job number to begin tracking time and costs, also called "cost accounting," including the effort it takes to take the project from being a prospect to a reality. In other words, even if the job does not proceed past the proposal stage, it is helpful to look back at the end of the year and calculate how many jobs were pursued and how many became active assignments. Additionally, while expenditures towards an unsuccessful bid may not be reimbursable, these expenditures can be tax-deductible as part of the firm's marketing costs. Some firms choose to use separate job numbers for projects that are in the marketing stage from those that are in production. The index may be organized in a number of ways: chronological, alphabetical by client, or by project type, such as residential, commercial, institutional, governmental, or corporate. Regardless of the method used to classify projects, this comprehensive index of projects is the simplest and clearest way of identifying all past and current projects, as well as who is managing them and how long they have been active, or when they were completed.

The "Project Number" index, or list, can begin with any number, but then should follow consecutively thereafter. The numbers may be keyed to start dates, such as "102203-52," or October 22, 2003, job number 52 (in the year 2003), but aside from how the numerical order is determined, it is best to keep the number uncomplicated and as brief as possible, since it will be used frequently. Always keep the numbers in sequence. Do not fill in the numbers in advance, since some assignments may need additional space. For jobs with several distinct subparts that need to be tracked separately for billing purposes, use one project number for the overall name of the assignment/client, and use sub-numbers or letters to indicate the different parts of the job (also, keep separate job sheets for such sub-numbers or letters). See example A.

Another way to establish job numbers is to use a code. Example A is based on the system shown in form 1. If jobs are unrelated, but have the same client and came in-house at the same time, use separate project numbers, as shown in example B.

Filling In the Form

In the "Date Opened" column, fill in the date the project is assigned to the firm. It may be the date of the signed project agreement, or it may be the date of the first client briefing, if your practice is to track precontract expenses. "Date Closed" is the date of the final payment received. In the "Client" column, fill in the client's name—regardless of whether it is an individual, a company, or some other entity. Under "Job Name," identify the job with a name that is clearly distinguished from other projects in the office.

Under "Project Lead," fill in the initials of the lead designer or project manager who will have primary responsibility for the assignment. Then, fill in the job number.

Using the Form

Use project numbers on all project-related forms, drawings, transmittals, and other correspondence. It is the central link to all information about a project.

Post the master Jobs Index near special printers—to track the numbers of copies billable to projects—the messenger desk, and other areas

Sample Numbering System

Project Number Codes	X	XX	–	XXX	XX	X
Commercial	C					
Residential	R					
Year		01				
Client Initials				TCN		
Job Number					1 to 99	
Sub-Job Number						A to Z
Eg: R01-TCN3A	R	01	–	TCN	3	A

Example A

Date Opened	Date Closed	Client	Job Name	Project Lead	Job #
7/1/02		Atlantis Group	Blue Oyster Restaurant	NB	C01-AG-1
"		" "	—Bar	SB	C01-AG-1A
"		" "	—Dining Rm.	SB	C01-AG-1B
"		" "	—Gift Shop	CD	C01-AG-1C
8/19/02		B. G. Smeet	Appleby's Farm Store	NB	C01-BGS-1

Example B

Date Opened	Date Closed	Client	Job Name	Project Lead	Job #
10/22/03		A. C. Paige	Cannes House	ZD	102203-11
"		" "	Park St. Apt.	SB	102203-12
"		" "	Aspen Cabin	ZD	102203-13

where employees can easily refer to it and be encouraged to use the job numbers consistently. It greatly simplifies record keeping.

Open job files, both computer and physical. Some firms use large, red, manila, string-tie envelopes; others use large, three-ring binders to keep all project materials organized. Label the files and project folders or envelopes with the job number, client, and job name, as well as the project start date.

Job files (digital and hard copy) are used to store copies of agreements, work change orders, receipts, and all other project materials. It is useful to separate correspondence and other nonfi-

nancial documents from materials that will serve as backup for billing purposes. (The most popular method of filing documents is in chronological order, most recent item on top.) If you know that you will be required to show backup for reimbursable expenses, a separate folder containing these receipts is a convenient place to gather these copies.

When the project is completed and billed, simply store its files and folders in either chronological or alphabetical order for future reference. Quite often, it is helpful to be able to check back to earlier proposals and contracts when estimating, negotiating, or planning new projects.

Jobs Index

Date Opened	Date Closed	Client	Job Name	Project Lead	Job #

Job Information Sheet

Cost accounting, or keeping track of time and costs expended on a project, is essential to maintaining a regular and accurate billing system, as well as a useful indicator of whether a project is profitable or not. The Job Information Sheet is the detailed record of all time and costs incurred during the course of a project. It is useful to record time and costs regardless of any fee arrangement, since even miscellaneous nonbillable time and expenses have an impact on profits when all real costs are fully known. Items such as special supplies, research time, and very long and frequent client meetings not originally calculated into the fee may significantly diminish what might have seemed to be an acceptably profitable job. The advantage of knowing all costs, including extras, is the possibility of more astutely negotiating time and fees of prospective assignments, or perhaps renegotiating a current one.

Job sheets can be used to analyze the following information:

Time. In addition to noting the time spent doing a job, this category can be further notated to indicate specific aspects or phases of jobs. For example, with design services for a hotel property with a variety of spaces, it may be necessary or useful to know how much time was spent on different types of guest rooms, separate from dining rooms, foyers, lobby, and other public spaces; or how much time was spent on design, separate from site supervision during installation.

Billable Costs. Depending upon the fee arrangement, some interior designers bill (and mark up or pass through discounts on) the cost of materials, hardware, furnishings, and other services they spec and supervise during construction and installation. Scale models, renderings (for brochures, client meetings, or other special needs), messengers, even toll calls are billable, depending upon negotiated arrangements with the client. Nonbillable items can be noted with an "NB" to the right of the "Total" column.

Profitability. Interior designers who are working on an hourly fee basis will find that accurate records are indispensable. However, when working on a flat-fee basis, it is still essential to be able to determine whether the fee charged is adequate for the time spent on the project. To examine profitability, subtract total actual costs from the total amount billed (not including taxes). For example:

Fee minus Nonreimbursable Project Costs = Gross Profit
$10,000 minus $1,500   = $8,500

Gross Profit minus Overhead Allocation = Net Profit
$8,500 minus $6,500   = $2,000

Net Profit divided by Fee = Per Cent Profit Margin
$2,000 divided by $10,000   = 20%

Overhead is the general cost of running your business. These items include, but are not limited to: rent, insurance, utilities, maintenance, general supplies, postage and subscriptions, bookkeeping and legal services, computers, leases, advertising/marketing, and nonbillable salaries and benefits for support personnel. While none of these items are billable to specific projects, they, along with a profit margin and contingency allowance, must be figured into the fee structure of every assignment.

The overhead factor must also be calculated into the hourly rates used to bill on the basis of time rather than on a flat fee. To calculate overhead expenses, add up all of the monthly business costs (which are not billable as reimbursable expenses), multiply by twelve to get the annual number, and divide this total by the number of jobs you expect to have in-house over the course of the year. The resulting number is the dollar amount that every job has to produce to cover the minimum cost of running your business.

For example:

Rent	$1,500
Utilities	$ 250
Leases	$ 125
Supplies	$ 200
Insurance	$ 225
Legal	$ 125
Advertising	$ 50
Marketing	$ 100
P/T Bookkeeper	$ 700
Principal's Salary	$8,125 (inc. approx. 38% for taxes and benefits in this $70,650 annual salary)
Total Monthly Overhead	$11,400 × 12 = $136,800 Total Annual Overhead Expenses

Above and beyond reimbursable expenses that are not included in the overhead items, the minimum amount of billings this business has to generate for this one year is $136,800 simply to stay in business—that is, *before* turning a profit. Any amount over this base is considered profit (unless there are unexpected costs that were not anticipated when calculating the overhead). It is generally a good idea to build a contingency factor into every project (between 5% and 20%) to cover nonbillable, unexpected costs.

Using this calculation for overhead expenses, this designer must produce $11,400 worth of gross profit every month, that is, $11,400 after all project expenses have been reimbursed. If there are three assignments in-house, each one should be generating approximately $3,800 apiece in monthly billings over nonreim-

bursable expenses (or some combination of this amount—larger projects will bring in more billings and cover projects with lower billings). The ideal strategy is to reduce as much as possible the nonreimbursable items on every project. That is, make sure that all time and costs are fully reimbursable. This tactic points to either billing on an hourly basis, or extremely accurate estimates for the time and materials that the project is expected to consume.

To calculate the minimum hourly rate needed to cover overhead expenses, divide the monthly overhead costs by the number of billable hours in the month. For example:

$$\$11,400 \text{ divided by } 150 \text{ billable hours per month} = \$76$$

The number of billable hours in an average work year is 1,800 hours (37.5 hours per week, less ten days of vacation and ten annual paid national holidays). Divide this by twelve to reach the monthly figure of 150 hours. Logic and experience will show that 100 percent billable time is generally not typical of most employees, particularly high-level managers, who spend considerable time on marketing, administration, and personnel chores. The calculation of billable time should be realistic.

In this example, $76 is the minimum hourly rate that can be charged in order to meet these monthly expenses, including salaries for the principal and a part-time bookkeeper. If there are other salaries in the business that are not billable to jobs, these salaries must also be considered as part of the overhead. Remember, however, that this calculation assumes all miscellaneous project costs are reimbursable and does not account for profit.

Calculating profit into fees and hourly rates is not an exact science. Generally, designers try to reach for an additional minimum 20 percent profit in the overhead figure. For example:

Minimum Hourly Rate	$76.00
Percent Profit Desired	×.20
Total Hourly Rate	$15.20 profit + $76.00 base rate = $91.20

Naturally, any hourly rate has to have a reasonable relation to what other professionals are charging for similar work and what the market will bear. Flexibility is important in determining fees and hourly rates—but you must never lose sight of the need to cover the ongoing expenses of your business. To cover slow periods, a business owner must either have a reasonable amount of savings or a credit line to cover overhead expenses while searching for new assignments. The ability to adjust expenses quickly in response to changes in the volume of work is also helpful, but so is a healthy amount of surplus savings. It is also generally recommended that no matter how busy you are with ongoing projects, you should never stop marketing for future ones.

In the event you are the principal of an interior design practice and most of your work is not directly accountable to project tasks, you will need to determine hourly rates for your employees who are working directly on projects. To do this, calculate the total cost of each employee: her salary and all her benefits, such as health, life, and disability insurance, and taxes that you are paying on her behalf, as well as miscellaneous "perks," such as commuting expenses, pension or profit-sharing programs, educational expenses, professional membership fees, etc. For example:

DESIGNER	
Base Salary	$50,000
Benefits and Taxes	$19,000
Other Benefits	$ 1,500
Total Annual Expenses	$70,500

$70,500 divided by 1,800 hours = $39.17 per hour (basic hourly rate)

To this hourly rate, add the *hourly overhead factor* to cover the costs of the business, as follows:

Targeted annual billing to cover $136,800 (annual overhead) plus 25% profit = $171,000

Divide the targeted annual billing amount by the individual personnel expense:

$171,000 divided by $70,500 = 2.43; this is the *hourly overhead factor* to be used to calculate this designer's basic hourly billing rate:

$39.17 × 2.43 = $95.18

Many firms simply determine hourly rate markups as three to four times billable personnel hourly rates; they also generally assign tiers of billing rates for different kinds of personnel. For example, senior personnel are all billed at one rate amount; mid-level at another, and lower level at still another. This simplifies billing and also reduces the chance of staff members discovering each other's earnings.

Project Types

In general, commercial projects command higher fees than residential projects. The requirements of commercial projects are usually more complex and take longer to complete, increasing the chances of unanticipated problems and cost overruns. On the other hand, commercial and institutional specialty areas may be more predictable than residential projects that involve the subjective nature of clients' tastes and their abilities to make firm decisions. The more experience an interior design firm has in niche areas, whether residential, commercial (retail stores, restaurants, offices), institutional (such as medical or educational facilities), or any other type of interior design, the greater its expertise in estimating costs, fees, and profits in these markets.

Filling In the Form: Page One, Side One

In the "Information" section, enter the job number, its name and location, as well as the client contact information indicated. Note different billing and shipping addresses, if necessary. Referral source information is useful in determining the effectiveness of your marketing or sales efforts. If the referral was a former client, it should signal a valuable source of future references, as well as a special note of acknowledgement to that client. Project team information is important to note, in that it is a quick reference for the person preparing periodic cost accounts and billing. Also fill in a brief description of the scope of work.

The "Dates" section is useful for cost accounting in several ways. First, if a project is billable at specific stages or completion dates, it is necessary to keep track of these dates. Second, since project deliverables are predicated upon specific approvals, it is important to be able to show the client a record of missed sign-off dates that affect deliverable dates. Additionally, a clear record of dates is very useful in understanding those areas of the project that were particularly efficient or inefficient and applying this knowledge to future project plans.

The "Billing" area of this form is the place to note the terms of the fees to be charged; whether fee plus costs, time plus materials, markups, discounts, and any other specific details of the fee agreement. Keep a record of billings under "Invoice Date", "Invoice Number," and "Invoice Amount" for a quick review of the project's billing history. It's handy to have all billing information available on one sheet. The "Work Change Orders" section is particularly important to keep up to date. It is a summary of the work changes approved by the client and spells out the amounts of additional (or reduced) billing, as well as changes in deliverable dates. A quick summary on this sheet will eliminate time wasted looking through stacks of paperwork.

Using the Form

Start a Job Information Sheet as soon as a job number has been assigned to the project from the Jobs Index (which can be a worksheet in your electronic project file).

Posting to page 2 should take place after time sheets have been collected and approved for payroll and when job-related bills are being paid. Indicating job numbers on time sheets and payable invoices makes it easier to post these items to individual job sheets.

Messenger, courier, and other service logs should have a jobs index nearby for easy reference to job numbers. When you receive bills for these services, it will be easy to assign these expenses to projects.

When a time-plus-cost-based project is ready for billing, using the information on page 2, side 1, tally all related items separately and post the totals onto page 1, side 2. For example, add messengers, samples costs, furnishings, hardware, and so on, separately. Add up project personnel time and/or total cost (if freelancer or contractor) separately. For billing, either itemize each cost type separately or combine under general headings by project areas or tasks. Remember to factor markups and/or discounts as appropriate.

You may or may not choose to show these calculations on your invoices, depending on the agreement you have with your client. Generally, discounts are indicated and markups are rolled into total numbers, although some interior designers clearly delineate both markups and discounts.

Filling In the Form: Page One, Reverse Side

The "Summary of Costs" is a comprehensive view of the project's estimated and actual job costs, as well as markup ("M/U") and discount factors, if applicable. Form 2 separates labor and materials expenses. You may wish to total both labor and materials expenses for each line item. Use this summary as a worksheet when calculating the total costs of the completed project. You can add additional "Actual" columns for interim summaries for partial billing, but do include a final total column.

Filling In the Form: Page Two and Continuing on Supplementary Pages

Uncomplicated, short-term assignments may only need a couple of these supplementary pages. When projects are complex and involve a great variety and frequency of services, or continue for long periods of time, there may be many supplementary pages to list the ongoing time and costs. This form allows for the listing of billables, line by line. The date that the item is posted on this sheet goes in the "Date" column. "Item" is the name of either the person (staff or freelance) or the vendor/supplier. Under "Description," fill in the invoice number and date; in the case of a staff person, fill in the date of the time sheet or the week-ending date and the project code. For staff, put the number of billable hours under "Hrs/Rate"; there is no need to show their rates here, since you have already included that in the project team section on page One. For freelancers, you can either indicate their hours and rates in this column, or put their invoice fee under "Total."

The "Material Expenses" column is for invoices received that separate labor from expenses. For example, a researcher might submit an invoice like this:

Restaurant theme research services:
18 hours @ $40.00/hour
Subtotal: $720.00

Expenses:
Library Reference Room Fees $ 12.00
Books $ 75.00
Transportation (NYC/Boston/NYC) $195.00
Subtotal: $282.00

Total: $1,002.00

For jobs that require periodic billing for fees and costs, draw a bold line or skip a space under the last item included in each separate invoice, and jot down the invoice number by this line, so that it will be easy to see where to start tallying for the next invoice. The form already includes subtotals for monthly billings.

Job Information Sheet

INFORMATION

Job Number _____

Job Name _____

Location _____

Client

    Name _____

    Address _____

    Phone _____

    Cell _____

    Fax _____

    Other Contact Information _____

    Bill To _____

        _____

        _____

    Ship To _____

        _____

        _____

    P.O. # _____

Referral Source

    Name _____

    Address _____

    Phone _____

    Sales/Marketing Source _____

Project Team Name

    Principal _____

    Design Director _____

    Senior Project Designer _____

    Designer _____

    Design Assistant _____

    CADD _____

    Consultant _____

    Other _____

Billing Rate

    _____

    _____

    _____

    _____

    _____

    _____

    _____

    _____

DATES

	Target Date	Actual Date	Notes
Contract Commencement	_____	_____	_____
Client Intake Meeting(s)	_____	_____	_____
Program Development Start			
Presentation (1)	_____	_____	_____
Presentation (2)	_____	_____	_____
Program Development Sign-Off	_____	_____	_____

	Target Date	Actual Date	Notes
Design Development—Phase One (Schematics) Start			
Presentation (1)	_____	_____	_____
Presentation (2)	_____	_____	_____
Design Development Phase One (Schematics) Sign-Off	_____	_____	_____
Design Development—Phase Two (Final) Start			
Presentation (1)	_____	_____	_____
Presentation (2)	_____	_____	_____
Design Development-Phase Two (Final) Sign-Off	_____	_____	_____
Contract Documents and Bids			
Project Implementation			
Purchasing—Stock Items	_____	_____	_____
Fabrication—Custom Orders	_____	_____	_____
Construction—Site Supervision	_____	_____	_____
Installation—Site Supervision	_____	_____	_____
Final Project Completion Items			
Walk-Through and Punch List	_____	_____	_____
Punch List Completion	_____	_____	_____

BILLING

Fee Information

Fee Amount _____

Time and Materials _____

Tax Percent _____

Invoice Date _____ Invoice Number _____ Invoice Amount _____

WORK CHANGE ORDERS

Date _____ Order Number _____ Item _____ Hrs/Rate _____ Expense _____ Total _____

SUMMARY OF COSTS

Item	Estimated Labor	Estimated Materials Expense	Estimated Total	Actual Labor	Actual Materials Expense	M/U or Discount	Actual Total
Program Development	_____	_____	_____	_____	_____	_____	_____
Design Development—Phase One—Prelim	_____	_____	_____	_____	_____	_____	_____
Design Development—Phase Two—Final	_____	_____	_____	_____	_____	_____	_____
Contract Documents and Bids	_____	_____	_____	_____	_____	_____	_____
Project Implementation							
Project Details							
Walls/Ceilings							
Paint	_____	_____	_____	_____	_____	_____	_____
Wallcoverings	_____	_____	_____	_____	_____	_____	_____
Mouldings	_____	_____	_____	_____	_____	_____	_____
Other	_____	_____	_____	_____	_____	_____	_____

Item	Estimated Labor	Estimated Materials Expense	Estimated Total	Actual Labor	Actual Materials Expense	M/U or Discount	Actual Total
Floors/Stairways							
Wood	___	___	___	___	___	___	___
Ceramic	___	___	___	___	___	___	___
Stone	___	___	___	___	___	___	___
Carpeting	___	___	___	___	___	___	___
Mouldings	___	___	___	___	___	___	___
Other	___	___	___	___	___	___	___
Window Treatments							
Shades/Blinds	___	___	___	___	___	___	___
Louvers	___	___	___	___	___	___	___
Drapery	___	___	___	___	___	___	___
Valances	___	___	___	___	___	___	___
Other	___	___	___	___	___	___	___
Millwork							
Fixtures and Hardware							
Bath	___	___	___	___	___	___	___
Kitchen	___	___	___	___	___	___	___
Lighting	___	___	___	___	___	___	___
Wall/Door	___	___	___	___	___	___	___
Other	___	___	___	___	___	___	___
Furniture							
Furniture—Purchase	___	___	___	___	___	___	___
Furniture—Commission	___	___	___	___	___	___	___
Furniture—Recondition/Special Finish	___	___	___	___	___	___	___
Furniture—(Re)upholstery	___	___	___	___	___	___	___
Audio/Video/Security/Other Electronic	___	___	___	___	___	___	___
Spa/Exercise Furnishings	___	___	___	___	___	___	___
Other Furnishings							
Linens	___	___	___	___	___	___	___
Rugs	___	___	___	___	___	___	___
Decorative Items (Objets d'art)	___	___	___	___	___	___	___
Miscellaneous							
Travel	___	___	___	___	___	___	___
Messengers	___	___	___	___	___	___	___
Insurance	___	___	___	___	___	___	___
Storage	___	___	___	___	___	___	___
Shipping and Handling	___	___	___	___	___	___	___
Project Total	___	___	___	___	___	___	___

				Material		
Date	Item	Description	Hrs/Rate	Expenses	Total	Billable/Nonbillable

COST ACCOUNT

Project Plan and Budget

There are a variety of ways to charge for interior design services, depending upon whether the design services are offered alone or with the sale of goods. Methods include: hourly rates plus expenses, flat fee, square foot factor, cost plus percentage markup of goods sold, percentage of total project costs, cost of retail, and percentage of retail items. Depending upon circumstances, one or a combination of these methods will apply.

The estimate form presented in this book is intended to help the designer accurately calculate every aspect of a proposed project, as well as serve as a comprehensive checklist of items to be considered. It is meant to be particularly useful in cases where the designer does not have a great deal of experience in the proposed project type or when detailed records of past projects are unavailable. With the results derived from these calculations, the designer may still choose any of the methods available for charging fees, but should be able to better anticipate the actual cost of producing the job.

Assuming that you are basing the project fee on a time-and-materials basis, here is a two-part form that lends itself to many purposes. You can use the Estimating Format internally to calculate all project expenses by labor and materials costs, phase by phase. Attach the "Summary Format" to client estimates or bids, using the information gleaned in the "Estimating Form" to show the client the detailed list of costs, also in phases, but without showing the labor rates and markups. You can also use the "Summary Format" to show the projected schedule.

Filling In the Form: "Estimating Format"

While this form is intended to be as complete as possible, to avoid confusion, it is better to use only those line items that apply to the project at hand. With the inclusion or deletion of specific column headings, this form may start out as the initial estimating spreadsheet used to determine detailed costs. Used as an estimating worksheet, it is most important to break down every aspect of the project into its separate components in order to determine how the complexity and scale of the job will determine the final costs.

Depending upon its intended use, check the appropriate box for the preferred title of the form. Fill in the client information, including name, addresses, and phone numbers. Include the project name, location, and description. In the event you have already assigned this project a number, fill it in. Most of this information is also found on the Job Information Sheet (which is not usually seen by the design staff); it is easy to simply copy and paste the information, as appropriate.

The "Estimating Format" is the area for breaking out the detailed project plan. Check the basis of rates, whether hourly, daily, or weekly. Regardless of which you select, make sure that all of the estimates are based on the selected span of time. If you select anything other than an hourly rate, such as daily or weekly, be careful to adjust for the percentage of time during which that individual will work on this project during the day or week. In many instances, designers are spread across several projects at the same time. So, if your lead designer is going to spend half his time on doing schematics for one week, and you are basing this estimate on weekly rates, show that as .5 (or 50%), not 1 (100%), for that week. On the "Rates" line, fill in each person's rate, depending on whether you have selected to estimate this project on an hourly, daily, or weekly rate.

For every task listed under the main groupings of activities, fill in the estimated amount of time each person will spend working on the project. This form has preset formulas that will automatically feed the rate times the time, per person, into the column for "Total Labor" amount. If you choose to add or delete lines or columns, make sure to check and adjust the formulas, as necessary. This form does not contain any macros; it is formatted for simple calculations. The form also has built-in calculations to add subtotals, and the final total is the sum of all the subtotals.

In the "Materials" column, put in the total cost of materials for each of the tasks listed; include all other costs in the "Misc." column for each task. In the "Cost" "section of columns, the "Budget" column has already been filled in by the automated formula. In the "To-Date" column, put in the total costs actually incurred at set intervals. These intervals may be weekly, monthly, or by periodic billings. The "Balance" column will automatically subtract the "To-Date" amount from the "Budget" amount to show how much money is left, or overspent. The "Schedule" column can show either the overall time allotted for each task, or it can track the amount of labor estimated and used. If it is going to be used to track labor time, a formula can be inserted that adds up all the time shown in the "Labor" columns. If the "Schedule" column is being used to show overall time, then that information will have to be inserted manually.

Using the Form

Microsoft Project, which is also discussed in the Comprehensive Production Schedule chapter, is a very useful software program that helps construct project schedules and budgets. It lends itself well to interior design productions and is also widely available for either PCs or Macs. While it requires a fair learning curve to master, and is somewhat rigid, it does provide a wide variety of reports that can be used for estimating, tracking time, money, and human resources.

Considered one of the safest ways of billing projects, estimates and billings based on the hourly rate method protect the designer from clients who may not make timely decisions or who require a great deal of personal attention. It requires accurate tracking of all personnel working on the project (using time sheets) and the calculation of hourly rates that include not only the base salary and all fringe benefits per person, but also markups for the firm's overhead costs and desired profit margin. (Overhead costs, billing rates, and profit margins are discussed in greater detail in the Job Information Sheet section of this book.) Additionally, all project-related expenses are billed separately, with or without markups, depending upon the terms negotiated for the project. It is customary to provide clients with copies of invoices for such items. Showing backup is not necessary for projects that are billed on a flat-fee and square-footage basis.

Whether a residential or commercial project, accurate estimating is the most important factor in assuring profitability. Key to estimating accuracy is understanding exactly what is involved in the successful completion of the job, starting with programming and schematic design, through design development, the preparation of contract documents and bidding, to finally doing the work, including commissioning of custom elements, purchasing, and completion supervision.

It is also important to have some familiarity with the client to be able to judge how much time it will take to turn around approvals, revisions, and final sign-offs. For repeat clients, this is made evident by past project experiences, documented by time sheets and job summaries. In the case of new and unfamiliar clients, a fair measure of the client may be based on the predesign phase. Otherwise, you can build in a contingency factor (a percentage applied to either hourly rates or total costs) to cover client delays leading to schedule "creep" (the slipping and extension of scheduled deliverables leading to additional costs for the design firm).

Painting, wallcovering, carpeting, drapery, upholstery, and other related trades have specific methodology for estimating costs. Estimates for these trades are usually based on the cost of labor plus materials. Here are the fundamental calculations: the area to be covered, which determines the amount of material that will be needed, which is multiplied by the unit cost of the material to be used (paint, wallpaper, fabric); the time (hourly, daily, or weekly) it takes to do the work by a set number of people, multiplied by their rate (make sure the rate and time calculations are consistent—hourly time by hourly rate, weekly time by weekly rate, etc.). It is very important to know the differences in work time incurred by different materials. For example, painting on drywall is different from painting on cabinets, water-base (latex) paint dries much quicker than oil-base (alkyd) paint and is generally easier to clean up, and so on. *Techniques for Estimating Materials, Costs and Time for Interior Designers*, by Carol A. Sampson (Watson-Guptill Publications, 1991) is a very handy book that provides clear and detailed instructions on how to calculate costs for these trades.

By hiding the columns used for calculating costs, it can then become the "breakout" estimate form that the client sees. In this instance, it is particularly useful to include the statement indicated at the bottom of this form to assure that the client recognizes that this is an estimate and not a contract.

Finally, as the job proceeds, it can be used either as the internal summary of ongoing costs vs. budget, or as a status report to the client, showing costs-to-date vs. budget on an item-by-item basis. As an internal document, use it to track how much time and money have been expended on specific job components and how much is left in the budget to complete the job. The routine monitoring of ongoing costs is very useful in detecting areas that are either signifi-

cantly over or under budget, allowing for budgetary and scheduling adjustments.

There is no standard requirement or practice about what interior designers report to their clients. Many would prefer to simply bill out a project at regular intervals against the agreed fee, making adjustments only for Work Change Orders (see form 20). Commercial clients often have more stringent reporting requirements, particularly for large projects, and find it assuring to receive status reports at regular intervals.

Filling In the Form: "Summary Format"

This is a form that can serve a variety of needs. It can be used either to show costs or time. It can be used alone or in conjunction with the "Estimating Format." It can be used to capture overall total costs, or those expenses that will come from sources outside of the design firm, such as paint, carpeting, furniture, appliances, fabrics, etc. It is flexible; therefore, make sure to give it the appropriate title, depending upon its use, and also include any assumptions upon which calculations are based.

Project Plan and Budget

CLIENT

Name _____

Address (Meetings) _____

Phone _____

Address (Billing) _____

Phone _____

Cell _____

Fax _____

Other Contact Information _____

ESTIMATING FORMAT   ASSUMPTION: RATES ARE PER   ☐ HOUR   ☐ DAY   ☐ WEEK

	LABOR			
	Principal	**Lead Designer**	**Designer**	**Design Assistant**
RATES	$	$	$	$
Program Development				
Client Intake Meetings				
Site Conditions: Measurements and Notes				
Research				
Schematics				
Preliminary Color/Materials ("Mood") Boards				
Preliminary Budget/Schedule Estimates				
Program Presentation				
Revisions				
Miscellaneous				
Subtotal				
Design Development—Phase One—Schematics				
Site Plan Base Drawings				
Traffic Patterns				
Space/Layout Plans				
Schematic Plans and Preliminary Selections				
Walls				
Floors				
Ceilings				
Window Treatments				
Millwork				
Fixtures and Hardware				
Furniture				
Audio/Video				
Spa/Exercise Furnishings				
Linens, Rugs, Decorative Items				
Presentation/Sample Boards				
Budget/Schedule Estimates				
Schematics Presentation				
Revisions				
Miscellaneous				
Subtotal				

☐ Estimate Form for Client
☐ Preliminary Budget and Schedule
☐ Budget and Schedule Status Review

Date ——————————————
By ——————————————

PROJECT

Job Number ——————————————

Job Name ——————————————

Location ——————————————

Description ——————————————

ESTIMATE FACTORS			COST			SCHEDULE		
Total Labor	Materials	Misc.	Budget	To-Date	Balance	Allocated	To-Date	Balance

ESTIMATING FORMAT   ASSUMPTION: RATES ARE PER   ☐ HOUR   ☐ DAY   ☐ WEEK

	Principal	Lead Designer	Designer	Design Assistant
RATES	$	$	$	$
Design Development—Phase Two—Final				
Final Site Plan Base Drawings				
Final Traffic Patterns				
Final Space/Layout Plans				
Final Plans and Selections				
Walls				
Floors				
Ceilings				
Window Treatments				
Millwork				
Fixtures and Hardware				
Furniture				
Audio/Video				
Spa/Exercise Furnishings				
Linens, Rugs, Decorative Items				
Final Presentation/Sample Boards				
Final Budget/Schedule				
Final Design Development Presentation				
Revisions				
Miscellaneous				
Subtotal				
Contract Documents and Bids				
Bid Drawings and Specs				
Bid Review				
Client Review of Bids				
Revisions				
Vendor Selection and Contracts				
Miscellaneous				
Subtotal				
Project Implementation				
Purchasing—Stock Items				
Wall Fabrics/Finishes				
Flooring Material				
Ceiling Materials				
Window Treatments				
Fixtures and Hardware				
Furniture				
Audio/Video				
Spa/Exercise Furnishings				
Linens, Rugs, Decorative Items				
Storage/Shipping/Handling				
Miscellaneous				
Subtotal				

LABOR

ESTIMATE FACTORS			COST			SCHEDULE		
Total Labor	Materials	Misc.	Budget	To-Date	Balance	Allocated	To-Date	Balance

ESTIMATING FORMAT   ASSUMPTION: RATES ARE PER   ☐ HOUR   ☐ DAY   ☐ WEEK

	Principal	Lead Designer	Designer	Design Assistant
RATES	$	$	$	$
Fabrication—Custom Orders				
Wall Fabrics/Finishes				
Flooring Material				
Ceiling Materials				
Window Treatments				
Millwork				
Fixtures and Hardware				
Furniture				
Audio/Video/Security/Other Electronic				
Linens, Rugs, Decorative Items				
Storage/Shipping/Handling				
Miscellaneous				
Subtotal				
Construction—Site Supervision				
Scheduling				
Walls				
Floors				
Ceilings				
Miscellaneous				
Subtotal				
Installation—Site Supervision				
Wall Painting/Coverings				
Floor Treatments				
Ceiling Treatments				
Window Treatments				
Millwork				
Fixtures and Hardware				
Furniture				
Audio/Video/Security/Other Electronic				
Spa/Exercise Furnishings				
Linens, Rugs, Decorative Items				
Miscellaneous				
Subtotal				
Final Project Completion Items				
Walk Through and Punch List				
Supervision of Punch List Completion				
Miscellaneous				
Subtotal				
Project Total				

ESTIMATE FACTORS			COST			SCHEDULE		
Total Labor	Materials	Misc.	Budget	To-Date	Balance	Allocated	To-Date	Balance

SUMMARY FORMAT   ASSUMPTION: FOR SCHEDULING, TIME SHOWN IS IN   ☐ HOURS   ☐ DAYS   ☐ WEEKS

	Program Development	DD/1—Schematics	DD/2—Final	Contract Docs and Bids
Project Details				
Walls/Ceilings				
Paint				
Wallcoverings				
Mouldings				
Other				
Floors/Stairways				
Wood				
Ceramic				
Stone				
Carpeting				
Mouldings				
Other				
Window Treatments				
Shades/Blinds				
Louvers				
Drapery				
Valances				
Other				
Millwork				
Fixtures and Hardware				
Bath				
Kitchen				
Lighting				
Wall/Door				
Other				
Furniture				
Furniture—Purchase				
Furniture—Commission				
Furniture—Recondition/Special Finish				
Furniture—(Re)upholstery				
Audio/Video/Security/Other Electronic				
Spa/Exercise Furnishings				
Other Furnishings				
Linens				
Rugs				
Decorative Items (Objets d'art)				
Miscellaneous				
Travel				
Messengers				
Insurance				
Storage				
Shipping and Handling				
Project Total				

Purchasing Stock Items	Fabrication Custom Orders	Construction Site Supervision	Installation Site Supervision	Final Project Completion	Total

Proposal Form

FORM 4

Reputation, recommendations, astutely targeted marketing and self-promotion all play their roles in capturing a client's attention. A critical final deciding factor in the client's selection process is a clear, concise, and accurate proposal outlining the scope and schedule of work, cost of materials, and fees.

Clients often use proposals to compare estimates by several designers being considered for an assignment. The ability to turn around a professional document in a timely manner is useful in winning projects. Consider each proposal as your final chance to persuade the client to hire you. It is concrete evidence of your creative and organizational skills. While it is not a promotional brochure, it is representative of your aesthetic sensibility; therefore, use your professional letterhead or a modified version of it, make sure it reads easily to a layperson, and that it is impeccably organized. Most important of all, respond directly to the client's request. Address all of the issues the client has raised up to this point proving that you understand his or her needs and preferences and can respond with ideas and recommendations that are creative and appropriate.

If information provided by the client is vague or incomplete, you are in a situation where you are expected to provide a "ballpark" proposal that gives the client an idea of approximately how much a project might cost. Such a proposal winnows out the designers to be considered seriously, at which point a more extensive proposal is usually requested. While ballpark proposals may be limited in detail, they should include a description of what is known about the assignment, approximate fee amounts, schedule, and expense policy. Schedules and specific terms can be generalized, but do clearly state that this is a preliminary proposal and that, if accepted, additional information reflecting updated specifications will be forthcoming. It is especially necessary to include a statement indicating that the proposal is predicated on available information and that additional information and changes will likely have an impact on the project's final cost and schedule.

The most important pieces of information to include in a proposal are: (1) the scope of work, i.e., an understanding of the assignment by means of a brief description; (2) your methodology, or an outline of your working process, including a list of the different trades to be involved; (3) fees and expense policy (billables, markups, schedule of billings, etc.); (4) time schedule; and (5) basic terms (changes, termination, payment schedule, etc.). Proposals can be standardized, such as the example shown in form 2, or they may be written in composition style in a letter. Generally, design professionals use their own standard formats with a personal cover letter, which is much like an "executive summary." This summary highlights the salient points of the scope of work, approximate overall fee or fee range and proposed completion date, along with a personal expression of the designer's interest in the project and desire to work with the prospective client.

When working with a new client, particularly on a project that is extensive or not well defined, it is best to draw up a Standard Contract, such as Form 29 or Form 30 or the contracts available from the American Society of Interior Designers.

Filling In the Form

Provide all of the client information indicated, the date of the proposal, who is writing it ("By"), and give the project an easily identifiable name, and its location. You may already have all this information if you have opened a job number and job information sheet for this project. In which case, it is simple to copy and paste this area. In the "Fee Information" section, specify how the design fee is being calculated. Under "Scope of Work," summarize the work to be done, including overall dimensions, number of rooms, and enough information to indicate the level of complexity of the proposed project.

In the "Work Plan" area, indicate costs and/or time for each phase of the proposed project. Design services are customarily billed on a phase-by-phase basis. In the event this is a flat-fee project, you may still want to break out the design fee in these phases. In case the project is canceled, it will be easier to collect the appropriate fee for completed work phases. For each relevant item under the "Work Plan – Detail" fill in any special notes, such as known brand names to be used, known or preferred vendors, or any other specific indicators that help identify the source of the costs. Under "Budget," fill in the expected cost of each item, (wherever known, include shipping, handling, and taxes— and indicate whether these items are included in the budget amount). For "Schedule," either indicate start and finish dates or expected length of time without start/finish dates. Total the "Budget" column and show either overall project start and finish dates or the total amount of work time the project will require, regardless of start and finish dates.

On the "Terms and Conditions" page, fill in or delete all of the blanks.

Using the Form

It is possible to use this form as a summary proposal for the entire space being designed and the total expenses, or it may be used to detail the work to be done space by space, particularly in residential projects. In this way, clients who may find themselves needing to limit their budget, may decide to have a couple of rooms designed rather than cancel the whole project. For commercial projects where rooms are designed in multiples (such as hotel rooms or identical offices), one form may be used for each kind of room that will be replicated and separate proposal forms may be used for unique rooms/spaces (e.g., the lobby, restaurants, meeting rooms, etc.).

In the case of a well defined, small-scale project, the proposal can be written so that if you are selected to do the job and the proposal needs no adjustments (assuming both the client and the designer are in complete agreement about the extent of the work to be done and its execution), the proposal can be signed by both parties and become a letter of agreement. To do this, make sure that there is a statement preceding the signature line to the effect that "If the content of this proposal meets with your (the client's) approval, in order to authorize (designer) to proceed with the assignment, please sign and date below and return a copy of this agreement to (the designer)." Additionally, the letter of agreement must contain both the client's and the designer's names in print and signature form, addresses and the signing date, as well as specific information about the number of preliminary sketches, billing for extras and changes, payment for materials, fixtures and furnishings, payment of sales tax, storage and transportation, liability, and a termination fee.

In a competitive situation, price is not always the sole determining factor in winning a project. It is better to be within the range of given price quotes than to be dramatically lower or higher. An extreme departure from the general range of price quotes signals a lack of understanding of the assignment, desperation, or indifference.

Proposal Form

Date _____

By _____

CLIENT INFORMATION

Name _____

Address (Meetings) _____

Phone _____

Address (Billing) _____

Phone _____

Cell _____

Fax _____

Other Contact Information _____

PROJECT

Name _____

Location _____

FEE INFORMATION

Flat Fee _____

Percentage (Square Feet) (Price of Goods) _____

Hourly Rates _____

SCOPE OF WORK

_____

_____

_____

_____

_____

_____

WORK PLAN SCHEDULE

	START-END DATES	BUDGET	TOTAL TIME
Program Development			
Design Development—Phase One—Schematics			
Design Development—Phase Two—Final			
Contract Documents and Bids			
Project Implementation			
Construction—Site Supervision			
Installation—Site Supervision			
Final Project Completion Items			

WORK PLAN—DETAIL

	NOTES	BUDGET	TOTAL TIME
Walls/Ceilings			
Painting			
Painting—Special			
Wallcoverings			
Mouldings			
Other			
Floors/Stairways			
Wood			
Ceramic			
Stone			
Carpeting			
Mouldings			
Other			
Window Treatments			
Shades/Blinds			
Louvers			
Drapery			
Valances			
Other			
Millwork			
Fixtures and Hardware			
Bath			
Kitchen			
Lighting			
Wall/Door			
Other			
Furniture			
Furniture—Purchase			
Furniture—Commission			
Furniture—Recondition/Special Finish			
Furniture—(Re)upholstery			
Audio/Video/Security/Other Electronic			
Spa/Exercise Furnishings			
Other Furnishings			
Linens			
Rugs			
Decorative Items			

	NOTES	BUDGET	TOTAL TIME
Miscellaneous			
Travel			
Messengers			
Insurance			
Storage			
Shipping and Handling			
Other			
TOTAL			

All information in this proposal is subject to the Terms and Conditions listed below.

TERMS AND CONDITIONS

Change Orders   Work change orders will be issued for additional work and changes requested after approval of plans or commencement of work. WCOs include a description of the change/addition requested, estimated additional costs, and changes to work schedules/project completion. Client's signature is required on WCOs to proceed with changes/additions.

Billable Items   In addition to the fees and costs estimated herein, costs incurred for insurance, storage, messengers, and shipping and handling are billable (at cost, with a markup of ____%). Wherever applicable, state and local sales taxes will be included in Billable Items.

Purchasing   All purchases made on client's behalf will be billed to client. In all cases, such prices will reflect a (discount) (markup) of ____%. Charges for sales tax, insurance, storage, and shipping and handling are additional to the price of each purchase. In the event client purchases materials, services, or any items other than those specified by the designer, the designer is not liable for the cost, quality, workmanship, condition, or appearance of such items.

Deposits   A 50 percent deposit is required on all orders made on behalf of the client, prior to the placement of such orders. The balance is due upon delivery. Any items canceled by the client more than 5 business days after designer has received client's approval to purchase will be billed at ____ percent of the price of the item.

Custom Orders   Client is fully responsible for paying all costs for custom orders canceled by client once manufacturing has started. The cost of special orders that are canceled by client following approval to purchase is fully dependent upon the terms and conditions put forth by the manufacturer, supplier, or vendor of the item(s).

Warranty   Designer makes no additional warranty, guarantee, or any other assurances, other than those provided by manufacturers, suppliers, or vendors of products and/or services.

Other Contracts   Designer is not responsible for any contracts that the client enters into directly with contractors, suppliers, manufacturers, or vendors for goods and/or services, whether or not such sources are recommended by the designer.

Purchase Orders   Designer is responsible for those purchase orders issued directly by designer. Client is fully responsible for all purchase orders issued by client. Responsibility includes, but is not limited to, errors, omissions, pricing, and scheduling.

Schedule of Payment   Hourly Rate: Regular billing periods (bimonthly, monthly) based on hours consumed or periodic approval points. Square Footage: Billing may be ____ percent upon project commencement, ____ percent following completion of design development, ____ percent upon completion of punch list items. Flat Fee: ____ percent of fee payable upon signing of contract, ____ percent upon approval of final design development phase, ____ percent upon completion of punch list items.

Termination Policy   Client and Designer may terminate project based upon mutually agreeable terms to be determined in writing, either prior to signing of this proposal or within the final Client-Designer Contract.

Terms of Proposal   The information contained in this proposal is valid for 30 days. Proposals approved and signed by the Client are binding upon the Designer and Client beginning on the date of Client's signature.

If the information in this Proposal meets with Client's approval, Client's signature below authorizes Designer to begin work. Kindly return a signed copy of this Proposal/Agreement to Designer's office.

Designer Signature _____   Print Designer Name _____   Date _____

Client Signature _____   Print Client Name _____   Date _____

Comprehensive Production Schedule

Interior design is a deadline driven profession that requires thoughtful planning and a keen understanding of logistics. Design managers are responsible for coordinating the activities of their staff, a variety of different trades, and the delivery of goods in order to complete assignments on time. In order to calculate the blocks of time needed to accomplish different tasks and make sure that the right people and resources are in place to meet deadlines, the designer should work out a production schedule as soon as possible after receiving the details of a new assignment; this exercise should already have been done during project estimating. A common practice is to calculate schedules by working backward from the final due date for completing the assignment. If the assignment is not driven by a final delivery date, the designer has the luxury of determining scheduling step-by-step starting at the beginning of the design process.

Two production schedule forms are offered in this section. The first gives an overall view of all the projects in the studio. It is meant to highlight top-level information, such as the timing of project phases, major event dates, personnel and special notes, if needed. Its special usefulness to a design manager is that it immediately reveals overlaps in the use of staff and other resources, particularly for important meetings, site or delivery supervision, and other critical events.

The second form is designed for individual project use. It lists the major phases of a project and within each phase the range of items that may be required. Please note that if your projects are less extensive (or more) that you may easily remove (or add) items that are irrelevant to your projects. These forms are customizable in order to be most useful for individual designers.

Filling In the Form (Form One—"All Projects")

List all the active jobs in the studio. You may wish to include those that are being marketed, but not yet contracted, to anticipate possible conflicts in staff scheduling and thereby adjusting start dates on new projects. List the project phases, their start and end dates, and the key due dates for each phase. List the names of the staff members working within each phase, as well as the consultants and the vendors (under "Sources"). In the "Notes" area, highlight any items that need special attention.

Using the Form

Keep the "All Projects" schedule up to date, if project phases shift, and remove old information. This form is not a record of past events; it is a living document that needs continual updating. It is the best way to prevent double-booking important meetings and avoid conflicts in scheduling staff, freelancers, and other resources.

Interior design is not a linear activity—phases and activities will overlap, particularly during implementation.

Charts and graphs are a simple visual aid to help track schedules. It is relatively easy to convert data from spreadsheet format to charts and graphs in Excel. Once you are familiar with this feature, track staff overlaps by using the bar graph feature. A more sophisticated visual tracking system is available in Microsoft Project. The application is not particularly intuitive, but once you become familiar with its features (and quirks), it does have several useful features. First of all, it presents scheduling data in Gantt and PERT chart formats. The Gantt chart presents your list of activities along with the scheduled start and completion dates via a horizontal bar chart. It also includes resource usage whereby you list the personnel required for each activity, their rates, and the percentage of time they will spend on each activity. It offers a wide variety of report views, some of which are standard, some of which can be customized. A simple calendar program may also serve to highlight project phases, due dates, and the use of personnel, but generally, there is limited space to provide all of this information at one time.

Filling In the Form (Form Two— "Individual Projects")

Fill in the "Job Name" and "Job Number" areas. List start and end dates under "Schedule." Include dates of presentations and deliverables under "Due Dates." Name the person who is responsible for providing the key deliverables ("By") and to whom ("To"), if applicable. Insert the date of completion under "Completed."

Using the Form

It is very important to either have experience or else thoroughly research the amount of lead time needed to manufacture custom-made items such as movable furniture, millwork, rugs and carpets, draperies, lighting, and special items like hardware, metalwork, and so on. These are the elements that the designer is dependent upon others to furnish. Lead time to acquire stock items (i.e., furniture, rugs, and other furnishings that are available from manufacturers' inventory) also needs to be considered, since availability and shipping times may vary. While it may be possible to rush orders, the added cost can be excessive.

The Individual Projects Production Schedule could be shared with the client, supplementing the Project Status Report (form 19). It provides baseline scheduling information that can be referenced when the client suggests changes that affect delivery dates.

Sample Time Sheet Code

Phase Codes	Phases	Activity Codes	Activities	Detail Codes	Detail Items
1	Program Development	C	Client Relations (Meetings/ Presentations)	00	Not a Detail Item
2	Design Development— Phase One (Schematic)	T	Travel	01	Walls/Ceilings
3	Design Development— Phase Two (Final)	B	Budget/Schedule/ Proposal	02	Floors/Stairways
4	Contract Documents and Bids	S	Site Visit/Inspection/ Supervision	03	Window Treatments
5	Project Implementation	R	Research	04	Millwork
6	Project Completion	D	Designing/Drawing	05	Fixtures and Hardware
		P	Presentation Drawing	06	Furniture
		M	Model Building	07	Audio/Video/Security/ Other Electronic
		W	Spec Writing and Drawing	08	Spa/Exercise Furnishings
		X	Spec Review and Selection	09	Other Furnishings
		Y	Shopping/Purchasing		
		Z	Coordination/Administration/ Meetings		

Sample Comprehensive Production Schedule

ALL PROJECTS

Job Name		Start Program Development	DD/Phase One	DD/Phase Two	Contract Docs and Bids	Fabrication—Custom Orders	Construction—Site Supervision	Purchasing Stock Items	Installation—Site Supervision	Final Project Completion
Blue Oyster —Bar	Dates	1-Sep	15-Oct	1-Dec	15-Jan	1-Feb	15-Feb	15-Mar	1-May	15-Jun
	Staff	SB (25%)	SB (25%)	SB (25%)	SB (25%)	SB (25%)	SB (25%)	EB (50%)	SB (25%)	
	F/L	AL (50%)	AL (50%)	AL (50%)	AL (50%)	AL (50%)	AL (50%)	AL (25%)	AL (25%)	
Blue Oyster —Dining Room	Dates	1-Sep	15-Oct	1-Dec	15-Jan	1-Feb	15-Feb	15-Mar	1-May	15-Jun
	Staff	SB (25%)	SB (25%)	SB (25%)	SB (25%)	SB (25%)	SB (25%)	EB (50%)	SB (25%)	
	Staff	NB (30%)	NB (30%)	NB (30%)	NB (30%)	NB (30%)	NB (30%)	NB (30%)	NB (30%)	
	F/L	AL (50%)	AL (50%)	AL (50%)	AL (50%)	AL (50%)	AL (50%)	AL (25%)	AL (25%)	
Blue Oyster —Gift Shop	Dates	1-Dec	15-Dec	1-Feb	1-Mar	15-Mar	1-Apr	1-Apr	1-May	15-Jun
	F/L	CD (100%)	CD (100%)	CD (100%)	CD (100%)	CD (100%)	CD (50%)	CD (50%)	CD (100%)	
Cannes House	Dates	15-Mar	15-Apr	15-Jun	15-Jul	1-Aug	15-Aug	1-Sep	1-Dec	15-Jan
	Staff	ZD (50%)	ZD (50%)	ZD (50%)	ZD (50%)	ZD (50%)	ZD (50J%)	EB (50%)	ZD (50%)	
	F/L	AL (25%)	AL (25%)	AL (25%)	AL (50%)	AL (100%)	AL (100%)	AL (50%)	AL (50%)	
Park Street Apartment	Dates	1-May	15-Jun	15-Aug	1-Sep	15-Sep	1-Oct	1-Nov	1-Dec	21-Dec
	Staff	SB (25%)	SB (25%)	SB (25%)	SB (25%)	NB (30%)	NB (30%)	EB (50%)	SB (25%)	
	Staff	NB (30%)								
	F/L									
Aspen Cabin	Dates									
	Staff	ZD (50%)	ZD (50%)	ZD (50%)	ZD (50%)			ZD (50%)	ZD (50%)	
Appleby's Farm Store	Dates									
	Staff									
	F/L									
	F/L									

Comprehensive Production Schedule

ALL PROJECTS

Job Name	Phase	Key Dates	Staff	Sources	Notes

INDIVIDUAL PROJECTS

CLIENT

Name _____

PROJECT

Job Name _____

Location _____

Job Number _____

Phase/Item	Schedule	Due Dates	By	To	Completed
Program Development					
Client Intake Meetings					
Site Conditions: Measurements and Notes					
Research					
Preliminary Color/Materials ("Mood") Boards					
Preliminary Budget/Schedule Estimates					
Program Presentation					
Revisions					
Client Sign-Off					
Design Development—Phase One—Schematics					
Site Plan Base Drawings					
Traffic Patterns					
Space/Layout Plans					
Preliminary Plans and Selections					
Walls					
Floors					
Ceilings					
Window Treatments					
Millwork					
Fixtures and Hardware					
Furniture					
Audio/Video					
Spa/Exercise Furnishings					
Linens, Rugs, Decorative Items					
Presentation/Sample Boards					
Budget/Schedule Estimates					
Design Development Presentation					
Revisions					
Client Sign-Off					

Phase/Item	Schedule	Due Dates	By	To	Completed
Design Development—Phase Two—Final					
Final Site Plan Base Drawings					
Final Traffice Patterns					
Final Space/Layout Plans					
Final Plans and Selections					
Walls					
Floors					
Ceilings					
Window Treatments					
Millwork					
Fixtures and Hardware					
Furniture					
Audio/Video					
Spa/Exercise Furnishings					
Linens, Rugs, Decorative Items					
Final Presentation/Sample Boards					
Final Budget/Schedule					
Final Design Development Presentation					
Revisions					
Client Sign-Off					
Contract Documents and Bids					
Bid Drawings and Specs					
Bid Review					
Client Review of Bids					
Revisions					
Client Sign-Off					
Vendor Selection and Contract Documents					
Project Implementation					
Purchasing—Stock Items					
Wall Fabrics/Finishes					
Flooring Material					
Ceiling Materials					
Window Treatments					
Fixtures and Hardware					
Furniture					
Audio/Video					
Spa/Exercise Furnishings					
Linens, Rugs, Decorative Items					
Storage/Shipping/Handling					
Miscellaneous					

Phase/Item	Schedule	Due Dates	By	To	Completed
Fabrication—Custom Orders					
Wall Fabrics/Finishes					
Flooring Material					
Ceiling Materials					
Window Treatments					
Millwork					
Fixtures and Hardware					
Furniture					
Audio/Video/Security/Other Electronic					
Linens, Rugs, Decorative Items					
Storage/Shipping/Handling					
Miscellaneous					
Construction—Site Supervision					
Scheduling					
Walls					
Floors					
Ceilings					
Miscellaneous					
Installation—Site Supervision					
Custom Wall Painting/Coverings					
Custom Floor Treatments					
Custom Ceiling Treatments					
Custom Window Treatments					
Millwork					
Fixtures and Hardware					
Furniture					
Audio/Video/Security/Other Electronic					
Spa/Exercise Furnishings					
Linens, Rugs, Decorative Items					
Miscellaneous					
Final Project Completion Items					
Walk-Through and Punch List					
Supervision of Punch List Completion					
Client Sign-Off					

Time Sheet

Regardless of whether a project is billed on a flat fee (percentage of cost or square footage) or an hourly rate basis, it is essential to know exactly how much time is spent by all staff members on every project. Additionally, it is useful to know how nonbillable time is being used. Naturally, it is important to have an accurate record for jobs billed by the hour, mostly to ensure that all billable time is reimbursed, and partly in the event that the client requests an audit of time-keeping records. However, this is more likely to be a requirement of institutional and governmental, rather than private, clients.

Time records should also be kept on projects that are billed on a nonhourly basis. A flat fee, whether based on a percentage of the cost of the project, a commission on purchases, or a square-foot rate, has to cover at least the amount of time to be spent on a project, with a markup to include profit and overhead expenses. (Non-billable costs such as rent, utilities, insurance, and other overhead items are discussed in the Job Sheet chapter.) To approximate the time to be spent on a project, the interior designer needs to think the assignment through all of its stages, its scope of work and complexity, and what, if any, kinds of outside services will be required, such as lighting, audio/video, or security consultants. Also, it is good to take into account the nature of the client—is it known to conduct numerous and lengthy meetings, does it require many sketches, does it sign off on designs in a timely manner, does it tend to request changes in midstream? Naturally, there are other factors in determining prices. Factors such as site conditions—will the piano be brought up in a freight elevator, or will it have to be lifted in through an exterior window by a crane? Also, the site's location—will site supervision incur extensive travel expenses? Is there potential exposure for the project and possible spin-offs? This may occur when designing a major company's corporate headquarters or the prototype for a franchise that may require interior design for nine other locations.

Time is the variable in determining fees and the most critical key to profitability on a flat-fee-based assignment. The more exact the understanding is of the technical aspects and client contact required, the more accurate the estimation of the time required. As a safety device, many interior designers customarily add 15 percent to whatever number of hours they estimate will be needed to complete the assignment; this is also called a contingency factor.

Filling In the Form

Each staff member fills in his name, the current month, dates covered by the time sheet (usually covering a week's activities), and the year. Fill in the "Project Number" column so that whoever is posting time sheets to job sheets does not have to refer to the Jobs Index every time a job name appears. Mid- to large-scale interior design firms now set up these tracking documents on their Intranets and can automate the transfer of data from time sheets to job sheets. You could also set up job sheets for non-project types of activities, to capture time spent on general administration, maintenance, sick days, etc.

Fill in the "Project Name" as listed on the Jobs Index. Indicate the day of the week or date under "Date." Specify activities using codes under the headings of "Phase Code," "Activity Code," and "Detail Code." Indicate the number of regular hours worked on each job every day. Fill in the number of hours that were overtime under "OT." It is important to note the "Total Billable" time, because project agreements may vary with regard to which activities are billable and which are not. The "Notes" area is useful for additional comments.

The "Totals" row is the place to capture the total amount of regular and overtime hours spent. You can also add "Subtotals" lines for each day of the week. The "Notes" column can be used to indicate the percentage of billable versus nonbillable hours spent, as shown in the sample form. Or it can be used to show other calculations, such as regular versus overtime hours, marketing versus project time, or other kinds of staff time information that the interior design firm would like to track.

The staff or project supervisor should sign or initial the "Approved" box. Whoever is responsible for transferring time sheet information to job sheets should indicate the posting date next to "Date Posted."

Using the Form

The coding system shown here is a suggested format that follows the system suggested throughout the business forms part of this book, including the estimate and job sheet forms. You may decide to either simplify, show greater detail, or use other coding symbols of your choice.

The advantage of this kind of breakout of phases, activities, and details in separate columns is that, in Excel, you can sort information by columns and analyze staff members' time spent on various activities.

For the most part, interior design firm employees do not get paid overtime. The reason you should track it anyway is that on hourly jobs, while you are billing the total time worked (regardless of whether it is regular or overtime), you are incurring additional costs for staff that is working overtime. These costs include overhead items, such as utilities, and variable costs, such as food and transportation for late-night work sessions. Knowing how much overtime is incurred is also helpful in determining if a staff person may be entitled to some additional time off, or "comp" time, particularly if the overtime is incurred to meet client demands rather than for poor working habits.

Everyone who is required to fill out a time sheet—and for the sake of billing, principals and other senior personnel need to be accountable—should fill out their time sheet daily. It is often hard to remember exactly how much time is spent on specific activities when the firm is busy and people are rushing to get work done.

Time sheets should be checked and signed by project leads or senior designers, as appropriate to the management style of your firm. Principals and senior staff usually turn over their time sheets directly to the person who does the posting.

Time sheets should be posted weekly, so that no more than a few days are needed to prepare billing when an assignment is complete or ready for the next phase of billing.

Also, some clients like to get weekly time accounts of their project's activities.

Sample Time Sheet

Name   Natalie Jaye
Month   12
Dates   1–7
Year   2002

Phase Codes	Phases	Activity Codes	Activities	Detail Codes	Detail Items
1	Program Development	C	Client Relations (Meetings/Presentations)	00	Not a Detail Item
2	Design Development—Phase One (Schematic)	T	Travel	01	Walls/Ceilings
3	Design Development—Phase Two (Final)	B	Budget/Schedule/Proposal	02	Floors/Stairways
4	Contract Documents and Bids	S	Site Visit/Inspection/Supervision	03	Window Treatments
5	Project Implementation	R	Research	04	Millwork
6	Project Completion	D	Designing/Drawing	05	Fixtures and Hardware
		P	Presentation Drawing	06	Furniture
		M	Model Building	07	Audio/Video/Security/Other Electronic
		W	Spec Writing and Drawing	08	Spa/Exercise Furnishings
		X	Spec Review and Selection	09	Other Furnishings
		Y	Shopping/Purchasing	10	Meetings
		Z	Coordination/Administration/Meetings		

							Time		Total	
Project Number	Project Name		Date	Phase Code	Activity Code	Detail Code	Reg	OT	Billable	Notes
C01-TCN-1A	Blue Oyster Restaurant—Bar		Mon	1	C	00	2		0	
C01-TCN-1A	Blue Oyster Restaurant—Bar			1	C	10	3		3	
C01-TCN-1A	Blue Oyster Restaurant—Bar			1	B	00	2		0	
C01-BGS-1	Appleby's Farm Store			PM	C	10	1	1	0	Internal Meeting—Plan Presentation
	Subtotal						8	1	3	
C01-TCN-1B	Blue Oyster Restaurant—Dining Room		Tues	3	D	01	2		2	
C01-TCN-1B	Blue Oyster Restaurant—Dining Room					02	2		2	
C01-TCN-1B	Blue Oyster Restaurant—Dining Room					03	1		1	
C01-TCN-1B	Blue Oyster Restaurant—Dining Room					04	3		3	
	Subtotal						8	0	8	
C01-TCN-1A	Blue Oyster Restaurant—Bar		Wed	1	S	00	2		2	
C01-BGS-1	Appleby's Farm Store			PM	P	00	3		0	
	Nonbillable			EA			3		0	Dentist Appointment
	Subtotal						8	0	2	
	Nonbillable		Thurs	SK			8	0	0	
C01-TCN-1A	Blue Oyster Restaurant—Bar		Fri	2	D	01	4		4	
C01-TCN-1A	Blue Oyster Restaurant—Bar					02	4		4	
	Subtotal						8	0	8	
			Sat							
			Sun							
	Totals						32	1	21 131%	

Approved _____

Date Posted _____

Nonbillable Codes	
General Administration	GA
Maintenance	MN
Promotion/Marketing	PM
Holidays	HD
Sick Days	SK
Excused Absences (Jury Duty, Bereavement, etc.)	EA

Time Sheet

Name _____

Month _____

Dates _____

Year _____

Project Number	Project Name	Date	Phase Code	Activity Code	Detail Code	Time Reg	OT	Total Billable	Notes
Totals									

Approved _____

Date Posted _____

Creative Log

Beginning with the program development phase of a project and carrying well through design development, it is customary to begin searching for examples of the elements that will appear in and/or influence the design of the project. These elements may be found in books, magazines, catalogs, and other publications. Such elements also include actual samples, swatches and chips of materials, and finishes. Any element that serves as inspiration for a project is useful to collect. The challenge is in finding them when you need them. It may not be possible to throw everything into a clipping file. A sample chair will not fit well into a file folder.

Here is a form that simplifies the task of locating creative elements when you need them, for example to put together a mood board for color selections or a style board showing recommended styles of movable furniture and ceiling and floor mouldings. Illustrating these concepts may be done with photographs, drawings, models, or actual samples.

Filling In the Form

Each project should have its own Creative Log. Under "Project," fill in the "Job Name," "Location," and "Job Number" of the project. Under "Creative Source Materials," fill in the item number—keep to a very simple numbering system if you decide to use anything other than straightforward descending numbers, starting with 1. Jot down a brief "Description" or a name of the item and what "Room" or space in which it will be located. Under "Location," indicate where the item can be found. If it is in a reference book in the library that cannot be checked out—specify the library name, the book's name and catalog number. If the material is a magazine clipping or catalog sheet that is being kept in a project file folder/binder, provide the name and location of the folder/binder. If the item is a full scale sample that is being stored, identify

the storage facility, its location and if it's a large storage facility, a more specific description of where the item is located.

Using the Form

Interior designers are constantly seeking inspiration and creative ideas, and sources can come from just about anywhere. It is a very common practice to collect clippings, samples, swatches, chips, and traditional design materials, but also to gather nontraditional sources of inspiration. These may be from nature, or they may be man-made (artwork, manufactured goods, remnants of industrial materials); whatever it is that gives an interior designer a fresh way to express his and his client's vision is valuable.

If it is your practice to collect such materials extensively, you might consider having a Creative Log that is not necessarily project-specific, but based on a thematic idea. So, if you are interested in a variety of themes, such as Art Deco, neo-Classical, and ultra-Modern materials and furnishings, you would have a Creative Log for each of these styles.

Creative Log

CLIENT

Name

PROJECT

Job Name

Location

Job Number

CREATIVE SOURCE MATERIALS

Item Number	Description	Room	Location

Initial Survey

At the beginning of the Program Development Phase of every interior design project, one of the earliest and most important tasks is to obtain an accurate picture of the site to be designed. If the project is to provide designs for an existing space for which accurate base plan drawings don't exist, then a complete set of plans and elevations will have to be drawn up for the assigned areas. Even if drawings do exist, it is important to verify the information in the drawings. It is possible that alterations may have occurred since the original plans were drawn up of which the client is not aware. It is the responsibility of the interior designer to make sure that he or she is working with correct dimensions and is aware of site conditions that may affect the proposed work.

If the assignment is a new construction or a renovation being led either by an architect or a contractor, then the interior designer is dependent upon the architect or contractor to provide as complete a set of plans as possible. Given even this circumstance, it is important for the interior consultant to keep in close contact with whoever is developing plans to make sure she is in the loop about changes.

Filling In the Form

Start with the "Client Name," then the project information, including the project's name, its location, and the job number.

Under "Site Dimensions and Conditions," provide all the necessary information about the site and its spaces, such as measurements and special and noteworthy conditions. Indicate the room and the item being detailed (e.g., floor plan, windows, staircase railing, etc.). Measurements should always be in drawing form; therefore a set of drawings should be given an identifying number and listed here. Photographs are useful as well and should be included here. All notations about the condition of the

space and any special features can be put under "Notes." Include the "Date" of the entry being made and the initials of the person responsible for the information contained in the drawings, photos, and notes, under "By."

In the "Inventory" section, include a list of the items in the current design scheme that will stay on in the new plan. If the client wishes to keep certain furniture or window treatments or anything else, then it is necessary to be aware of exactly what they are, their dimensions and condition and other useful notes. Fill in the listed areas, as described in the "Site Dimensions and Conditions" section above.

Using the Form

The rule of thumb with all numbering systems is to keep them simple and easy to understand. One approach is to use the job number (or an abbreviated version of it, if it is long) with the addition of "sD" for site drawings and "sP" for site photographs, and start with number one and continue in order. For example, TCN-1A-sD1 stands for the Atlantis Group's Blue Oyster Restaurant, the Bar area, site drawing number 1.

The "Notes" area is the place to highlight things such as the existence of fine architectural details, or the pristine condition of the parquet floors, or the water damage you suspect under the wallpaper, and so on. For the "Inventory," also note what pieces will require refurbishing, reupholstering, new paint, and so on.

Initial Survey

CLIENT

Name_____

PROJECT

Job Name _____

Location _____

Job Number _____

SITE DIMENSIONS AND CONDITIONS

Room	Item	Drawing Number	Photograph Number	Notes

INVENTORY

Room	Item	Drawing Number	Photograph Number	Notes

Date _____

By _____

Project Drawings Log

The practice of interior design tends to breed vast amounts of paperwork and other free-floating materials. The bane of many interior designers is keeping their paperwork in order. One of the ways to keep projects organized is to have logs for various elements, such as sketches, designs, presentations, working or spec drawings of floor and ceiling plans, sections, elevations, and other details. Some of these elements will be stored in files on computer hard drives and/or portable media, such as disks; others will require physical filing and storage. The purpose of this log is to provide a quick reference to their location.

The Project Drawings Log is the record of the plans and design drawings developed by the interior designer for a project. It is particularly helpful when there are different designers working on different aspects of a project. Ultimately, a complete set of physical drawings should be assembled and bound for archiving purposes, along with a digital copy of all computer-generated drawings placed on a portable disk.

Filling In the Form

For all active projects that have a job number and a job sheet, open a Project Drawings Log. Fill in the client name, project name, project's location, and the project job number. Under "Room," identify the room or space that is the subject of the drawing. Note the general focus of the drawing under "Item." Note the phase in which the drawing was made—whether it was design development/preliminary, design development/final, or contract document for bidding. Use the drawing number you used on the drawing (see below for numbering schemes). Identify the location of the drawing (file/directory name or physical location), the date of the drawing, and include any special comments under "Notes."

Using the Form

Logs are only as useful as they are accurate and up-to-date. To ensure that these logs (and other studio records) are updated regularly, develop the habit, for yourself and your staff, of reserving about fifteen to twenty minutes at the end of each work day to update logs, file documents and drawings, and fill in time sheets and other project records. Another scenario is to allow ten minutes midday and ten minutes before quitting time for these tasks. The key to preventing paperwork chaos is regular and consistent record keeping.

The easiest elements to file and store are those created on the computer. Just the act of opening a document or file requires you to name it and decide where to store it on your computer, and in some instances to also save the document or file on either a portable or hard disk.

Files may be organized by industry types (residential, commercial, industrial, institutional, governmental) or, more specifically, by trades (private residences, housing developments, restaurants, hotels, retail stores, schools, hospitals, etc.). If your firm practices in a niche market, you may decide to use project or client names.

Interior design firms that make extensive use of computer-aided drafting and design (CADD) programs usually also have a separate file server that is used expressly to store or "back up" project materials on a regular basis. The basic rules of physical filing also apply to digital filing. Whatever system works best for you and is easiest for you to update is the one to use. When you do select a method, keep it consistent. Make sure all staff members are familiar with the system and use it.

To keep things simple, decide whether you want to keep all project-specific documents in one overall file or if you prefer to keep all similar documents in separate files. In other words, you can have one file for the Smith Residence, in which you can find all of the correspondence, contract, specs, drawings, etc. relating to this project. Or you can have separate folders for contracts, correspondence, drawings, etc., in which you can place different project materials. My personal preference is to keep all project materials in one file, with redundant files for documents like contracts and proposals. The reason for the second copy is that, while I find it easier to look for everything in one file that is related to a specific project, when I am writing a new proposal or contract, it is handy to be able to refer to my folder of existing contracts and proposals.

Developing nomenclature, or a naming system, for computer documents and files is easy and important. Decide what kind of names and sequences to use and stick to them. One approach is to use an abbreviated form of the project name that is on the Job Index. You may wish to identify document *types* by abbreviated name or code. For example, for the Smith Residence, you will have *text* documents: Smith_prpsl (proposal), Smith_cntrct (contract), and Smith_sr (status report). There will be *spreadsheet* documents: Smith_est (estimate), Smith_bdgt_v2 (budget, version 2), and Smith_wco (work change order). Design *drawing* files may be called: Smith_flpln (floor plan) and Smith_dr_elev (dining room, elevations).

In the event this is one of a series of jobs for the Smiths, a further identifier may be needed, such as Smith_Aspen_prpsl, Smith_Miami_bdgt, Smith_Miami_renov3_wco (renovation, number 3), or Smith_Miami_guesths_cntrct (guesthouse contract).

A different approach is to use project numbers instead of names. Project numbers may be less intuitive, but easier to keep consistent. For example, 01R-JTS03 (2001, residential, J. T. Smith, project number 3—J. T. Smith's Miami House) and 01R-JTS04 (J. T. Smith's Miami House, project number 4—J. T. Smith's Miami Guest House Addition).

Project Drawings Log

CLIENT

Name

PROJECT

Job Name

Location

Job Number

Room	Item	Phase	Drawing				Notes
			View	Number	Location	Date	

Contractor Log

In many instances, interior designers work with their own team of crafts and trades people. Often clients will select a designer who is known to have teams of workers who are excellent and/or unique in their trades. In this sense, interior designers act not only as creative directors, but also as general contractors. They are responsible for the selection of contractors, establishing secure contracts with them, and for supervising their work. The purpose of the Contractor Log is to have one place to look for the list of all of the contracts generated by a project.

This log is meant to be used only for items requiring construction, fabrication, and special custom treatment. This is not intended to be a list of purchases.

Filling In the Form

Fill in the client name, project name, project's location and the project job number. Indicate the trade or specific element for which the contractor is engaged under "Item." List the contractor's company name, and the name of the primary contact, including his or her phone/fax numbers. In the "Bid Documents" area, indicate what specs and drawings were provided (refer to the drawing number from the Project Drawings Log), and the date and number (if applicable) of the contract. Under "Pricing," list the "Purchase Order Number" and its total amount, if one was issued. List any work change order numbers and the final agreed price under "Invoice Total." For "Schedule," list the date the work was ordered (this could be the date of the purchase order), the delivery or due date, and when the work was received or completed.

Using the Form

While the Estimate Log (form 14) is a list of all of the bids received for the project, the

Contractor Log contains only the information about the selected contractors.

The Contractor Log is also a good reference for future projects that require similar items and services. It is also helpful to be able to look up pricing and scheduling for special custom items.

Contractor Log

CLIENT

Name_____

PROJECT

Job Name _____

Location _____

Job Number _____

| | | | BID DOCUMENTS | | |
Item	Contractor	Contact	Specs	Drawings	P.O. Number

PRICING			SCHEDULE			
P.O. Total	Change Orders	Invoice Total	Start	Inspection	Delivery/Due	Received/Completed

Purchase Log

The Purchase Log is the center for information about all purchases made on behalf of your client. It is a way to keep track of what's been ordered in a more comprehensive way than by purchase orders. While it does not have the level of detail about individual items that the purchase order will, it is a one-stop overview of necessary information.

It cannot be overstated that a regularly updated log that provides a quick view of what has been ordered, from whom, at what price, when, as well as its current status, is a great time-saver. Rather than sifting through piles of purchase orders, contracts, specs, and drawings, you can have the most salient information immediately at your fingertips. The key, of course, as with all tracking, logging, and accounting systems, is to input information on a regular basis and make sure to update changing elements. Another helpful detail is to devise a system of identification for project drawings, photos, swatches, and other samples. More detail is presented about identifying systems in the Project Drawings Log (form 9) and the Initial Survey (form 8).

Filling In the Form

Fill in the client name, project name, project's location, and the project job number. List the items ordered for each room. Fill in information about the vendor and order contact information; an account of the bidding information, including a very brief note of the specs, drawings, catalog information, and available samples or photos; pricing information, such as the purchase order number and amount, change orders, if any, and the final cost. A brief history of the order dates is provided to give an at-a-glance history of the original order date, due date, and actual completion or delivery date. If the item is completed, but the site is not yet ready and it has to be stored, fill in the storage information.

Using the Form

Throughout the business forms section of this book, we strongly recommend that forms are intended to be used either as is or customized for the reader's particular requirements and needs. It is easy to add, delete, and replace headings and items.

While the sample below is organized by rooms, it could just as easily be grouped by item types, such as furniture, window treatments, hardware, and so on, with a column added for "Location."

If it is necessary for you to track tax information, add a column for the tax amount, and the same for shipping, handling, and freight, if you prefer to see that separately. Here, this has been abbreviated, because the detail about this information is available on the purchase order issued for each item.

If the project fee is based upon either markups on purchases, or conversely, if there is a separate project fee and the designer's discount is meant to be passed through to the client, it might be a good idea to include a column showing these amounts or percentages.

On complex and large-scale projects, items may arrive at different times, and sometimes before the site is ready for them. In this case, it is necessary to arrange for storage, particularly with delicate and fragile items. Use this form to indicate where the items are being stored, when they arrived, and when they were picked up or shipped to the site. Additionally, it is useful to indicate the storage ticket number.

Sample Purchase Log

CLIENT
Name — Smith Residence
PROJECT
Job Name — Park Street Apartment
Location — 152 Park Street
Job Number — 102203-12

			Bid Documents				Pricing				Schedule			Storage			
Item	Vendor	Order Contact Info.	Specs	Drawings	Catalog Info.	Swatches/ Samples	P.O. Number	P.O. Total	Change Orders	Invoice Total	Order Date	Delivery/ Due	Received/ Completed	Location	Ticket Number	In	Out
Dining Room																	
Wall Covering	Schlumberfest	Alex Bolton 245-3245	16 rolls; #D560-GN	no		#S12	247	$1,589.50	no	$1,589.50	19-Feb	12-Apr	15-Apr	AFC Storage	SB152	17-Apr	15-Jun
Window Louvers	Orleans Window Co.	Bud Casper 313-222-5876	Custom; Spec#44	#D15-17		no	251	$5,799.00	no	$5,799.00	19-Feb	29-Apr	27-Apr	AFC Storage	SB153	29-Apr	15-Jun
Window Drapes	Baxter Drapes	Sally Bea 277-4500	Custom; Spec#37	#D22-23		S#13, 14	255	$3,200.00	CO#33	$4,500.00	19-Feb	29-Apr	15-May	no—sent to site			
Floor Treatment	ZZ Flooring	Max Abel 552-1301	#772+4 coats water-base polyurethane	no		Stain— S#27	280	$1,700.00	no	$1,700.00	1-May	22-Jun	22-Jun	NA			
Table	Bentleywood	Natalie J. 212-331-2903	42x104; #FXN337104	no		Photo #4	259	$6,770.00	no	$2,770.00	2-Feb	2-May	17-May	AFC Storage	SB191	17-May	14-Jul
Chairs	Bentleywood	Natalie J.	10; #FXN537999	no		Photo #5	259	$5,000.00	no	$5,000.00	2-Feb	2-May	17-May	AFC Storage	SB192	17-May	14-Jul
Sideboard	Bentleywood	Natalie J.	28x60; #FXN437060	no		Photo #6	259	$2,800.00	no	$2,800.00	2-Feb	2-May	29-May	AFC Storage	SB193	29-May	14-Jul
Area Rug	Arden Co.	Spencer Delanie 516-222-6799	Custom; Spec #37	#D45		S#17	262	$8,000.00	CO#37	$9,500.00	2-Feb	12-Jun	22-Jul	no—sent to site			

Purchase Log

CLIENT

Name

PROJECT

Job Name

Location

Job Number

			Bid Documents				Pricing		
Item	Vendor	Order Contact Info.	Specs	Drawings	Catalog Info.	Swatches/ Samples	P.O. Number	P.O. Total	Change Orders

Invoice Total	Schedule			Storage			
	Order Date	Delivery/ Due	Received/ Completed	Location	Ticket Number	In	Out

Final Survey

At the conclusion of every project, the interior designer should follow up with a last survey of the completed work. The purpose of this form is to briefly note the actual color, material, fabric selections, furnishings, and the list of contractors and vendors who worked on the job. It is not a detailed list of information about contractors and purchases (which can be found in the Contractor Log (form 10) and the Purchase Log (form 11).

Filling In the Form
Start with the client name, then the project information, including the project's name, its location, and the job number. Indicate who prepared the survey and the date it was done. List the rooms/spaces being detailed and the items and photographs, if applicable. Under "Material Specs," list any relevant, specific information that may be needed in the future—whether by the client or by the designer for repair or additional work. List the contractors' and vendors' names and enter any special notes that would be useful to have when the project is no longer fresh in the memory.

Using the Form
If the client wishes to buy additional paint or fabric, or retouch a scratched chair, the designer need not dig around stacks of purchase orders and look for detailed specs in old design drawing files. She can glance at this list and rattle off the paint manufacturer and color, or fabric supplier that was used and the fabric names, and so on.

Well-documented projects are a joy on several levels. There is less time spent fumbling around in the middle of a project looking for catalogs, swatches, documents, and drawings when the designer has a handy system of logs. Later, when it would be good to know which faux paint specialist was able to capture exactly the right patina for a panel, it is great to be able to quickly find his name and look up his contact information.

Final Survey

CLIENT   Date _____

Name _____   By _____

PROJECT

Job Name _____

Location _____

Job Number _____

Completed Site Survey

Room	Item	Photo Number	Colors	Materials	Other	Contractors	Other Vendors
				Material Specs			
____	____	____	____	____	____	____	____
____	____	____	____	____	____	____	____
____	____	____	____	____	____	____	____
____	____	____	____	____	____	____	____
____	____	____	____	____	____	____	____
____	____	____	____	____	____	____	____

Notes _____
_____
_____

Inventory

Room	Item	Photo Number	Colors	Materials	Other	Contractors	Other Vendors
				Material Specs			
____	____	____	____	____	____	____	____
____	____	____	____	____	____	____	____
____	____	____	____	____	____	____	____
____	____	____	____	____	____	____	____
____	____	____	____	____	____	____	____

Notes _____
_____
_____

Estimate Request Form

Whenever clients and designers prefer or need to have a variety of choices in the selection of sources and services (such as special effects painting, custom made furniture, drapery, carpeting and hardware, or any other kind of nonstandard items), it becomes necessary to request estimates from eligible and appropriate suppliers. To avoid confusion in evaluating these estimates, it is useful to provide the competing suppliers with exactly the same description of the work to be performed.

This form may also be used to back up a verbal quote when the supplier has been selected without preliminary screening. Although it is clearly a quotation of approximate fees and costs, the estimate request helps to control significant variations in vendor bids. As noted elsewhere in this book, the difference between an estimate and a bid is that an estimate is an approximate calculation, and a bid is a specific proposal whose numbers are binding, unless the specifications (specs) that led to the bid change.

Filling In the Form

Fill in the name of the client and project, the date, the job number, the name of the person requesting the estimate and her contact information. Fill in the name and address of the vendor/supplier. Fill in "Specifications/Description" as completely as possible; include as much information as necessary to accurately estimate the work to be done, or items to be purchased. Leave blank the spaces for estimate, subtotal, shipping/handling, tax, total and deposit required. These spaces are for the vendor/supplier. Fill in the delivery date. The vendor/supplier should sign the estimate, provide his contact information and include the date he signed the form.

Using the Form

When requesting an estimate, fill in the heading and the specifications/description part of the form; make as many copies as needed to distribute to the prospective bidders (plus one for your files, of course); and customize the vendor/supplier information individually as appropriate. This way it is certain that everyone has exactly the same instructions on which to base his or her estimates.

If necessary, send a copy of all the completed estimate requests to the client. Include information that will have an effect on the estimate, even though it is not included in the technical spec. For example, if there are complicated shipping requirements, or if the assignment will require the vendor to travel, or any other significant service or condition that is in addition to the basic work requested.

Keep this form in the job file. Jot down the selected estimate in the Summary of Costs area on the project's Job Sheet.

Estimate Request Form

Client _____   Date _____

Project Name _____   Request By _____

Project Number _____   Phone _____

Fax _____

E-mail _____

Supplier Name _____

Address _____

Phone _____

Fax _____

E-mail _____

SPECIFICATIONS/DESCRIPTION

Item Number	Detailed Item Description	Quantity	Unit Price	Total
_____	_____	_____	_____	_____
_____	_____	_____	_____	_____
_____	_____	_____	_____	_____
_____	_____	_____	_____	_____
_____	_____	_____	_____	_____
_____	_____	_____	_____	_____
_____	_____	_____	_____	_____
_____	_____	_____	_____	_____
_____	_____	_____	_____	_____

Delivery Date _____

Subtotal _____

Shipping/Handling _____

Tax _____

Supplier Signature

Total Estimate _____

Deposit Required _____

Print Supplier Name

Date _____

This is not a purchase order. The information contained in this form is to provide a basis for estimating the cost of the services requested. It is understood that while the estimated costs are approximate, final billing will be adjusted according to specific instructions provided in a purchase order or contract. Kindly fill in the information requested in the shaded area under Estimate, sign, date and return a copy of this form by _____.

Thank you.

Estimate Log

The Estimate Log is the place to list the results of the estimate requests made for the manufacture, fabrication, or purchase of special items for which there are no standard prices that can be found in catalogs and other product information sources. The Estimate Request (form 13) is recommended here to use in gathering multiple estimates.

Filling In the Form
Fill in the client name, the project information, including the project's name, its location, and the job number. List the date the estimate is being logged (it is a good idea to log these as soon as they come in), the name of the supplier (or contractor, vendor, etc.), the date the original Estimate Request (form 13) was sent. Include the item number from the Estimate Request form, the item's name and the quantity requested. From the supplier's response, list the unit price quoted, as well as the subtotal of all the items and any other costs such as shipping and handling and taxes, if applicable. Make sure to note if, and how much, of a deposit is required, as well as the delivery date quoted. In the last column, place a check mark next to the supplier that was chosen for the assignment.

Using the Form
When there are several contractors and vendors who can provide similar products and services, and the designer does not have a favorite to work with, it is time to solicit estimates. Or, if the designer is unfamiliar with the cost of a special item, it is very helpful to learn the possible ranges in price, quality, and delivery schedules of such items.

Certain clients, most often institutional, corporate, and governmental, will require a minimum number of bids for the manufacture and purchase of all project items. It is very important to be familiar with the guidelines provided by these clients as they are usually quite stringent in maintaining these standards and occasionally audit records, if they do not request such documentation to be included with the required package of project correspondence.

In the event similar items or services are required later for other projects, and a known contractor or vendor is no longer available, here is a quick way to look up possible alternatives or replacements.

Estimate Log

CLIENT

Name_____

PROJECT

Job Name _____

Location _____

Job Number _____

Log Date	Supplier Name	Estimate Request Date	Item Number	Item	Quantity	Unit Price	Subtotal	Shipping/ Handling	Tax	Total Estimate	Deposit	Delivery Date	Selected Vendor (✔)

Purchase Order

The Purchase Order serves as a written notice to vendors, manufacturers, and other suppliers, including special consultants, to begin work on a specific assignment or to deliver goods. Most vendors will not proceed without a written purchase order. For the interior design firm, the Purchase Order form is handy in two ways. First, it is a record of when goods and services have been ordered, from whom, pricing, and when the items are expected to be delivered or installed. Second, when invoices are received from vendors, purchase orders are useful for verifying precisely what was ordered and at what price. In the event the supplier is in error, either in her product or her invoice, the purchase order serves as verification of the original order.

As with job numbers and invoice numbers, purchase orders can be based on any numbering system, but then should continue in numerical order. While a purchase order index has not been included in this book, it is strongly recommended that one be created. The following sample is suggested:

Purchase Order Index

Date	Vendor	Project Number	Total	P.O. Number
12/2	Acme Flooring, Ltd.	102202-1A	$15,700	2002-001
12/5	Trimmings USA, Co.	091702-1	$2,500	2002-002
12/17	Stuart Upholstering, Inc.	102202-1A	$8,750	2002-003
12/19	Specialty Fabrics by Spencer, Ltd.	110402-3	$1,022	2002-004

Whether the designer uses preprinted purchase order forms or creates electronic copies, it is absolutely essential to have the following information included: the designer's business name, address, and contact information, including the name of the person generating the form, her telephone, fax, and e-mail address, if applicable. These details should be clearly visible on the form. Miniscule type, or almost any shade of gray, does not fax well.

It is also strongly suggested that the designer maintain both digital and hard copies of every purchase order. A simple three-ring binder is a handy place to keep these forms together. In large studios, it is useful to provide separate copies of purchase orders to the design team and the bookkeeping department. In some companies, designers forward requests for purchase orders to the bookkeeper; in others, they simply request a purchase order number, and then supply the client with a copy of the completed purchase order.

Filling In the Form

Fill in the project number, the purchase order number, and the date of the order. In the space under "To," fill in the name of the vendor, their address, the name of the contact or sales representative, and his or her phone, fax, and e-mail information. In the area marked "Schedule," fill in the date the item must be received or installed completely. In the space under "Specifications," fill in the item number as it pertains to this list, not to any other list or number—start always with "1" and continue numerically down the list. In the space for "Description," fill in either the name of the item or instructions for the work to be done or the goods to be delivered. It is necessary to communicate exactly what is being ordered. If a drawing is attached, make reference to that information here. If using a catalog to order from, give the specific item codes, catalog page numbers, descriptions, colors, finishes, and so on. Be absolutely precise. Include the quantity being ordered and unit price. List discount or special pricing information under "Other." Add shipping/handling charges, taxes, and deposit, if any. The subtotal, total, and balance due amounts should be computed. In the space for "Ship to," fill in the name and address where the goods are to be delivered and/or installed. In the space for "Bill to," fill in the name and address where the supplier is to send his or her invoice, if other than to the designer. Purchase orders should always be signed by the person authorized to issue them, and include her direct voice or fax contact information, so that the vendor can quickly communicate questions or concerns.

Using the Form

Purchase orders are legally binding documents. A vendor is entitled to full payment on an item she delivers that conforms to the specifications listed in the purchase order, even if the designer has made an error in the specifications. Further, if a purchase order is cancelled after the vendor has begun work on an item, even if the cancellation is fairly early, the vendor is still entitled to at least partial payment, if not full—depending upon the terms of the purchase negotiated with the vendor.

It is strongly recommended that the designer receive a sign-off or approval notice (in some form of writing) from the client for the proposed purchase *before* the designer issues a purchase order for the item. The client does not need to sign each purchase order; it may be sufficient to tie his approvals to project-phase written approvals or drawings showing the elements to be purchased.

Remember that both rush and overtime work usually incur additional costs. It is best to check what these will be in advance. Markups for rush and overtime orders can be as much as 100 percent and more. Overtime refers to work that must be completed outside of regular business hours, including weekends and holidays.

Provide drawings, sketches, swatches, as appropriate, to convey a full understanding of the order. The more precise and descriptive an order, the less chance there is of having to accept and pay for mistakes.

Most suppliers prefer to bill the designer directly and usually are not pleased to have to bill a third party. This scenario should be worked out in advance. The supplier will often require a deposit. In many instances, suppliers will also require bank and business references before committing to a large order with a designer (or client, if billing to the client).

If the designer uses Purchase Order forms to contract freelance artists, who create original paintings such as murals, it is important to remember to include information pertaining to copyright, future uses, and what, if any, rights the artist has to show the work in her portfolio or marketing materials. It is also necessary to obtain the freelancer's social security or federal identification number, so that Form 1099 can be completed (as required by the Internal Revenue Service for any payments of $600 or more to independent contractors).

Purchase Order

Job Number _____   P.O. Number _____

To: _____   Date _____

Vendor _____   Phone _____

Address _____   Fax _____

Contact _____   E-mail _____

Schedule   Delivery Due: Installation Completed:

SPECIFICATIONS

Item Number	Description	Quantity	Unit Price	Other	Total
_____	_____	_____	_____	_____	_____
_____	_____	_____	_____	_____	_____
_____	_____	_____	_____	_____	_____
_____	_____	_____	_____	_____	_____
_____	_____	_____	_____	_____	_____
_____	_____	_____	_____	_____	_____
_____	_____	_____	_____	_____	_____
_____	_____	_____	_____	_____	_____
_____	_____	_____	_____	_____	_____

NOTES _____

_____

_____

_____

_____

Subtotal _____

Shipping/Handling _____

Tax _____

Total _____

Deposit _____

Balance Due _____

Ship to: _____

_____

_____

Bill to: _____

_____

_____

Ordered by

Signature _____   Phone _____

Print name _____   Fax _____

Transmittal Form

The Transmittal Form is most frequently used as a kind of cover letter for enclosures, attachments, and any other kind of material being disseminated within or outside of the design firm. The advantage of having one multiuse transmittal form is that it eliminates the need to create individually written cover notes every time material needs to be circulated. Also, the information on the form is comprehensive, thereby uniformly communicating the necessary facts about the accompanying items. These forms may be printed in hard copy on the designer's letterhead or kept as a digital document that is generated as needed. Make sure your firm's name, address, telephone, and fax numbers are easily readable. Run a test copy through your fax machine to make sure that the copies it generates are sharp and clear. Avoid the temptation to use tiny type and soft colors on this form.

Filling In the Form

Fill in the name of the recipient, his or her company's name, and telephone and fax numbers. Include the name of the person sending the transmittal ("From"), the date, and the job number, if applicable. List the names of additional people who will also be receiving a copy of this form next to "Copies to." Next to "For," check the reason for sending the enclosed or accompanying material. In the "Via" section, check or circle the means by which this communication is being sent. For "Enclosed," mark the type of attachment or enclosure. Under "Media," indicate whether you're sending hard copy or a digital file, and include the name of the file next to the appropriate file type. In the "Disposition" area, indicate whether the material is to be replied to, returned, kept, or distributed. Use the space left for "Remarks" for additional messages and instructions.

Using the Form

Keep copies of transmittals having to do with active project work. It may be helpful for identifying the location of missing items or paperwork.

If the enclosed material being transmitted is valuable, indicate who is responsible for loss or damage—including the time during shipment. If the material is of significant value (such as expensive samples), obtain adequate insurance to cover loss and damage in shipment.

Transmittal Form

To _____   From _____

Company _____   Date _____

Phone _____   Job Number _____

Fax _____

Copies to: _____

For: _____

❏ Review   ❏ Files   ❏ Information

❏ Approval   ❏ Distribution   ❏ As Requested

Via: _____

❏ Fax (Number of pages, including transmittal) _____

❏ Messenger   ❏ UPS   ❏ Interoffice

❏ Courier Service ❏ Freight Forwarder

❏ US Mail (regular) ❏ US Mail (express)

Enclosed: _____

❏ Drawings—Originals   ❏ Catalog   ❏ Correspondence

❏ Drawings—Blueprints   ❏ Swatch/Chip   ❏ Promotion Package

❏ Photographs   ❏ Model   ❏ Article

❏ Color Copies   ❏ Other Samples ❏ Book

❏ Other

Media: _____

❏ Hard Copy

❏ Digital   **Type**   **File Name(s)**

                   ❏ Floppy Disk (Mac) (PC)   _____

                   ❏ Zip Disk (Mac) (PC)   _____

                   ❏ Jaz Disk (Mac) (PC)   _____

                   ❏ CD-ROM   _____

                   ❏ External HD   _____

                   ❏ Other   _____

Disposition: _____

❏ Kindly Reply   ❏ Return   ❏ Keep   ❏ Distribute

Remarks: _____

_____

_____

Traffic Log

It is a basic need of every design office to know the whereabouts of materials that have left the premises. In a relatively small interior design firm, it may be enough to have one overall traffic log to track the comings and goings of documents, drawings, models, samples, and so on. The Traffic Log form is designed to meet this kind of need. With very minor adjustment, it can also be adapted for use on individual large, complex, and long-term projects. To do this, simply include the following information in the space under the form's title:

CLIENT

Name

PROJECT

Job Name

Location

Job Number

Then, continue with the rest of the headings, as provided in this form.

Filling In the Form

Fill in the date the item is sent, to whom (include both the name of the company and the street address shown on the shipping label or envelope), and, very briefly, what the item is. Note the media, as indicated on the transmittal form, and what other enclosures are included, if any. If the item is supposed to be returned, place a check mark under "Return." If applicable, fill in the job number and who requested that the item be sent, if that person is not managing the log.

Using the Form

Transmittals (form 16) do not take the place of this log. Digging through copies of transmittals does not provide the information you need to quickly locate where an item was sent, when, and by whom.

This form should be located in or near the design office's traffic area. It can be filled in by individual staff members, or it can be the responsibility of one person, such as a receptionist. In the latter case, all staff members need to transmit the necessary information to this person. In large firms, individual departments maintain their own traffic logs.

Traffic Log

Date Sent	To (Name and Address)	Item	Via

Media	Enclosure	Return	Job Number	By

Inventory Log

This form is being included because there may be times when a designer has the opportunity to purchase some special items at a good price and turn them over at a desirable profit.

In the event your practice includes the resale of goods, then it is important to keep track of what you have and where it is. Remember also, that for accounting purposes, inventory is considered a tangible current asset and must be included with the firm's bookkeeping documents.

Filling In the Form

Fill in the date that each entry is made. List the item in stock and under "SKU/Color/Size" indicate specific details. You may need to add extra columns to this form if you have a large variety of items in different styles, sizes, and colors. Indicate the location of the items, if you have more than one place of storage, the storage ticket number, and the dates that the items were received in storage and removed.

Using the Form

The timely turnover of inventory goods is important, since styles can become dated quickly and may suffer damage in storage.

"Signature" goods, or those products that are designed by or otherwise exclusive to the design firm, may be a source of secondary income. In this case, it is helpful to protect the individuality of such items with either a patent or copyright notice, if applicable.

Remember to include all inventory items under the firm's general liability insurance in the event of damage, theft, or other loss.

Inventory Log

Date	Item	SKU/Color/Size	Quantity	Location	Storage Ticket Number	Shipping Dates	
						In	Out

Project Status Report

Interior designers use project status reports for long-term and complicated projects, because they are invaluable in keeping clients informed of the project's progress, particularly if the client is not easily accessible to the designer. Additionally, commercial, institutional, and similar clients may require this kind of documentation on a regular basis, particularly if there are teams of people assigned to the project on the client side. This report includes information about what is presently going on, who is waiting for what, from whom, and when. Used regularly, these reports help smooth communications between designer and client and may also be helpful in keeping subcontractors tuned in to the rhythm and direction of the project. For short-term, uncomplicated assignments, project status reports can be used to prod a client out of a stalled situation.

This report can also be particularly useful to nonvisual or inexperienced clients, because it gives them a clear picture of what is expected to happen and in what order. Using standard professional terminology in these reports also allows the client to become familiar with the language as well as the process of interior design. Finally, when dealing with a team of people on the client side, a status report helps to identify those individuals who have responsibility to carry out specific tasks. It is a clear, but nonthreatening way of getting people to respond to specific issues and needs.

Filling In the Form

Fill in the name of the person(s) who will be receiving this report or the corporate name of the client, if it is to be circulated widely, along with the names of additional people who will be receiving a copy of this report. Fill in the name of the project, the job number; and the date of the report. (This format may also be used for summarizing the minutes of meetings, in which

case, the date of the meeting can be included here.)

There are two ways to use this form: 1) For short, specific tasks that correspond to the list of phases, checkmark the applicable phases, and fill in the items and other information in the spaces provided; 2) If the need is to discuss one or two topics in greater length and detail, check the phase appropriate to the discussion, and use the entire space available on the sheet to outline the points to be made. In this instance, do not include any other phases or items that do not require discussion.

Using the Form

Someone on the design team should take notes during client meetings. The ability to articulate the client's needs and ideas briefly, along with a written record of critical decisions, serves as a great advantage in conceptualizing and moving a project along.

When it is useful to keep subcontractors (such as freelance consultants, vendors, and manufacturers) apprised of project developments, this form can be addressed either directly to them or they can be included in the general distribution of copies. Very often, subcontractors are either directly affected by specific changes on a project or they simply need to know whether the work is proceeding according to schedule.

Most interior design projects have critical deadlines, and it is important for everyone involved to know how their contribution fits into the overall scheme. It cannot be overstated that clear, timely, and accurate communications are essential to the success of group projects.

Project Status Report

To _____ Job Number_____ Date _____

Copies _____ Job Name_____

Phase	Item	Status	Action Required	From	To	Date Due
Program Development						
Design Development—Phase One—Schematics						
Design Development—Phase Two—Final						
Contract Documents and Bids						
Implementation						

Work Change Order

In the course of virtually every interior design assignment, it is almost inevitable that clients will request some changes. Whether such changes occur early in the life cycle of the project or later, it is very important to document those requests that affect either the project budget or schedule for completion. In particular, any changes to items that were previously approved should be noted, first, to verify the exact nature of the change, and second, to justify any additional (or reduced) billing and scheduling that the change in work necessitates.

A brief and simple form is easier for clients to read, sign, and return than addenda to contracts, or even letters outlining the new client instructions. It is important to follow through on obtaining signed copies of this form.

Filling In the Form

Fill in the name of the client and the project. Include the name of the person who has initiated the change request. Also, include the job number, the date, and a number for the change order. The work change order number can be linked to the individual project number, or there could be an office-wide work change order system, like purchase orders.

Check the stage during which the change is being requested. In the "Work Change Description" area, describe what is being changed. Under "Cost Change," indicate the additional or reduced amount. In general, negative numbers in bookkeeping are indicated by parentheses ( ). Also, fill in the change to the schedule—expanded or collapsed. If a lengthy description is required, attach additional pages to this form. Make sure to indicate if a drawing is attached, in case one is needed. At the bottom, fill in the name of the person to whom the form is to be returned.

Using the Form

Keep close track of all additional time and costs incurred by changes in the project's scope or specifications. If the client questions additional changes, these Work Change Orders serve as proof that additional work took place, either at the client's behest or with the client's approval for changes initiated by the designer.

Keep this form in the job file. Jot down the form's date, number, and amount on the Job Information Sheet (form 2).

Work Change Order

Client _____   Change Order Number _____

Project _____   Date _____

Work Change Requested By _____   Job Number _____

Phase

Program Development ☐

Design Development—Schematics ☐

Design Development—Final ☐

Contract Documents and Bids ☐

Implementation ☐

Work Change Description	**Cost Change**	**Schedule Change**

This is not an invoice. Revised specifications on work in progress represents information that is either different from that which the original project budget and schedule were based upon, or follows after client's approval to the stage of work in which this (these) item(s) appear(s). Changes in time and cost quoted here may be approximate, unless otherwise noted. Your signature below will constitute authorization to proceed with the change(s) noted above. Kindly return a signed and dated copy of this form to:

Authorized Signature _____

Print Name _____

Date _____

Billing Index

The Billing Index is the list of all monies billed to clients for ongoing or completed work. Knowing the amount and timing of expected revenue is critical for any business.

Bookkeepers and accountants are familiar with "accounts receivables" and keep a separate ledger of all outgoing invoices, among several other types of ledgers. It is helpful on the studio level to be able to quickly and easily check when jobs have been billed, whether or not they have been paid, and how long bills have been outstanding (not paid).

The Billing Index is also the source of all invoice numbers. Invoice numbers are to billing what job numbers are to cost accounting. An invoice number is an identifying "tag" that serves to keep track of invoices within both the designer's and the client's bookkeeping systems. When assigning invoice numbers, begin with any number, and then follow consecutively thereafter. It is best not to link invoice numbers to job numbers or purchase order numbers. An uncomplicated, independent, sequential list of numbers is less likely to create confusion for both manual and computerized billing systems. More information about creating numbering systems is given in the Jobs Index section (form 1).

Filling In the Form

Fill in the date that will appear on the invoice, the invoice number, and the job number of the assignment being billed. For "Billed To," list the name of the client as it appears on the job sheet. Fill in the job name, as designated on the Jobs Index. Fill in the fees, total cost of goods sold ("Products"), the amount of reimbursable expenses and tax, if applicable, in the designated columns. If this invoice is for a deposit on a project, or a purchase item, fill in the deposit amount in the "Deposit" column only. Fill in the total amount of the invoice, even if it is just for a deposit. The "Paid" columns are for the date and check number when the payment is received.

Using the Form

The Billing Index is used for generating invoices for consulting fees and costs. It is also used for the sale of goods that pass through the designer's hands. In some instances, these goods are sold wholesale to the designer, and the client pays the retail price to the designer, leaving the designer with the markup. Other times, the designer may pass through the discount and earn consulting fees to capture the time and effort expended on the project.

Projects may be based on a flat fee, for example, as a percentage of the cost of construction per square foot. In this, and in most other instances, billing is phased over the course of the project. It is customary to collect a 50 percent deposit prior to starting schematic development and, most certainly, prior to placing any orders for purchases. For long-term projects and those with very large fees, phased billing may be on a basis of one-third to start, one-third upon approval of final design development drawings, and one-third upon project completion. Another option would be one-quarter to start, one-quarter upon approval of schematic design development drawings, one-quarter upon approval of final design development drawings, and one-quarter upon completion of the assignment.

Use this index together with the project's job sheet and work change orders (a summary of which should be on the job sheet) when preparing invoices. First, determine the amount to be billed, based upon either a percentage of the job completed or hourly rates, or whatever arrangement is in place. Tally up all the reimbursables, and include whether there is a deposit already in place (or whether this invoice is for a deposit). Assign a number to the invoice from the Billing Index. Write up the invoice, and fill in the rest of the information indicated on the Billing Index. On the job sheet, jot down the invoice number, date, and amount. Use the Work Change Order number on the invoice to reference any changes to the expected billing.

Invoice 1

Date _____

Invoice Number _____

Job Number _____

To _____

_____

_____

Attention _____

Purchase Order Number _____

Work Change Order Number(s) _____

Project Title _____

Description	Fees	Costs	Deposit	Total
_____	_____	_____	_____	_____
_____	_____	_____	_____	_____
_____	_____	_____	_____	_____
_____	_____	_____	_____	_____
_____	_____	_____	_____	_____
_____	_____	_____	_____	_____

Subtotal $ _____

Tax _____

Total $ _____

Terms: Invoices are payable upon receipt.

Design documents including, but not limited to, drawings, renderings, models, specifications, sample boards, and all other design documents are the exclusive property of Designer. Exclusive copyright of these materials is reserved by the Designer; upon full payment of all fees and costs, Client is granted the right to use the designs contained in these materials for the location specified in project contract only. All others rights remain the exclusive property of the designer.

Billing Forms

Billing is the financial pipeline of the interior design studio. Considering that the turnaround time for payment can be anywhere from thirty to ninety days and more, it is imperative that billing be done quickly and regularly. In the project contract, establish a payment schedule, even for small assignments. At the least, arrange for an advance payment against the total fee, with the balance and reimbursable expenses to be due upon completion of the work. If the job is based on a one-time final payment, it should be billed immediately upon completion. More information about payment schedules is available under Billing Index (form 21).

Two different sample invoice forms are shown here. Although the total billing information contained may be identical, the second form is much more detailed than the first and is intended to be a preprinted and possibly two-sided form. If forms are preprinted for filling in manually, it is a good idea for them to be printed in multiples to save time and expenses making copies. It is better not to have preprinted forms numbered in advance. Forms of any kind are generally more useful when they allow for flexibility in the numbering process, saving the bookkeeper and/or accountant trouble with voided numbers. The Billing Index (form 21) is the running log and source of all invoice numbers. Of course, forms in digital format allow for easy customization and outputting as needed.

Compensation Structures

Several different compensation models have been discussed throughout this book. To summarize:

Flat Fee

This is an overall fee for the project, as determined and specified in the project contract. Billing may be phased by either percentages correlated with work/phases completed or by regular time intervals (e.g., monthly, quarterly, etc.). Depending upon the project contract, the flat fee may be only for the interior design consulting services, with reimbursable items listed separately, or a project may have one entire flat fee that includes all reimbursables.

Square Footage Fee

The cost of the project is calculated by the predetermined cost per square foot multiplied by the gross square feet (sq. ft.) area of the project, as follows: _____ total area in gross sq. ft. × $_____ per sq. ft. = $_____ total fee. The cost-per-square-foot allowance is based upon careful calculations of the time and costs for the scope of work to be performed. Naturally, the more extensive the work, the greater the demand for high-end materials, finishes, and furnishings, and the more demanding the nature of the client, the greater this allowance has to be. The square footage fee is supposed to cover interior design services, as well as the cost of materials, goods, construction, installation, and all other costs and services agreed to in the project contract. Incidentals such as travel may be billed separately, as per prior agreement.

Percentage of Project Cost

In this case, the interior design consulting services fee is based on a percentage of the overall cost of the project. Calculations may be based on the cost of construction, fixtures, finishes, installation, movable furniture, and other goods and furnishings.

In the event the client does not purchase the specified construction, goods, and materials, the designer has to arrange for other compensation, based on time already spent on the project (usually an hourly or weekly rate that was agreed to in the project contract).

Hourly Fee

Billing based on hourly fees is calculated for time actually worked. The hourly (or weekly) fee may be per individual rates, or on a tiered rate for different levels or types of personnel. (See Job Information Sheet for discussion about rate structures.) Time sheets should be available for clients to see, if they so wish, at regular intervals or upon billing. Reimbursable expenses are included in these invoices, but listed separately.

Hourly Fee with a Cap (Preset Maximum)

This follows billing based on an hourly rate structure (as above), but with a specified maximum limit. This structure usually has predetermined rates and a specified maximum number of hours or maximum amount for the total fee. It is important to include a caveat in the project contract that allows for additional billing dependent upon various contingencies, such as work change orders.

Cost Plus (Percentage of Markup)

This structure is similar to the percentage-of-project-cost method. In this scenario, individual costs of construction, furnishings, goods, installation, and so on are marked up at a predetermined percentage rate. The term "designer's cost" is the amount the designer pays to his or her manufacturers and suppliers; the "client's cost" is the price that the client pays to the client's suppliers and vendors. It is important to know that the designer is entitled to the markup even if the client makes purchases directly from his or her own sources.

Retail

Designers who work with vendors and suppliers who offer them substantial designer discounts use the retail method. The designer uses the difference between his or her cost and the full retail price (which may range anywhere from 20 percent to 60 percent and maybe more, depending upon the volume the designer generates with the supplier/vendor) to cover his or her time and costs in the consulting aspects of their service. Using the retail method, the fee for services is based on the client paying the designer the full retail price of all goods and services incurred by the project. The retail price is that which is determined and specified by the manufacturer and/or suppliers, also known as the "suggested retail price."

Filling In the Form: Invoice 1

Use this form for billing simple fees and/or a limited number of reimbursable items. Fill in the date of the invoice, its number (from the Billing Index), and the job number (from the Jobs Index). Fill in the complete billing "To" information, including company name, if applicable, and the billing address. "Attention" is usually used with corporate or institutional entities and may be either the project contact, the purchasing agent, or simply "accounts payable." State the name of the assignment next to "Project Title." If a purchase order has been issued by the client, fill in that number. If the billing is in response to, or affected by, one or more work change orders, fill in that number or numbers.

The easiest way to write the "Description" for an invoice is to copy from, or summarize with a list, the language used in the assignment's proposal, letter of agreement, or contract. If the agreement contains a schedule of payment, the invoice can be a direct copy of that schedule. If the invoice is based on an overall flat fee, list the services performed, but do not assign dollar amounts to each service; just summarize the list with an all-encompassing phrase, such as "Design and Development Fee." Reimbursable items should be grouped by type, with one total number for each. If this form is used to bill staff time, use the individual person's name and/or title, her hours, her rate, and the total. (For extensive, detailed lists, use Invoice 2.) Subtotal all the items, and indicate the amount of tax, if applicable. Remember to indicate, and deduct from the subtotal, any paid deposits or retainers that are applicable to this invoice, and fill in the total for the entire bill. In the "Terms" statement, indicate if the invoice is payable "upon receipt" or whatever time frame has been agreed to with the client. Even if clearly noted in the contract, it is advisable to reiterate the terms of copyright and usage rights that the designer wishes to retain.

Filling In the Form: Invoice 2

Use Invoice 2 for billing that is based upon a variety of factors, such as percentage fees, hourly rates for personnel, and reimbursable items. Fill in the complete billing "To" information, including company name, if applicable, and the billing address. "Attention" is usually used with corporate or institutional entities and may be either the project contact, the purchasing agent, or simply "accounts payable." State the name of the assignment next to "Project Title." If a purchase order has been issued by the client, fill in that number. If the billing is in response to, or affected by, one or more work change orders, fill in that number or numbers.

Check the project phase being billed, if applicable. Include any relevant detail under "Notes," and include the fee amount next to "Fee Subtotal." To bill the cost of personnel, list either names and titles (Spencer, B., Senior Designer), or only titles (Junior Designer), or tiered task descriptions (executive, senior, junior, etc.); indicate the hours, the hourly rates, and the total for each line. Tally the personnel costs next to "Personnel Subtotal."

The reimbursable expenses included in this form are suggested items. The list may be inapplicable to your purposes, or it may be incomplete. Feel free to adjust these items as needed. Include any relevant notes, if needed under "Notes," and specify item quantities, unit costs, shipping/handling, freight, and storage costs, if applicable. Fill in the amounts for the tax and total for each item.

In the case of something like construction or installation costs, it is not necessary to list the cost of each item in the contractors' bills. If you are passing through the contractors' invoices, treat the invoice in its entirety; do not break it out for the client in your invoice. You can or should include these invoices as backup, depending upon your arrangement with the client on this issue. For example, if a cabinetmaker sends you a bill that itemizes all the materials used, only list the kinds of cabinets, the quantity, their unit price, etc., or, more simply, the total amount of the invoice. If you have purchased different kinds of chairs on behalf of the client from one source, then it is useful to list the kinds of chairs, the quantities, their unit prices, and so on. If this level of detail is too great, remove the quantity, unit price, shipping/handling/freight columns, and simply list the total amount for each line item, attaching the invoices if backup scrutiny is expected. Subtotal the reimbursable items, and finally, add up the fees, personnel costs, and reimbursables for a complete invoice total. Be sure to indicate, and deduct from the subtotal, any paid deposits or retainers that are applicable to this invoice.

Using the Form(s)

One of the inevitable snags in producing bills quickly is that suppliers and freelancers often do not submit their bills in time to be approved and posted to project job sheets. This results in incomplete backup information. First, it is necessary to urge all outside providers to be timely in their billing, and second, billing may be broken out, separating fees from costs. An invoice for the fee or billable time and all available costs may be billed with a notice on the invoice, clearly written in an obvious location, stating, "Additional production/reimbursable costs to follow." When all such costs have been received, approved, and posted, a second invoice can follow, with a notation under "Description":

Additional production costs, as per invoice #____, dated ____.

For prearranged markups on hourly rates and/or reimbursable items, the invoice should automatically reflect the marked-up rates.

While it is not necessary to itemize every markup computation on reimbursable items, it is recommended that the backup bills for each grouping of items be stapled together, with an adding machine tape showing both the tally of the attached bills and the markup computation. This is a courtesy to the client's bookkeeper and should help move invoices along smoothly.

Invoice 2

To _____ Date _____

_____ Invoice Number _____

Attention _____ Job Number _____

Project Title _____ Purchase Order Number _____

Work Change Order Number (s) _____

Project Phase

❏ Program Development   ❏ Contract Documents and Bids

❏ Design Development—Phase One—Schematics   ❏ Project Implementation

❏ Design Development—Phase Two—Final

Fee Subtotal _____

Personnel	**Hours**	**Rate**	**Total**

Personnel Subtotal _____

Reimbursable Expenses	**Quantity**	**Unit Price**	**Shipping/Handling**	**Freight**	**Storage**	**Tax**	**Total**
Renderings/Illustrations							
Models							
Purchases							
Appliances							
Artwork							
Decorative Goods							
Electronic							
Exercise/Spa Equipment							
Hardware							
Linens							
Movable Furniture							
Rugs							
Other							
Travel and Lodging							
Courier Services							
Portable Media (computer disks)							
Telecommunications							
Photocopies, Blueprints, and Other Printing							
Other							

Reimbursable Expenses Subtotal _____

Total _____

Notes

_____

_____

_____

Terms: Invoices are payable upon receipt.

Design documents including, but not limited to, drawings, renderings, models, specifications, sample boards, and all other design documents are the exclusive property of Designer. Exclusive copyright of these materials is reserved by the Designer; upon full payment of all fees and costs, Client is granted the right to use the designs contained in these materials for the location specified in project contract only. All others rights remain the exclusive property of the designer.

Statements and Collection Letters

Clients may be requested to pay invoices within any reasonable amount of time, but in reality, it is more likely that clients will pay according to their own payment cycles. However, once payment for an invoice is overdue (anywhere from ten to thirty days, depending upon the specific time frame established in the proposal or agreement for the assignment), the designer has two options. He or she can call the client, mention the possibility of an oversight, and ask the client, or client contact, to look into the matter. And/or, the designer can send the client a billing statement, such as form 23. Such statements are routinely sent by vendors and credi-tors, usually monthly, and are merely a summary of the amounts due for payment.

In the unfortunate event that there is no response to the first statement or call, another call can be placed to the client or the designated contact. If this does not yield satisfaction within a very short time, a second notice, such as the one below, should be sent. This notice is a virtual copy of the statement, with slightly different language. Some designers simply stamp a copy of the original invoice with the statement "Second Notice," or "Overdue," but with this method, the service charge on overdue invoices is disregarded.

Second Notice   Date _____

To _____

Attention _____

Reference _____
_____
_____

Please be advised that payment for the following has not been received as of the date of this statement.

Date of Invoice	Invoice Number	Invoice Amount Due	Service Charge	Total Due
_____	_____	_____	_____	_____
_____	_____	_____	_____	_____
_____	_____	_____	_____	_____
_____	_____	_____	_____	_____

This is the second notice you have received about this overdue account. If you cannot make immediate payment in the full amounts shown, please contact us right away.

Contact _____   Telephone Number _____
_____   Fax Number _____
_____   E-mail Address _____

By the time of the Final Notice (form 24), the Statement, should be sent in a way that the client has to sign a receipt acknowledging its delivery: messenger, telegram, registered mail, UPS, or some other courier service would serve this purpose.

Filling In the Forms

Fill in the date, the name of the client (individual or corporate), the address, and the name of the contact on the assignment or the head of accounts payable next to "Attention." If the statement concerns one specific assignment, next to "Reference," fill in the name of the project, its job number, and the client's purchase order number, if applicable. If several assignments are involved, state the overall name of the account (this may be the client's name or the name of the corporate entity). List the unpaid invoices. Calculate the amount of the service charge, and fill in the name and contact information of the person whom the client should contact in the designer's office. For form 24, Final Notice, in the "Reference" area, list the overdue invoice number(s), date(s), and total amount(s).

Using the Forms

There is no guaranteed way of successfully collecting payment on late bills. It is critically important to have all of the financial details of a project detailed in a clearly-written letter of agreement or contract. It is very important for the designer to have a copy of such a document with the client's signature. It is also necessary to bill projects promptly and/or regularly.

Establishing advance payments in the form of retainers and deposits and a schedule of payments is also extremely useful. It is better to spot payment problems while the designer still has some leverage, or hasn't invested too much into the project.

The last recourse is to turn the account over for collection, either by a reputable agency or attorney. Fees for this service range from 25 to 40 percent (and more) of the monies collected. Keep in mind that collection agencies can only ask for money. They are not licensed to practice law and cannot bring lawsuits. If the client is unlikely to pay, retaining an attorney at an hourly fee might be the best approach.

For amounts of less than a few thousand dollars, depending upon locale, small claims court may be a viable option. Local court offices provide information about filing claims.

Tenacity is important to the success of collecting, but in some cases, it may be necessary to be flexible in accepting partial payment with a revised payment schedule.

Statement

Date _____

To   _____
       _____
       _____
       _____

Attention _____

Reference _____

_____

_____

Please be advised that payment for the following has not been received as of the date of this statement.

Date of Invoice	Invoice Number	Invoice Amount Due	Service Charge
_____	_____	_____	_____
_____	_____	_____	_____
_____	_____	_____	_____
_____	_____	_____	_____

Total Due _____

Your prompt attention and earliest payment would be greatly appreciated. Please contact us if you have questions about this statement. Please note that invoices not paid according to terms are subject to a 1½ percent monthly service charge.

Contact _____

Telephone Number _____

Fax Number _____

E-mail Address _____

Final Notice

Date _____

To _____

_____

_____

_____

Attention _____

Reference _____

_____

_____

This account is now seriously in arrears. We have repeatedly requested payment and have neither received payment nor have we been contacted with an explanation.

We must collect immediately, and, if payment is not received within _____ days of the date of this notice, we have no choice but to turn this account over for collection. Be aware that this process may result in additional legal and court costs to you and may damage your credit rating.

It is not too late to contact us:

Contact _____

Telephone Number _____

Fax Number _____

E-mail Address _____

Receipts Log

This is a very simple form that is useful to design firm employees in keeping track of the piles of miscellaneous little receipts that litter their busy work areas. The Receipts Log is designed for use by either individuals to track their out-of-pocket expenses or for the person in charge of petty cash disbursements. Some firms have petty cash accounts, and many companies issue corporate credit cards to employees that the employee first has to pay and then request reimbursement—showing all receipts. It is easy for these expenses to slip between the cracks and, in many instances, make it difficult to be reimbursed for legitimate expenditures.

Filling In the Form

Fill in the date of the receipt, name of the vendor, merchant, or supplier, the receipt number, and its total amount. Indicate if the expenditure was paid in cash or by credit card in the appropriate column, and then jot down the job number, if applicable. For travel and entertainment items, the employee should specify the names of the people involved and the business purpose of the expense, since the Internal Revenue Service requires this information for the expense to be eligible for a tax deduction.

Using the Form

Although the Internal Revenue Service does not require proof of purchase for items below $75, it is highly recommended that receipts exist for as many of these kinds of purchases as possible. It is easier to substantiate missing receipts when there is evidence of regular record-keeping practices, backed up by significant proof.

Expenditures made by employees out-of-pocket and via petty cash disbursements should be regularly recorded on job sheets, whether reimbursable or not. If they are reimbursable, such expenses must be recorded; if they are not reimbursable, they will still have an impact on the true cost (and profitability) of the project.

Receipts Log

Date	Supplier/Vendor/Merchant	Number	Amount	Cash	Credit Card	Job Number

Payables Index

The Payables Index is used to track all incoming invoices, whether or not they are related to billable jobs. It is handy for checking monthly statements and determining whether or not bills have been approved and posted to Job Information Sheets (form 2). It also contains all of the necessary information to relocate lost bills.

Incoming invoices should be gathered on a daily or biweekly basis (depending upon the volume of incoming bills). After recording the required information to the Payables Index, distribute the bills to those who will be approving them. (Closed-sided manila file folders with each person's name on the tab are handy for this purpose.) This is assuming, of course, that purchasing and placing orders is not a centralized function in the operation. Some firms invest design teams with the responsibility of placing and tracking orders; other firms prefer to have a purchasing agent handle all of these kinds of needs. Either way, there should be a system to check purchases during each step of the process—first, upon placing the order, then to check the delivery against the order specifications, and finally, to examine the invoice against both the purchase order and the condition of delivery, if any adjustment is required.

Filling In the Form

In the first column, fill in the date the bill was received, the name of the vendor or supplier, the invoice number, its date, and the total amount due. Under "Attention," list the person within the firm who is responsible for approving this particular bill. Write the date it was returned in the "Approved" column. Job-related bills are now ready for posting to Job Information Sheets, after which they can be paid and filed. Bills not related to jobs can be paid and filed directly. Check the "posted" column when the bill has been posted.

Using the Form

Every bill for expenses incurred by any specific job or for general supplies for the firm should be checked by the individual who ordered the corresponding material or services. (Generally, project managers on large assignments have the responsibility of reviewing such invoices.)

Whoever is responsible for approving invoices should indicate the following on each one:

❏ The project job number (if it was an expense incurred for the project, but not a billable item, indicate it as such with an "NB" next to the job number).

❏ If the bill is for a studio expense and not related to any specific job, simply indicate "studio" or give a department number.

❏ Her initials and the date.

❏ If the bill is for more than one job, divide the sum appropriately, and indicate the amounts applicable to the separate jobs.

If the bill is incorrect, this is the time to make adjustments with the vendor. Ask the vendor to reissue a correct invoice, if possible, rather than making the corrections by hand.

File a copy of all invoices billable to projects in file folders (or three-ring binders) identified on the outside by individual job names and numbers. Every job should have this "backup" file to collect copies of all reimbursable expenses (which are then sent to the client when the job is billed, to substantiate the listed expenses).

Payables Index

Date	Vendor/Supplier	Invoice Number	Date of Invoice	Amount Due	Attention	Approved	Posted

Credit Reference

New and unknown clients are naturally a welcome challenge to every interior design firm. They may bring stimulating opportunities for interesting design solutions. They may develop into long-term creative and financially rewarding relationships. They may also bring financial havoc. Whether a client is simply new or entirely unknown, a serious look at the newcomer's financial history would be a prudent first step toward deciding whether or not to spend the time and effort needed to produce an excellent proposal.

In the case of a new, but not unknown client, a call or two to the vendors and individuals known to have business relationships with the client might produce the necessary information.

In the case of an entirely unknown prospective client, the only way to obtain financial information is to ask the prospect for a list of credit references. Designers are often reluctant to go to this extent to protect their interests; however, they should remember that they have to furnish the same information to obtain credit with vendors and suppliers. Large or small, vendors and suppliers rarely, if ever, open accounts without first verifying creditworthiness.

It is not enough simply to ask the client to fill out this form. It is necessary to actually contact the references and ask about the prospect's credit status. Some credit agencies may require a fee for this service. Generally, neither banks nor individuals will comment on the exact dollar worth of the prospect (which, in any case, is not the issue). However, they are able to provide information about the prospect's cycle of payments and general financial history. Be prompt in starting credit inquiries, since the references may take some time to respond or require a written request. At the same time, the client may want to move ahead.

In case the prospective client is unable to furnish any credit information and the designer chooses to take the assignment, the only recourse in protecting him or herself is to require that the client pay a substantial portion of the fee in advance as a retainer, with the balance due at regular billing intervals. Reimbursable items should be billed with regular frequency, and payments should be received within a specified number of days. It is also advisable to have all clients pay deposits on all purchases the designer makes on their behalf.

Filling In the Form

Fill in the date, the name of the company or individual, the billing address, telephone and fax numbers, and contact name.

The client fills in the information about her company or herself, as applicable. The client also fills in the names, addresses, telephone and fax numbers, account numbers, and/or contact names of the references he or she prefers to list. The client or an authorized representative signs and dates the form on the bottom, below the statement, granting the design firm permission to run a credit check. The "Notes" column is reserved for internal use—for whoever in the design firm is running this process to jot down information as it is received, whether by phone or credit report. If it is a written report, positive or negative responses can be indicated generally in the "Notes" column and a copy of the letter attached to this form. File the completed copy of this form.

Using the Form

The most important questions to ask the reference when checking the prospect's credit:

❑ How long has the reference done business with the prospect?

❑ What type of business relationship has the reference had with the prospect?

❏ Has the reference extended credit to the prospect? How much? When?

❏ What is the maximum amount of credit the reference would extend to the prospect?

❏ How many days does the prospect take to pay reference's bills?

❏ Does the prospect pay all invoices in full as presented, or does it pay on account (in small, but regular payments over an extended period of time)?

❏ Would the reference have any reservations about extending credit to the prospect now and in the amount of the anticipated project billing?

Credit Reference Form

Individual or Company Name _____   Date _____
Billing Address _____   Phone _____
_____   Fax _____
_____   Contact Name _____

Companies

Years in business _____
Number of employees _____
Number of locations _____
Business type _____
    Private _____
    Incorporated _____
    Partnership _____
Federal ID Number _____

Individuals

Employer Name _____
Address _____
Telephone _____
Years with current employer _____
Home: own / rent _____
Years at current home address _____

Credit Agencies (Name and Address)	Telephone Number	Fax Number	Reference Number	Notes
1.				
2.				

Banks (Name and Address)	Telephone Number	Fax Number	Account Number	Contact
1.				
Notes				
2.				
Notes				

Trade References (Name and Address)	Telephone Number	Fax Number	Account Number	Contact
1.				
Notes				
2.				
Notes				

Personal References (Name and Address)	Telephone Number	Fax Number	Notes
1.			
2.			

By the signature below, authorization and permission is granted to contact the references listed above for the purpose of verifying available credit information about the company and/or individual named above.

_____   By _____   Date _____
Company Name   Authorized Signatory

Marketing Checklist

Logic would dictate that talent, experience, sensible business practices, and the ability to manage people and endless project details are all key prerequisites to a successful interior design practice. In fact, these are useful attributes, but without the constant pursuit and flow of new projects, no independent firm can stay in business. Even an in-house interior design studio has to maintain a level of productivity that justifies its existence within a larger organization. Every interior design firm should have a realistic and well-thought-out plan to promote its capabilities. There have to be funds for some reasonable expenditure on marketing materials, including, stationery, brochures, photography, and perhaps a Web site. It also requires the investment of time by both principals and staff members.

Firms that are founded by two or more partners are usually at an advantage in this area, because it is very likely that one of the partners is well suited to the marketing and promotion needs of the business. It is also possible that a sole proprietor is someone with a strong vision and force of personality that is able to drive the business in directions that will reap new sources of work. Given the advantage of personality, vision, and drive, with a plan and regular procedures, the chances for long-term success are much greater. If there is not someone within the firm that can devote the time and resources needed to develop such a plan, it may be necessary to hire a marketing consultant. Be sure to select someone who either understands your business very well or has extensive experience, and proven success, in those markets in which you wish to develop a presence.

With all the promotion tactics and techniques that are available (see Using the Form, below), the most immediate and most valuable source of new work can be found in your client list—past and present. Word-of-mouth, personal introductions, and references are the cheapest and most reliable sources of new business that exist. There is no more credible recommendation than from former or current clients. Endeavor to understand their design needs and their personal choices, and help them realize their vision by delivering the best quality possible for the price. Do all you can to mitigate problems, and be flexible and creative in solving them. Do all that can be done, within reason, to make clients feel that they have received the best possible design services that you can offer.

Filling In the Forms

The first part of this form is the Calls Log, form 28A. This form can be copied and repeated endlessly as a separate log, or it can be combined with the second part, the Qualifying Checklist. The Qualifying Checklist can stand on its own or, as noted, be attached to the individual Calls Log that generated the need for further information.

Calls Log

Fill in the date of the call and who made the call (next to "By"). Jot down the name and title of the contact that was reached and any comments that may be useful to follow-up. Under "Results/Next Steps," check the appropriate box and the recommended date for the action to be taken. Make sure to follow through, either personally or transmit the needed information to the person who is supposed to follow up.

Qualifying Checklist

Fill in the date the form is being generated and who is filling in the form (next to "By"). Fill in all of the information about the prospective client, including company and contact name, address, and all contact information, such as phone, cell, and fax numbers, and e-mail address. For project information, fill in the prospective location, type of structure/facility/client. Check what kind of construction project is planned (new, existing, etc.) and, if known, who the builder, developer, architect, and/or proposed contractors are. Also indicate, if known, when the project might start and/or is proposed to be completed under "Proposed Schedule." Check the known history, and list possible competitors. Include any special remarks and other information under "Notes." Finally, check the applicable "Results/Next Steps" and the dates they should be taken.

Using the Form

Here is a brief outline of the steps, questions, and actions involved in developing a marketing plan:

Self-Assessment

❑ **Mission:** Why are we in business? What do we hope to accomplish? What do we want to be known for?

❑ **Strengths:** What kinds of special skills and unique experiences do we have? Are we in a highly specialized niche?

❑ **Experience:** Develop a case history sheet for every significant project.

❑ **Capabilities:** What is the range of skills we have? At what relative levels?

❑ **Capacity:** How much work can we do well at one time?

❑ **Client list:** Develop a client list that has the dates, names, and notes for all projects worked on with each client.

❑ **Competitors:** Who are the closest competitors in our market? How do they promote themselves?

Market Assessment

❑ Using resources such as newspapers, trade and government journals, local newsletters, industry reference guides, and trade association resources, study possible sources of work in:

- Niche markets—specific trades and industries
- Local area—look for areas of growth

- Regional area—look for areas that are underserved

Action Plans

❑ Identity and Visibility

- Develop logo, stationery, business cards, brochures, signage, leave-behinds, Web site, and other image materials that give a clear message of the firm's professionalism and expertise
- Enter completed work in competitions
- Enter showcase events—charity-sponsored, trade shows, and other opportunities to raise visibility in the community, trades, and local industry
- Appear/speak at lectures and industry and trade events
- Serve on design juries
- Write articles and send pictures to local newspapers, newsletters, and consumer, trade, and industry magazines
- Send press releases to announce special events
- Hire a public relations firm
- Consider paid advertising

❑ Lead Generation

- Former clients—reference list and quotes that may be used as endorsements
- Industry and trade contacts—reference list and quotes that may be used as endorsements
- Develop/buy call and mail lists—cull qualified leads into a database
- Institute regular system of cold calling and follow-up
- Institute regular mailings and follow-up

❑ Lead Qualification and Pursuit

- Cull warm leads and institute process for follow through
- Have boilerplates ready of initial estimates and proposals for quick response to RFPs (requests for proposal) (see forms 3 and 4)
- Develop presentation materials and skills
- Selling and closing—study the art of persuasion

Marketing Checklist

CALLS LOG

Date _____   By _____
Contact: Phone _____
Name _____
Title _____

NOTES
_____
_____

Results/Next Steps

❏ No Lead   ❏ Will call   ❏ Call back   ❏ Research   ❏ Send materials   ❏ Appointment
                    Date   Date   Date   Date   Date

Date _____   By _____
Contact: Phone _____
Name _____
Title _____

NOTES
_____
_____

Results/Next Steps

❏ No Lead   ❏ Will call   ❏ Call back   ❏ Research   ❏ Send materials   ❏ Appointment
                    Date   Date   Date   Date   Date

Date _____   By _____
Contact: Phone _____
Name _____
Title _____

NOTES
_____
_____

Results/Next Steps

❏ No Lead   ❏ Will call   ❏ Call back   ❏ Research   ❏ Send materials   ❏ Appointment
                    Date   Date   Date   Date   Date

QUALIFYING CHECKLIST

Date _____   By _____

PROSPECT INFORMATION

Company _____   Phone _____

Contact Name _____   Cell _____

Address _____   Fax _____

_____   E-mail _____

PROJECT

Location _____   ❏ New Construction

Type _____   ❏ Existing—Structural & Interior

Size _____   ❏ Existing—Interior Only

Estimated Value _____

Potential Fee _____

Architect/Developer _____

Builder/Contractor _____

Proposed Schedule

      Q1   Q2   Q3   Q4

CLIENT HISTORY   COMPETITION

❏ No prior contact   ❏ _____

❏ Aware of firm   ❏ _____

❏ Knows firm well   ❏ _____

❏ Other   ❏ _____

NOTES

_____

_____

_____

Results/Next Steps

❏ Call back   ❏ Send materials   ❏ Research   ❏ Send letter   ❏ Proposal   ❏ Appointment

             Date   Date   Date   Date   Date

Designer-Client Agreement for Residential Project
Designer-Client Agreement for Commercial Project
Contract Summary Sheet

Being able to craft workable contracts with clients is crucial to the success of an interior design business. Likewise, the agreement between the designer and the client is vital to a successful project. This agreement may take many forms, from a simple letter that the client countersigns beneath the words "Agreed to" to a complex, formal document running for many pages and supplemented by numerous attachments. Residential projects are likely to be on the more informal, simpler end of the spectrum, while commercial projects will tend to require more complex contracts. While oral contracts may be valid, it is certainly wise to use a written contract as proof of the terms of the understanding. This will make disagreements less likely and increase the likelihood of a positive outcome for the project and future business with the client.

More than any other forms in this book, form 29 and form 30 must be shaped to fit your business and the particular client with whom you are dealing. To suggest that an interior design firm can make do with a single contract form would be misleading. Even if a firm only does residential work, or only does commercial work, each project is likely to have many variables. Using only one contract form might put the firm at a disadvantage. For example, a residential designer might usually bill on a retail/list basis, but this form of billing won't make sense if the job is to redo the design scheme of a previous designer hired by the client. In that case, most of the items have already been purchased, so the designer will have to bill in a different way to be fairly compensated for design services. Like the god Proteus, the contract must be capable of shifting into many shapes to meet the needs of the firm and its clients. The advantage of the CD-ROM is the greater ease of customization of the forms. Nor is it enough to customize the form once for

the firm. It should really be customized for each client. The help of a knowledgeable attorney is invaluable in facilitating this customization process.

Form 29 and form 30 are similar in many ways. However, form 29 is a letter of agreement addressed to the client. In residential projects, this informality is likely to be appreciated. Form 29 anticipates three phases for the project (in fact, project phases may not be necessary for simpler projects). And form 29 assumes that the designer will be compensated based on the expenditures for the project. On the other hand, form 30 is intended for use with businesses doing commercial projects. It is set up as a formal contract. It anticipates that the scope of work will divide into five phases (plus a catch-all of other services). It includes payment provisions for billings based on time, a flat fee, or a retainer plus a markup on expenditures. If a residential project comes along that should be done with a flat fee, that payment provision can always be imported from form 30 to form 29 by using the CD-ROM. Or if a commercial project would lend itself to being done on a retail/list price basis, that could be imported from form 29 to form 30. What the forms offer is a starting point, an armature that can be fleshed out according to the unique needs of each project. Particularly for commercial projects, the breakdown of the scope of work into phases is likely to take the form of a lengthy attachment to the agreement.

Form 29 and form 30 begin with a description of the project. It details the location of the project, which areas are to be designed, the square footage, and the likely number of occupants. Precision about which areas are to be designed avoids the client changing the scope of work by adding new areas. The scope of work is then set forth and broken down into phases. The description of the scope of work should be exacting, since the designer and client should be in agreement throughout the project with respect to the designer's duties. The project phases have to be closely reviewed and supplemented to make certain they fit the actual project at hand.

Scheduling is crucial, but in many cases the designer is not in control of the schedule. The client may cause delays by vacillating or changing the plans. Custom items may come late from fabricators. Contractors may fail to meet their deadlines. The designer must be careful never to guarantee a move-in date. At best, the designer can agree to move the design work forward promptly. Beyond the risk of delays by clients or suppliers is the possibility of delays due to floods, earthquakes, strikes, riots, and similar unforeseeable contingencies, all of which the design firm must protect itself from by contract.

Purchases for the project are important in many ways and have to be carefully handled. If the designer is charging retail/list prices or cost plus, the designer's fee will depend on the amount of the purchases. The designer will want to limit financial exposure and potential liability by having the client purchase directly insofar as that is possible. This is true with respect to furnishings and especially true with respect to construction, although some showrooms will only deal with designers. Another approach, especially for large projects, is for the designer to purchase as the agent of the client and disclose this on all purchase orders. For commercial projects, the expectation would be for the client to contract directly for merchandise and construction. If the designer is preparing purchase orders (and this is certain to be the case if the design firm is using its own credit), the purchase orders should be approved by the client (see form 32). When the purchase orders are approved, the firm should obtain a sufficient deposit prior to placing orders to protect itself if it is buying directly.

The designer has to navigate a careful course with respect to furnishings, custom work, and construction. On the one hand, the designer must reassure the client that the designer will work toward a good outcome. On the other hand, the designer must create protection against claims based on the failures of other parties. So, for example, the designer certainly shouldn't guarantee the results of fabricators, contractors, or even furniture ordered from a catalog. A much better approach is to warn the client that the designer will not guarantee or accept liability for failures by other parties, but will assign to the client whatever rights the designer may have against those parties. The designer can certainly make efforts to right such failures, but should always be clear with the client that the designer is doing this as a courtesy and not because of any assumption of responsibility that might be taken as a guarantee.

If fees are based on purchases, it becomes important to define both exclusions and inclusions. The designer would expect to benefit from all purchases necessary to realize the interior design. However, if an architect is involved in the project there may be a gray area in which both the designer and architect want to claim fees based on expenditures. This might apply, for example, when the designer has prepared drawings or made selections that might overlap the work of the architect, such as for custom plumbing fixtures, lighting, window treatments, flooring and floor coverings, interior painting or wall coverings, and cabinetry. Such a conflict should be resolved in the agreement with the client by listing any purchases that will be excluded from the designer's fee. At the same time, the designer must protect against the client purchasing items that the designer would have been expected to provide. The agreement can indicate that purchases by the client are to be treated as purchases by the designer for purposes of computing the designer's fees. If the client already owns furniture that will be used in the newly designed interior, these items can be listed and excluded from the fee computation.

The agreement should certainly make clear that the client is responsible for paying for shipping, sales tax, and any similar charges on purchases, especially since the purchase orders approved by the client will not show these charges. If the designer is not preparing the purchase orders, it will be important for the designer to receive copies (especially since the fee may be based on the purchases). And every document that the client reviews and approves should be initialed or signed to reflect that approval, including purchase orders, plans, drawings, and renderings (or be referenced in an approval form such as form 32). The designer should have a strong paper trail to document that what has been done is in accord with the client's desires in case of a later dispute.

The agreement should also clarify that the client has certain responsibilities, such as cooperating with the designer, providing certain information, promptly reviewing anything that may require an approval, and, if necessary, designating someone to act as liaison with the designer. If the client is to provide floor plans or related information, the agreement should indicate that this is at the client's expense and that the designer may rely on the accuracy of the information. The client should have to let the designer know immediately if any problem arises with respect to the project. Also, the parties should ascertain who will receive, inspect, and store items for the project.

The remuneration of the designer may be based on a number of different approaches, from retail/list price to cost plus to flat fee to time basis to a hybrid. If we examine why so many approaches are used, it becomes clear that the method of determining the fee has to fit the situation presented by the project. Using retail/list or cost plus would be common for residential work and, if the budget for purchases is sufficient, should yield far more than would working on a time basis. On the other hand, designers doing commercial projects will frequently use a flat fee or charge on a time basis. If a flat fee is used, the designer has to be particularly careful to limit the scope of the work. When charging on a time basis, some firms like to show in the agreement that their fees are a multiple (such as 2½ or 3 times) of their DPE (direct personnel expense). In any event, the designer must be certain that the gross profit from the project will be sufficient to carry overhead plus bring in a profit.

In addition, the designer should seek a nonrefundable retainer that will, ideally, be applied to the final payment due on the project. If work is cancelled early, the retainer guarantees that the designer will be compensated for the effort expended on the project. In setting the method of computation for the fee and its amount, the designer should carefully consider circumstances special to the project, such as conditions on the project site that may require additional preparation, circumstances that might cause high delivery cost, costs due to a distant project location, additional time that may be required on account of coordination with consultants and other professionals working on the project, clients who can't make up their minds, and related factors that use the designer's time and increase costs.

A sensitive issue, particularly for commercial projects, is how much work the design firm will do when competing to obtain a project. Once a client retains the designer, revisions may become an issue. In some way, whether by specifying a certain number of revisions or limiting revisions to a reasonable amount, the designer must be protected from having to make limitless changes without compensation. Also, more generally, if the services requested exceed the scope of work, there must be a provision for increasing the design fee.

Unless the design fee has been set high enough that the designer can absorb project-related expenses, these expenses should be reimbursed to the designer. These might range from messengers to long-distance phone calls to overnight delivery charges. The designer may choose to mark up these expenses. If certain expenses are likely to be substantial, such as travel to a distant project site, a provision should be crafted to detail which expenses are covered, to what degree (such as whether air tickets can be first class), and what markup, if any, will be used. If expenses will be substantial, the designer may want the client to give an advance against expenses. If the advance is not used up during the project, the remaining balance is either applied to fees or returned to the client at the end of the project.

The designer needs to be assured of prompt payment, especially if the design firm is buying on its own account for resale to the client. The contract can specify an interest charge for late payments. The interest charge should not violate state usury laws. While these interest charges are only rarely applied to balances owed, they do serve an intimidation function in encouraging clients to pay in a timely manner. If the designer has a concern over possible collection problems, the agreement can provide that if the designer sues and wins then the client will also have to pay attorney's fees and court costs. Such a provision is only of value if the client has assets that can be reached.

Termination is an important provision. At the least, the designer must be protected by having a right to compensation for all work done through the point of termination. Indeed, this may not be sufficient when a client breaches an agreement. The designer may prefer to sue for the reasonably foreseeable consequences of the breach, such as lost profits. Especially for simpler projects, the designer may prefer that both parties have a right to terminate on notice to the

other party. At the least and certainly in this case, the client must be responsible to make payments for purchase orders approved by the client plus any additional billable work and expenses.

The designer will want to own the designs. The client is merely using the designs for a particular application, but the designer should control any reuse of the designs that might be practicable. If, for example, an item designed for a project might be marketable as merchandise, the designer would certainly want to own any copyrights, design patents, or trademarks, and benefit from selling the item or licensing it to a manufacturer (see form 37).

The designer should require that other professionals, such as architects, be hired and paid by the client. The designer should never practice in an area for which the designer is not properly licensed. Likewise, the agreement with the client should not hold out that the designer will render services that the designer cannot legally provide without appropriate licensing. And code compliance should be the responsibility of the various licensed professionals in their areas of specialty.

The designer will want to be able to publicize the project, which most clients welcome. This would require that the client permit photography of the project both in progress and when complete. In addition, the designer will want credit for the interior design if the client garners public attention for the project.

The nature of the relationship between the parties should be made clear. The designer is an independent contractor and not an employee of or a joint venturer with the client. Also, there should be a restriction on the parties' rights to assign the contract. The designer does not want to be faced with a new client in the middle of the project. And the client has hired the design firm because of its reputation and unique skills, so the client certainly does not want the designer to pass the project off to a different designer whose work the client may not know or may dislike. At the same time, the designer may want the right to assign portions of money due the designer to other parties. Since, unlike design, money is fungible, the client should usually find this provision acceptable.

In general, it is wise to have an arbitration provision in the agreement with the client. While the benefits of this should be discussed with an attorney familiar with the court system in the design firm's locality, arbitration tends to achieve a speedier, less costly resolution of disputes. Mediation, in which a neutral party hears both sides in a dispute and make nonbinding recommendations, might also be considered as a supplementary first step before proceeding to arbitration, which is binding.

If words have special meanings in the agreement, they should be carefully defined. For example, it may be important to define "merchandise" or "construction" if the agreement bases the designer's remuneration on expenditures and applies differing rates to merchandise and construction. This might also be significant if the designer doing a residential project commits to buy merchandise on the design firm's account, but prefers that construction be contracted for directly by the client with a markup as the design firm's fee. If the designer is to be reimbursed for expenses, it would be important to exclude expenses for overhead (e.g., expenses that the design firm would incur for items such as rent, salaries, health insurance, and other items that relate to the ongoing operation of the office).

The agreement should also encompass a number of typical or "boilerplate" provisions. It should be binding not only on the parties, but on those who may stand in place of the parties, such as an estate or an assignee. The agreement should be the whole agreement and subject to amendment only by a written agreement. If a

breach is forgiven once, this should not mean that the agreement can with impunity be breached again and again in the same way. And, since laws may vary from state to state, it should be specified which state's laws will govern the agreement.

Finally, authorized signatories sign for both the design firm and the client. Because a great deal depends on the agreement being valid, it is important to know that the person signing for the client is authorized to do so. If the designer has any doubts about this, the question should be raised with the client and resolved prior to undertaking the project.

After the contract has been negotiated, a summary should be prepared (form 31) so that everyone in the design firm who needs to know the contractual terms can have easy access to the key points in the agreement.

There are a number of helpful references to supplement the discussion of contracts. The American Society of Interior Designers offers for sale Interiors Documents Collection A (commercial) and Interiors Documents Collection B (residential), which can be purchased from their Web site (*www.asid.org*) or by calling their office at (202) 546-3480. *Business Guide for Interior Designers* by Harry Siegel (Whitney Library of Design, Watson-Guptill Publications), *A Guide to Business Principles and Practices for Interior Designers* by Harry Siegel with Alan M. Siegel (Whitney Library of Design, Watson-Guptill Publications), *Interior Design Law and Business Practices* by C. Jaye Berger (John Wiley & Sons, Inc.), and *How to Prosper as an Interior Designer* by Robert L. Alderman (John Wiley & Sons, Inc.) all offer discussions and insights of value with respect to the designer's contracts with clients.

Filling In Form 29

Fill in the date and the name and address for the client. In Paragraph 1 check the box if the plan will be attached as Schedule A. Otherwise, fill in the project location and other information, the scope of work to be done by the designer, edit the work descriptions for the various phases and add additional services to be provided by the designer to each phase and the overall scope of work. Also, indicate whether an estimated budget will be prepared in the initial phase of the project. In Paragraph 2 specify what the designer is to prepare and how long the designer has to do this. Check the box to indicate whether the designer shall make reasonable efforts to move the project forward or shall commit to a schedule that would then be filled in along with the target occupancy date.

In Paragraph 3 check the applicable box with respect to the manner in which purchases will be handled and, if using the CD-ROM, delete the provisions that are not applicable. If appropriate, fill in a hybrid variation under "Other arrangement." Then specify how much of a deposit must be made if the designer is paying on its own account for merchandise or construction.

If the client has to designate a project liaison, give the name of this person in Paragraph 5. Also, in Paragraph 5, indicate if the designer will play a role with respect to receiving, inspecting, or storing deliveries.

In Paragraph 6 check the applicable box as to the method of remuneration and, if using the CD-ROM, delete the provisions that are not applicable. With respect to whichever method of remuneration is chosen, fill in the blanks and specify the amount of the initial nonrefundable payment. If the fee is based on the amount of purchases, indicate whether any purchases are to be excluded from the computation of the designer's fees, give a markup to be paid to the designer on purchases by the client, and, if the client is going to exclude any items already owned by the client, attach a list of these items to the agreement. If an estimated budget is to be prepared in the initial phase of the project, check

the box if an additional fee will be payable and state how much the fee will be. In addition, indicate how the designer will charge if design services are required beyond the agreed on scope of work.

In Paragraph 7 specify how the designer will charge for revisions beyond a reasonable amount or after the client has approved what is to be changed. In Paragraph 8 fill in any markup for expenses as well as how travel or other large expenses will be handled. If an advance against expenses is to be paid, fill in the amount. In Paragraph 9 state when the client must pay invoices and what interest will be charged for late payments. In Paragraph 10 give the ending date for the initial term and specify how long renewal terms will be. State what length of postponement will allow the designer to terminate the agreement.

If the client doesn't want the client's name or the project location revealed in publicity about the project, fill in the client's restrictions in Paragraph 13. With respect to arbitration in Paragraph 16, show who will arbitrate and where. If the designer can easily sue in the local small claims court, fill in the maximum amount that can be sued for in the last sentence. Indicate which state's laws will govern the agreement in Paragraph 17. Then have an authorized signatory for each party sign the agreement.

Filling In Form 30

Fill in the date and the names and addresses for the client and designer. In Paragraph 1 check the box if the plan will be attached as Schedule A. Otherwise, fill in the project location and other information, the scope of work to be done by the designer, detail the scope of work in each of the phases (refer to the discussion for Paragraph 1 in the Negotiation Checklist for an overview of the types of entries to be included in the various phases), and add additional services to be provided by the designer. Also, indicate whether an estimated budget will be prepared in the Design Concept phase of the project.

In Paragraph 2 specify what the designer is to prepare and how long the designer has to do this. Check the box to indicate whether the designer shall make reasonable efforts to move the project forward or shall commit to a schedule that would then be filled in along with the target occupancy date.

In Paragraph 3 check the applicable box with respect to the manner in which purchases will be handled and, if using the CD-ROM, delete the provisions that are not applicable. If appropriate, fill in a hybrid variation under "Other arrangement." Finally in Paragraph 3, indicate whether or not the designer will be preparing the purchase orders.

If the client has to designate a project liaison, give the name of this person in Paragraph 5. Also, in Paragraph 5, indicate if the designer will play a role with respect to receiving, inspecting, or storing deliveries.

In Paragraph 6 check the applicable box as to the method of remuneration and, if using the CD-ROM, delete the provisions that are not applicable. With respect to whichever method of remuneration is chosen, fill in the blanks and specify the amount of the initial nonrefundable payment. If the fee is based on the amount of purchases, indicate whether any purchases are to be excluded from the computation of the designer's fees, give a markup to be paid to the designer on purchases by the client, and, if the client is going to exclude any items already owned by the client, attach a list of these items to the agreement. If an estimated budget is to be prepared in the Design Concept phase of the project, check the box if an additional fee will be payable and state how much the fee will be. In addition, indicate how the designer will charge if design services are required beyond the agreed on scope of work.

In Paragraph 7 specify how the designer will charge for revisions beyond a reasonable amount or after the client has approved what is to be changed. In Paragraph 8 fill in any markup for expenses as well as how travel or other large expenses will be handled. If an advance against expenses is to be paid, fill in the amount. In Paragraph 9 state when the client must pay invoices and what interest will be charged for late payments. In Paragraph 10 state how long a postponement will allow the designer to terminate the agreement.

If the client doesn't want the client's name or the project location revealed in publicity about the project, fill in the client's restrictions in Paragraph 13. With respect to arbitration in Paragraph 16, show who will arbitrate and where. If the designer can easily sue in the local small claims court, fill in the maximum amount that can be sued for in the last sentence. Indicate which state's laws will govern the agreement in Paragraph 17. Then have an authorized signatory for each party sign the agreement.

Filling In Form 31

The Contract Summary Sheet incorporates information that will save staff from having to refer to the more complex designer-client agreement. It should be customized around the type of agreement most frequently used by the designer, which depends on the nature of the design firm and its clients.

Fill in the name, address, telephone, e-mail, and contact person for the client. Indicate who is representing the design firm. Describe the project, checking the box to indicate whether a complete description appears in the agreement or in an attachment to the agreement. Give the commencement date of the agreement, any schedule for the project, and any projected occupancy date.

Indicate how purchases of merchandise or construction will be handled, including which party will pay, who will prepare purchase orders, and what provisions are in place regarding substitutions, exclusions, and deposits or working funds. Give the method for computing the designer's remuneration. Indicate whether an estimated budget is to be done for presentation of the design concept, whether an additional fee will be charged, and how that fee will be computed.

As to billings, set out how revisions and expenses will be handled as well as when the client must make payment and the interest rate for late payments. Give the term of the agreement. Indicate whether the client has placed any restrictions on publicizing the project. State the position of the person signing the agreement for the client.

Check the boxes to show whether the designer's standard provisions are included, then specify whether any of these provisions have been changed and whether any new provisions proposed by the client have been added. Fill in who completed the Contract Summary Sheet and the date on which it was completed.

Negotiation Checklist

❏ Unless the designer is certain the client has good credit and pays promptly, it would be wise to run a credit check.

❏ Specify the project location, which areas will be designed, the square footage, and how many people are likely to use the area. (Paragraph 1)

❏ Carefully delineate the scope of work, indicating exactly what the designer will and will not do. (Paragraph 1)

❏ For a residential project, set forth whether the scope of work includes aspects such as initial studies; plans with room layouts;

measuring; discussions as to client's budget and taste; drawings for suggested designs; drawings and samples to show color combinations, floor surfaces, wall coverings, and window and ceiling treatments; layouts for movable furnishings; lighting plans; drawings for cabinets and closets; and meetings with other professionals hired by the client. (Paragraph 1)

❏ For a residential project, consider whether it is necessary to break the project into phases. (Paragraph 1)

❏ If phases are necessary for a residential project, determine how the scope of work should be divided into phases. (Paragraph 1)

❏ For a complex commercial project, decide the number of phases into which the project should be subdivided. For example, there might be the following phases—programming (covering scheduling, functional and organizational requirements, feasibility studies, and program establishment); design concept (covering layout, detail plans, preliminary design, estimated budget, presentations to be made, and corporate identity programs); decoration (such as furniture, art, and cabinet drawings); contract documentation (including plans for flooring, furnishing, ceilings, electric, and telephone; schedules for finish, hardware, and doors and windows; special conditions; any engineering studies that may be required; purchase orders and the need for bidding or negotiation); contract administration (including such aspects as coordination, scheduling, inspections, handling of change orders, contract interpretation, revisions, overseeing the move-in, and working up the punch-list); and other services (such as manuals or a post-occupancy or annual audit). (Paragraph 1)

❏ Clarify who is responsible for measurements.

❑ Clarify who is responsible for shop drawings.

❑ Specify whether the designer will prepare an initial budget and, if so, whether there will be a separate fee for doing so. (Paragraphs 1 and 6)

❑ If an initial budget is prepared, make clear that it is only estimated and not definitive or binding. (Paragraph 1)

❑ If the client has a proposed budget, clarify in the agreement that such a budget cannot be binding and the designer does not guarantee prices in any event.

❑ Indicate who will select suppliers. (Paragraph 1)

❑ Limit to what degree the designer will supervise (as opposed to consult), and make certain the client does not expect more supervision than the designer expects to provide. (Paragraph 1)

❑ Make clear that suppliers and contractors are responsible for the quality and supervision. (Paragraph 1)

❑ Decide the nature of the schedule commitment the design firm can make, keeping in mind that the designer should only commit to a schedule within the control of the design firm and its staff, since the client and third parties often derail even the best efforts to meet a fixed deadline. (Paragraph 2)

❑ Among the dates that might be included in a schedule are the starting date; the approvals for survey information, layouts, preliminary budgets, design concepts, the final design and budget, and purchase orders; the issuance of construction documents; the beginning of construction; and occupancy.

❑ If a schedule or occupancy date is specified, make certain that the designer's time to perform is extended for delays on the part of the client, suppliers, and acts beyond the control of the parties. (Paragraph 2)

❑ Determine whether the designer will purchase for the designer's own account and, if so, whether this will include construction. (Paragraph 3)

❑ If the amount of merchandise and construction to be purchased is too large an amount for the designer to risk, either have the client purchase directly or have the designer act as agent for the client. (Paragraph 3)

❑ If the designer is to expend money, require that the client approve the expenditure in advance and give either full payment or an appropriate deposit. (Paragraph 3)

❑ When the designer is to expend money on behalf of the client, require the client to maintain working funds that the designer can draw against for deposits and other outlays.

❑ If the designer expends money, state that orders placed by the designer may not be cancelled by the client. (Paragraph 3)

❑ If the designer expends money and the client has in turn made a partial deposit, require full payment prior to delivery and installation or the completion of construction. (Paragraph 3)

❑ If the designer is paying for purchases or acting as agent for the client, make written approvals by the client a requirement prior to any purchase. (Paragraph 3 and 4)

❑ If the designer is paying and rebilling to the client, the client may request the right to have an accounting of money spent. The designer should be willing to do this, but should not have to go beyond what is necessary to document placement of orders and should not have to reveal the actual prices paid by the designer.

❑ Indicate whether the designer shall prepare purchase orders. (Paragraph 3)

❏ Disclaim the designer's liability and responsibility with respect to lateness or defects in merchandise, purchases, or construction. (Paragraph 3)

❏ Provide that changed circumstances with respect to purchases, including changes in price, are the responsibility of the client. (Paragraph 3)

❏ If the designer is disclaiming liability for lateness or defects, give the client the right to receive an assignment of the designer's rights against suppliers. (Paragraph 3)

❏ If the client requests that the designer use best efforts to guard the client against defects, consider whether the designer is comfortable with this requirement.

❏ If the designer is asked to be the arbiter when issues arise between the client and suppliers or contractor, consider whether the time and stress of this makes sense.

❏ In terms of acting as an intermediary between the clients and suppliers or contractors, it would be better for the designer not to undertake to secure faithful performance by those parties to the contract between them.

❏ If the designer is not preparing purchase orders, have the client supply the designer with copies of purchase orders and invoices. This is especially needed if the designer's fee is based on expenditures. (Paragraph 3)

❏ Make clear that the client must pay sales tax, packing, shipping, and related charges, despite the fact that such charges do not appear on the purchase orders. (Paragraph 3)

❏ If the client can make substitutions, require that the designer's approval be obtained and the substitutions fit with the aesthetics of the design.

❏ Give the designer the right to make substitutions when the original items cannot be obtained or have increased in price, although it would be best to obtain client's approval prior to making any substitution.

❏ Require the client to make a paper trail of approvals. (Paragraphs 3 and 4)

❏ Specify the responsibilities of the client, such as giving information, arranging interviews, providing access to the project site, promptly making approvals, aiding communications among the designer and other professionals, and, if needed, designating a liaison as the designer's regular contact. (Paragraph 5)

❏ Insofar as the client provides materials to the designer, make the client responsible for the accuracy of these materials. (Paragraph 5)

❏ If the client becomes aware of any problem with the project, such as a supplier giving items that do not meet specifications, require that the designer be given prompt written notice. (Paragraph 5)

❏ Determine the client's responsibility with respect to receiving, inspecting, and storing deliveries. (Paragraph 5)

❏ Set forth the method by which the designer will be remunerated. (Paragraph 6)

❏ Whichever method of remuneration is chosen, require that the client pay a nonrefundable fee to start the project. (Paragraph 6)

❏ Apply any retainer to the last payments owed by the client to the designer, rather than the first payments, unless the billing method allows the designer to stay ahead of fees owed by the client. (Paragraph 6)

❏ If billing is based on retail/list price, determine whether this can apply to construction or whether construction should be billed directly to the client with a markup payable to the designer. (Paragraph 6)

❏ If the designer's fee is based on expenditures, specify whether any items are to be excluded from the fee because they are supplied by other professionals. This should include any services that might be overlapping, such as specifications and selections that could be done either by an interior designer or an architect. (Paragraph 6)

❏ If the designer's fee is based on expenditures, make certain that if the client purchases substitute items this does not reduce the fee. (Paragraph 6)

❏ If the designer's fee is based on expenditures and the client already owns certain items to be used in the new design, attach a list of those items to the agreement so both parties are aware that only those items are exempt from the design fee. (Paragraph 6)

❏ Particularly if the client may have contacts that will allow obtaining the construction for less than it would usually cost and the designer's fee is based in part on a percentage of construction costs, include a requirement that for purposes of computing the designer's remuneration, the construction costs will be based on the fair market costs of such construction when done by licensed contractors.

❏ If the designer is being paid a flat fee, indicate that additional amounts will have to be paid if the project continues beyond a certain date. (Paragraph 6)

❏ If a flat fee is to be paid, keep in mind the danger of the project taking too much time and be very careful in setting the amount.

❏ If a project, especially a commercial project, is billed on a square footage basis, carefully establish the correct square footage and apply the billing rate to ascertain the total.

❏ If fees are based on square footage, consider charging more for heavily decorated areas (such as executive offices, reception areas, and board rooms) than for staff areas that are less heavily decorated.

❏ In determining the method and amount of setting the fee, carefully consider special circumstances, such as conditions on the project site that may require additional preparation, circumstances that might cause high delivery cost, costs due to a distant project location, additional time that may be required on account of coordination with consultants and other professionals working on the project, clients who can't make up their minds, and related factors that use the designer's time and increase costs.

❏ If the project is to have an upset fee—that is, a maximum amount for the designer's fee, specify the amount.

❏ If the project is to take place over a long period of time, such as several years, consider having the fees adjusted for inflation.

❏ If the client asks for services beyond the scope of work, indicate how the designer will charge for this. (Paragraph 6)

❏ Depending on how the designer computes fees and whether differing percentages apply to differing categories, consider whether definitions of such terms as "cost," "retail," "list," "merchandise," "custom," "out-of-pocket," and related terms might defuse potential disputes and help the client better understand the designer's business practices.

❏ Specify how many revisions the designer will do before making additional charges and set forth how the designer will charge when changes are requested in materials that have already been approved. (Paragraph 7)

❏ Indicate how many rounds of changes are included in the fee.

❏ Consider whether a certain number of renderings should be included in the scope of work, after which a charge would be specified for additional renderings.

❏ Require the client to reimburse the designer for expenses. (Paragraph 8)

❏ Determine whether to mark up expense reimbursements. (Paragraph 8)

❏ Decide if large expenses, such as for travel, should be treated differently from other expenses. (Paragraph 8)

❏ Set forth whether an advance will be paid by the client against expenses. (Paragraph 8)

❏ Specify how long the client has to make payments after receipt of invoices. (Paragraph 9)

❏ Give an interest rate to be charged on late payments by the client. (Paragraph 9)

❏ Since the most likely lawsuit is one for money owed to the designer, state that if the designer wins a lawsuit the client must also pay attorney's fees and court costs. (Paragraph 9)

❏ Give a term for the project, which should be enough time for the design firm to complete its work. (Paragraph 10)

❏ Consider whether to have automatic renewals after the initial term, since certain rights such as to payment should not be lost if the client's delays cause the project not to be completed until after the end of the term. (Paragraph 10)

❏ Provide that notice will be given prior to termination for cause. (Paragraph 10)

❏ Indicate what causes are grounds for termination. (Paragraph 10)

❏ Consider whether to give either party the right to terminate without cause at any time, providing that full payments will be made through the point of termination.

❏ Allow for termination for cause. (Paragraph 10)

❏ Specify without limitation what causes would be grounds for termination. (Paragraph 10)

❏ Consider requiring notice to the other party and allowing a time to cure any breach, prior to having the right to terminate. (Paragraph 10)

❏ Allow the designer to terminate the contract if the project is postponed for longer than a certain time period. (Paragraph 10)

❏ If the project is postponed, give the designer the right to bill for work through the postponement date.

❏ Reserve all rights in the contract, so that, if termination is the fault of the client, the designer can consider whether to sue for breach of contract rather than simply billing for work done to the point at which work halted. (Paragraph 10)

❏ In the event of termination, make the client responsible not only for the designer's fees but also for any purchases and expenses already incurred. (Paragraph 10)

❏ If the client requests the right to terminate after the presentation of the design concept, make certain that an appropriate fee, often in the form of a nonrefundable initial payment, has been obtained.

❏ Stipulate that the designer owns the designs, including intangible property rights therein. (Paragraph 11)

❏ If the client has an opportunity to reuse a design (perhaps as licensable merchandise), require that the designer's permission be obtained and compensation paid. (Paragraph 11)

❏ Require that the client retain and pay professional consultants, such as architects, landscape architects, and engineers. (Paragraph 12)

❏ Agree to cooperate and coordinate with other professionals. (Paragraph 12)

❏ Under no circumstances should the designer provide or appear to provide services for which the designer is not licensed.

❏ If the designer is to hire other professionals, be aware of the risks of this in terms both of losing money if the client doesn't pay their fees and the possibility the designer will be perceived to be offering to perform the services for which these other professionals are licensed.

❏ Make certain that appropriately licensed professionals handle all code compliance requirements.

❏ Give the designer the right to pay for documentation of the project for promotional purposes. (Paragraph 13)

❏ If the client consents to the designer's promotional use of the project, indicate how the project and client will be identified in those promotions. (Paragraph 13)

❏ If the client documents and publicizes the project, require that credit be given to the designer. (Paragraph 13)

❏ Specify that the relationship of the parties is that of independent contractors, not employer-employee or joint venturers. (Paragraph 14)

❏ Compare the standard provisions in the introductory pages with Paragraphs 15–17.

Designer-Client Agreement for Residential Project

[Designer's Letterhead]

Date

Ms. Alice Client
123 Main Street
Greenwich, CT 06830

Dear Ms. Client:

We are delighted to have been selected by you for your interior design project (the "Project"). This letter is to set forth the terms under which we will work together.

1.   Description. We agree to design the Project in accordance with ❑ the following plan ❑ the plan attached hereto as Schedule A and made part of this agreement.

Project location, including identification of areas, square footage, and likely number of occupants:

_____

_____

_____

Scope of work to be performed:

_____

_____

_____

_____

Scope of work set forth in project phases:

Program plan. We shall consult with you to ascertain your goals, interview the people who will use the space, visit the premises and make measurements, prepare designs and renderings, and offer recommendations for purchases of merchandise and construction (including sample materials, when helpful). Other services we will render during this phase include:

_____

_____

_____

_____

❑ If this box is checked, Designer shall prepare an estimated budget to include in the presentation, but you acknowledge that this budget is subject to change and is not a guarantee on our part with respect to the prices contained therein.

Design documents. After your approval of the presentation, we shall prepare interior architectural drawings for the following areas _____ _____, which, after your further approval, shall be submitted for competitive bids to contractors selected by you after consultation with us. In addition, we shall prepare purchase orders for merchandise and construction for your approval. Other services we will render during this phase include:

_____

_____

_____

_____

Design implementation. We shall visit the Project with the following frequency _____,
discuss the status of the work with you, and be available to consult with you with respect to whether what is being delivered or constructed is in conformity with specifications and of suitable quality. However, the quality and supervision of merchandise or construction shall be the responsibility of the suppliers or contractors. Other services we will render during this phase include:

_____

_____

_____

_____

Services to be rendered by us in addition to those described above:

_____

_____

_____

_____

2.   Schedule. We agree to make our presentation within _____ days after the later of the signing of this Agreement or, if you are to provide reference, layouts, measurements, or other materials specified here_____,

_____

after you have provided this to us.

After approval of the presentation, we shall ❑ make reasonable efforts to progress the Project; or ❑ shall conform to the following schedule: _____

_____

based on an intended occupancy date of _____.

You understand that delays by you, suppliers, or contractors may delay performance of our duties, and our time to perform shall be extended if such delays occur. In addition, if we or you are unable to perform any obligations hereunder because of fire or other casualty, strike, act or order of a public authority, act of God, or other cause beyond our or your control, then performance shall be excused during the pendency of such cause.

3.   Purchases of merchandise and construction shall be handled in the following manner:
❑ We shall pay for purchases of merchandise, and you shall pay for construction.
❑ We shall commit to purchases of merchandise and construction as your agent, but you shall make payment directly to the suppliers or contractors.
❑ You shall pay for purchases of merchandise and construction.
❑ We shall pay for purchases of merchandise and construction.
❑ Other arrangement _____

_____

If we are paying for either merchandise or construction, you shall give advance approvals by signing written authorizations. You shall pay us in full for lighting fixtures, fabrics, wallpaper, plants, flatware, crystal, linen, china, and other household items, pay a deposit of ____ percent for other merchandise; and pay a deposit of ____ percent for construction. You understand that we shall not place any order until after receipt of the signed approval with appropriate payment. Once we place such an order, it cannot be cancelled by you. If a deposit has been made, the full balance due shall be paid by you prior to delivery, installation, or completion of construction.

If we are acting as your agent, you shall approve all purchases of merchandise or construction by signing a written authorization.

We shall prepare purchase orders for purchases of merchandise or construction and shall advise you as to acceptability, but shall have no liability for the lateness, malfeasance, negligence, or failure of suppliers or contractors to perform their responsibilities and duties. In the event that, after your approval for purchases of merchandise or construction, changed circumstances cause an increase in price or other change with respect to any such purchases of merchandise or construction, we shall notify you in writing, but shall bear no liability with respect to the changed circumstances, and you shall be fully responsible with respect to the purchases of merchandise or construction. We make no warranties or guarantees as to merchandise or construction, including but not limited to fading, wear, or latent defects, but will assign to you any rights we may have against suppliers or contractors, and you may pursue claims against such suppliers or contractors at your expense.

If you pay directly for purchases of merchandise or construction, you shall make certain that we receive copies of all invoices.

You shall be responsible for the payment of sales tax, packing, shipping, and any related charges on such purchases of merchandise or construction.

4.   Approvals. On our request, you shall approve plans, drawings, renderings, purchase orders, and similar documents by returning a signed copy of each such document or a signed authorization referencing such documents to us.

5.   Your Responsibilities. You shall cooperate throughout the Project by promptly providing us with necessary information; arranging any interviews that may be needed; making access available to the project site; giving prompt attention to documents to review and requested approvals; facilitating communications between us and other professionals, such as architects and engineers whom you have retained; and, if necessary, designating the following person _____ to act as liaison with us. If you are to provide specifications, floor plans, surveys, drawings, or related information, this shall be at your expense, and we shall be held harmless for relying on the accuracy of what you have provided. If at any time you have knowledge of a deviation from specifications or other problem with the Project, you shall promptly give notice in writing to us. You shall be responsible for receiving, inspecting, and storing all deliveries, except that we shall assist in this as follows:

_____
_____
_____

6.   Remuneration. You agree to pay us on the following basis, as selected by a check mark in the appropriate box or boxes:

❏ Retail/list price plus a percentage of construction costs. We shall purchase merchandise at retail/list price and shall be compensated through the discount customarily allowed designers from such retail/list prices. If construction is required, we shall be paid a markup of _____ percent of construction expenditures. You shall pay us a nonrefundable retainer of $_____ on the signing of this Agreement, which retainer shall be applied to reduce the last payments due to us from you or, if insufficient purchases of merchandise and construction are made for the retainer to be so applied, shall be retained as a design fee.

❏ Flat fee plus a percentage of costs. Our compensation shall be a nonrefundable design fee of $_____, paid by you on the signing of this Agreement, plus an additional markup of _____ percent of the expenditures for merchandise and _____ percent of the expenditures for construction, except that the following budget items shall not be included in this calculation:

_____

_____

_____

Regardless of whether payment is made by us or you, all purchases of merchandise and construction for the Project shall be included for the purpose of computing remuneration due us, except for the following exclusions:

_____

_____

_____

In addition, you may append to this Agreement a list of items owned by you prior to commencement of the Project and use these items without any additional fee being charged by us.

❏ If an Estimated Budget is required by you, an additional fee of $_____ shall be charged for its preparation.

In the event that design services beyond the scope of work for this Project are requested by you and we are able to accommodate your request, we shall bill for such additional services as follows:

_____

_____

_____

7.   Revisions. During the development of the Project, we shall make a reasonable amount of revisions requested by you without additional charge, but if the revisions are requested after approvals by you, an additional fee shall be charged as follows:

_____

_____

8.   Expenses. In addition to the payments pursuant to paragraphs 6 and 7, you agree to reimburse us for all expenses connected to the Project, including but not limited to messengers, long-distance telephone calls, overnight deliveries, and local travel expenses. These expenses shall be marked up _____ percent by us when billed to you. In the event that travel beyond the local area is required, the expenses for this travel shall be billed as follows:

_____

_____

At the time of signing this agreement, you shall pay us $_____ as a nonrefundable advance against expenses. If the advance exceeds expenses incurred, the credit balance shall be used to reduce the fee payable or, if the fee has been fully paid, shall be reimbursed to you. Expenses shall in no event include any portion of our overhead.

9.   Payment. You agree to pay us within _____ days of receipt of our billings for remuneration, expenses, or purchases of merchandise or construction. Overdue payments shall be subject to interest charges of _____ percent monthly. In the event that we are the winning party in a lawsuit brought pursuant to this agreement, you shall reimburse us for the costs of the lawsuit, including attorney's fees.

10.   Term and Termination. This agreement shall have a term that expires on _____, 20___ The term shall automatically renew for additional _____ periods unless notice of termination is given either by us or you thirty (30) calendar days in advance of the renewal commencement. In addition, this agreement may be terminated at any time for cause by either party notifying the other party in writing of that party's breach of the Agreement and giving ten (10) business days for a cure, after which the notifying party may terminate if there has been no cure of the breach. Causes for termination shall include, but not be limited to, failure to perform any duty pursuant to this agreement in a timely manner and postponements of the Project for more than _____ business days in total. While reserving all other rights under this Agreement, in the event that the Project is terminated, we shall have the right to be paid by you through the date of termination for our work, for any purchases by us of merchandise and construction pursuant to purchase orders approved by you, and for our expenses.

11.   Ownership of Design. We shall retain ownership of the design, including any drawings, renderings, sketches, samples, or other materials prepared by us during the course of the Project. Our ownership shall include any copyrights, trademarks, patents, or other proprietary rights existing in the design. You shall not use the design for additions to this Project or for any other project without obtaining our permission and paying appropriate compensation.

12.   Consultants. If outside consultants, including but not limited to architects, structural engineers, mechanical engineers, acoustical engineers, and lighting designers, are needed for the Project, they shall be retained and paid for by you, and we shall cooperate fully with these consultants. Such consultants shall be responsible for code compliance in the various areas of their expertise.

13.   Publicity. We shall have the right to document the Project in progress and when completed, by photography or other means, which we may use for portfolio, brochure, public display, and similar publicity purposes. Your name and the location of the Project may be used in connection with the documentation, unless specified to the contrary _____. If we choose to document the Project, we shall pay the costs of documentation. In addition, if you document the Project, we shall be given credit as the designer for the Project if your documentation is released to the public.

14.   Relationship of Parties. We and you are both independent contractors. This agreement is not an employment agreement, nor does it constitute a joint venture or partnership between us and you. Nothing contained herein shall be construed to be inconsistent with this independent contractor relationship.

15.   Assignment. Neither our nor your rights and duties may be assigned by either party without the written consent of the other party, except that we may assign payments due hereunder.

16.   Arbitration. All disputes arising under this Agreement shall be submitted to binding arbitration before _____ in the following location _____ and settled in accordance with the rules of the American Arbitration Association. Judgment upon the arbitration award may be entered in any court having jurisdiction thereof. Disputes in which the amount at issue is less than $_____ shall not be subject to this arbitration provision.

17. Miscellany. This agreement shall be binding on both us and you, as well as heirs, successors, assigns, and personal representatives. This agreement constitutes the entire understanding. Its terms can be modified only by an instrument in writing signed by both us and you. Notices shall be sent by certified mail or traceable overnight delivery to us or you at our present addresses, and notification of any change of address shall be given prior to that change of address taking effect. A waiver of a breach of any of the provisions of this agreement shall not be construed as a continuing waiver of other breaches of the same or other provisions hereof. This agreement shall be governed by the laws of the State of _____.

If this agreement meets with your approval, please sign beneath the words "Agreed to" to make this a binding agreement between us and you. Please sign both copies and return one copy for our files. We look forward to working with you.

AGREED TO

Sincerely yours,
XYZ Interior Design, Inc.

By: _____   By: _____
            Alice Client   Authorized Signatory, Title

Designer-Client Agreement for Commercial Project

Agreement as of the _____ day of _____, 20_____, between _____, located at _____ (hereinafter referred to as the "Client") and _____, located at _____ (hereinafter referred to as the "Designer") with respect to an interior design project (hereinafter referred to as the "Project").

Whereas, Designer is a professional interior designer of good standing;

Whereas, Client wishes the Designer to design the Project described more fully herein; and

Whereas, Designer wishes to design this Project;

Now, therefore, in consideration of the foregoing premises and the mutual covenants hereinafter set forth and other valuable considerations, the parties hereto agree as follows:

1. Description. The Designer agrees to design the Project in accordance with ❑ the following plan ❑ the plan attached hereto as Schedule A and made part of this agreement.

Project location, including identification of areas, square footage, and likely number of occupants:

_____

_____

Scope of work to be performed by Designer: _____

_____

_____

Designer's scope of work set forth in project phases:

Programming _____

_____

_____

Design Concept _____

_____

_____

Decoration _____

_____

_____

_____

Contract Documentation _____

_____

_____

Contract Administration _____

_____

_____

_____

❏ If this box is checked, Designer shall prepare an estimated budget to include with the Design Concept for presentation to Client, but Client acknowledges that this budget is subject to change and is not a guarantee on the part of the Designer with respect to the prices contained therein.

As the work is in progress, the Designer shall visit the Project with the following frequency _____, discuss the status of the work with the Client, and be available to consult with the Client with respect to whether what is being delivered or constructed is in conformity with specifications and of suitable quality. However, the quality and supervision of merchandise or construction shall be the responsibility of the suppliers or contractors.

Services to be rendered by Designer in addition to those described above: _____
_____
_____
_____

2. Schedule. The Designer agrees to make its presentation within _____ days after the later of the signing of this Agreement or, if the Client is to provide reference, layouts, measurements, or other materials specified here _____ _____, after the Client has provided same to the Designer. After approval of the presentation, the Designer shall ❏ make reasonable efforts to progress the Project; or ❏ shall conform to the following schedule _____
_____
_____

based on an intended occupancy date of _____.

The Client understands that delays on the part of the Client or suppliers may delay performance of the Designer's duties, and Designer's time to perform shall be extended if such delays occur. In addition, if either party hereto is unable to perform any of its obligations hereunder by reason of fire or other casualty, strike, act or order of a public authority, act of God, or other cause beyond the control of such party, then such party shall be excused from such performance during the pendency of such cause.

3. Purchases shall be handled in the following manner:
  ❏ The Client shall pay for purchases of merchandise and construction.
  ❏ The Designer shall commit to purchases of merchandise and construction as the agent of the Client, who shall make payment directly to the suppliers or contractors.
  ❏ Other arrangement _____
_____

If the Designer is acting as agent for the Client, the Client shall approve all purchases by signing a written authorization.

The Designer ❏ shall ❏ shall not prepare purchase orders for purchases of merchandise or construction and shall advise Client as to acceptability, but shall have no liability for the lateness, malfeasance, negligence, or failure of suppliers or contractors to perform their responsibilities and duties. In the event that, after Client's approval for purchases of merchandise or construction, changed circumstances cause an increase in price or other change with respect to any such purchases of merchandise or construction, the Designer shall notify Client in writing, but shall bear no liability with respect to the changed circumstances, and Client shall be fully responsible with respect to the purchases of merchandise or construction. The Designer makes no warranties or guarantees as to merchandise or construction, including but not limited to fading, wear, or latent defects, but will assign to Client any rights Designer may have against suppliers or contractors, and Client may pursue claims against such suppliers or contractors at its own expense.

The Client shall make certain that Designer receives copies of all purchase orders and invoices.

The Client shall be responsible for the payment of sales tax, packing, shipping, and any related charges on such purchases.

4. Approvals by Client. On Designer's request, the Client shall approve plans, drawings, renderings, purchase orders, and similar documents by returning a signed copy of each such document or a signed authorization referencing such documents to the Designer.

5. Client Responsibilities. The Client shall cooperate throughout the Project by promptly providing Designer with necessary information; arranging any interviews that may be needed; making access available to the project site; giving prompt attention to documents to review and requested approvals; facilitating communications between the Designer and other professionals, such as architects and engineers whom the Client has retained; and, if necessary, designating the following person _____ to act as liaison with the Designer. If the Client is to provide specifications, floor plans, surveys, drawings, or related information, this shall be at the Client's expense, and the Designer shall be held harmless for relying on the accuracy of what the Client has provided. If at any time the Client has knowledge of a deviation from specifications or other problem with the Project, the Client shall promptly give notice in writing to the Designer. The Client shall be responsible for receiving, inspecting, and storing all deliveries, except that the Designer shall assist in this as follows:

_____

_____

_____

6. Remuneration. Client agrees to pay the Designer on the following basis, as selected by a check mark in the appropriate box or boxes:

❏ Hourly or per diem rate. The Designer shall bill its usual hourly or per diem rates. The Client shall pay a nonrefundable design fee of $_____ on the signing of this Agreement. Thereafter, the Client shall pay a monthly retainer on the first day of each month in the amount of $_____ until _____. The Designer shall render billings on a _____ basis, applying the design fee and retainer payments thereto, and the Client shall pay any balance due on the billings within _____ days of receipt.

❏ Flat fee plus a percentage of costs. The Designer's compensation shall be a nonrefundable design fee of $_____ paid by Client on the signing of this Agreement, plus an additional markup of ____ percent of the expenditures for merchandise and ____ percent of the expenditures for construction, except that the following budget items shall not be included in this calculation: _____

_____

_____

❏ Flat fee. The Designer's compensation shall be a design fee of $_____, which shall start with a nonrefundable payment of $_____ by the Client, with the balance paid in installments of $_____ on the following schedule:

_____

_____

If the Project continues beyond _____, an additional fee of $_____ shall be paid each month until completion.

In the event that the Designer's remuneration is based, in whole or in part, on the amount expended for the Project, all purchases of merchandise and construction for the Project shall be included for the purpose of computing remu-

neration due the Designer, except for the following exclusions: _____
_____
_____
_____

In addition, the Client may append to this Agreement a list of items owned by Client prior to commencement of the Project and use these items without any additional fee being charged by the Designer.

❏ If an Estimated Budget is required by the Client, an additional fee of $_____ shall be charged for its preparation.

In the event that design services beyond the scope of work for this Project are requested by the Client and Designer is able to accommodate Client's request, the Designer shall bill for such additional services as follows:
_____
_____

7. Revisions. During the development of the Project, the Designer shall make a reasonable amount of revisions requested by the Client without additional charge, but if the revisions are requested after approvals by the Client, an additional fee shall be charged as follows: _____
_____.

8. Expenses. In addition to the payments pursuant to Paragraphs 6 and 7, Client agrees to reimburse the Designer for all expenses connected to the Project, including but not limited to messengers, long-distance telephone calls, overnight deliveries, and local travel expenses. These expenses shall be marked up ____ percent by the Designer when billed to the Client. In the event that travel beyond the local area is required, the expenses for this travel shall be billed as follows: _____.

At the time of signing this Agreement, Client shall pay Designer $_____ as a nonrefundable advance against expenses. If the advance exceeds expenses incurred, the credit balance shall be used to reduce the fee payable or, if the fee has been fully paid, shall be reimbursed to Client. Expenses shall in no event include any portion of Designer's overhead.

9. Payment. Client agrees to pay the Designer within ____ days of receipt of Designer's billings for purchases, remuneration, or expenses. Overdue payments shall be subject to interest charges of ____ percent monthly. In the event that the Designer is the winning party in a lawsuit brought pursuant to this Agreement, the Client shall reimburse the Designer for the costs of the lawsuit, including attorney's fees.

10. Term and Termination. This Agreement shall have a term that expires on _____, 20___. The term shall automatically renew for additional _____ periods unless notice of termination is given by either party thirty (30) calendar days in advance of the renewal commencement. In addition, this Agreement may be terminated at any time for cause by either party notifying the other party in writing of that party's breach of the Agreement and giving ten (10) business days for a cure, after which the notifying party may terminate if there has been no cure of the breach. Causes for termination shall include, but not be limited to, failure to perform any duty pursuant to this Agreement in a timely manner and postponements of the Project for more than ____ business days in total. While reserving all other rights under this Agreement, in the event that the Project is terminated, the Designer shall have the right to be paid by the Client through the date of termination for the Designer's work, for any purchases by the Designer of merchandise and construction pursuant to purchase orders approved by the Client, and for the Designer's expenses.

11. Ownership of Design. The Designer shall retain ownership of the design, including any drawings, renderings, sketches, samples, or other materials prepared by Designer during the course of the Project. The Designer's ownership shall include any copyrights, trademarks, patents, or other proprietary rights existing in the design. The Client shall not use the design for additions to this Project or for any other project without the permission of the Designer and appropriate compensation.

12. Consultants. If outside consultants, including but not limited to architects, structural engineers, mechanical engineers, acoustical engineers, and lighting designers, are needed for the Project, they shall be retained and paid for by the Client, and the Designer shall cooperate fully with these consultants. Such consultants shall be responsible for code compliance in the various areas of their expertise.

13. Publicity. The Designer shall have the right to document the Project in progress and when completed, by photography or other means, which the Designer may use for portfolio, brochure, public display, and similar publicity purposes. The name of the Client and location of the Project may be used in connection with the documentation, unless specified to the contrary _____. If the Designer chooses to document the Project, the Designer shall pay the costs of documentation. In addition, if the Client documents the Project, the Designer shall be given credit as the designer for the Project if the Client's documentation is released to the public.

14. Relationship of Parties. Both parties agree that the Designer is an independent contractor. This Agreement is not an employment agreement, nor does it constitute a joint venture or partnership between the Designer and Client. Nothing contained herein shall be construed to be inconsistent with this independent contractor relationship.

15. Assignment. This Agreement may not be assigned by either party without the written consent of the other party hereto, except that the Designer may assign payments due hereunder to other parties.

16. Arbitration. All disputes arising under this Agreement shall be submitted to binding arbitration before _____ in the following location _____ and settled in accordance with the rules of the American Arbitration Association. Judgment upon the arbitration award may be entered in any court having jurisdiction thereof. Disputes in which the amount at issue is less than $_____ shall not be subject to this arbitration provision.

17. Miscellany. This Agreement shall be binding upon the parties hereto, their heirs, successors, assigns, and personal representatives. This Agreement constitutes the entire understanding between the parties. Its terms can be modified only by an instrument in writing signed by both parties. Notices shall be sent by certified mail or traceable overnight delivery to the parties at the addresses shown herein, and notification of any change of address shall be given prior to that change of address taking effect. A waiver of a breach of any of the provisions of this Agreement shall not be construed as a continuing waiver of other breaches of the same or other provisions hereof. This Agreement shall be governed by the laws of the State of _____.

In Witness Whereof, the parties hereto have signed this Agreement as of the date first set forth above.

Designer _____   Client _____
           Company Name   Company Name

By _____   By _____
    Authorized Signatory, Title   Authorized Signatory, Title

Contract Summary Sheet

Client _____

Address _____

Telephone _____ Fax _____
Cell phone _____ E-mail _____

Contact at Client _____

Representative for Designer _____

Description of Project _____
_____
_____

Full description appears in ❑ the agreement, or ❑ schedule attached to the agreement

When does the agreement commence? _____

What is the schedule for the Project? _____

Is there a projected occupancy date? _____

How will purchases of merchandise or construction be handled in terms of which party is paying, which party is preparing purchase orders, substitutions, exclusions, and what deposits or working funds will be made available?
_____
_____
_____

How will remuneration be handled, including requests for work beyond the scope of the Project?
_____
_____
_____

Has an estimated budget been requested for inclusion with the presentation of the design concept? ❑ Yes ❑ No

If such estimated budget has been requested, will an additional fee be charged and, if so, how will it be computed?
_____
_____

When will revisions be billable? _____

What expenses are billable? _____

How long does the client have to pay billings after receipt of invoices? _____

What interest rate can be charged on overdue invoices? _____

What is the term of the agreement? _____

Has the client placed any restrictions on publicizing the project? _____

What is the position of the person signing the agreement for the Client? _____

Does the agreement include the Designer's standard provisions as follows:

That the quality and supervision of merchandise or construction shall be the responsibility of the suppliers or contractors? ❑ Yes ❑ No

That delays caused by the Client, suppliers, contractors, or acts of God, etc. shall extend the designer's time to perform? ❑ Yes ❑ No

The Designer shall have no liability for the lateness, malfeasance, negligence, or failure of suppliers or contractors to perform their responsibilities and duties? ❑ Yes ❑ No

That Designer shall have no liability if changed circumstances cause a change in price or other change after Client's approval for purchases of merchandise or construction? ❑ Yes ❑ No

That Designer makes no warranties or guarantees as to merchandise or construction, including but not limited to fading, wear, or latent defects, but will assign to Client any rights Designer may have? ❑ Yes ❑ No

The Client shall be responsible for the payment of sales tax, packing, shipping, and any related charges on such purchases? ❑ Yes ❑ No

That Client must sign approvals on Designer's request? ❑ Yes ❑ No

That Client must meet the usual client responsibilities? ❑ Yes ❑ No

Does the Designer own all rights in the designs? ❑ Yes ❑ No

Is the Client responsible for retaining and paying other professional consultants? ❑ Yes ❑ No

Is there an arbitration provision? ❑ Yes ❑ No

Is there a standard "Miscellany" provision? ❑ Yes ❑ No

Has any standard provision been altered, and have any provisions been added to the agreement at the request of the Client?
_____
_____

Person completing this Contract Summary Sheet _____

Date completed _____

Client Approval

Much confusion and error can be avoided by instituting a process that gives clients the opportunity to sign off on both general and specific project elements. Additionally, if changes are made following client approvals, the designer is in a significantly better position to issue Work Change Orders (form 20) and to defend changes in billing and scheduling. It is also an opportunity to catch issues that need additional attention and possible redesign. It is always better to have a client that is in sync with the project details and can offer clear guidelines at appropriate times. It is important to stipulate in the project contract that changes following client approvals and sign-offs are subject to changes in budget and schedule.

Filling In the Form

Fill in the client and project names, as well as the location of the project and its job number. If you are using the form in its entirety and will keep it as a running approval list, then instruct the client (or highlight the appropriate rows) as to which items you are requesting to have approved. Show the client where to place his or her initials and the date. If you prefer to have separate forms for different phases or items, delete the unnecessary information, and proceed to have it signed and dated. If you are mailing the form, make sure to keep a copy indicating when you sent it out. Attach a note to the form specifying when you need to have sign-off or approval in order to be able to proceed in time to stay on schedule.

Using the Form

While this form is very comprehensive, it is easy to reformat it by deleting all the rows that are either irrelevant to the project or do not require client approval. It may just be enough to maintain the "Approval to Proceed to Next Phase"

lines in each phase, along with the final project sign-off.

The trick, of course, is to get clients to sign off. Some client representatives are loath to sign their names to anything. The best approach to this problem is to state in the project contract that written client approvals to proceed from phase to phase is a condition of bringing the project in on schedule. It may also help to note on the Project Status Reports (form 19) that client sign-off is pending.

If the client or the client contact is unwilling to physically sign the approval form, it may be necessary to issue a note to the effect that, "In the absence of written client approval, the information contained in the attached Client Approval form is assumed to be correct and acceptable to the client unless the designer is notified in writing within ____ days of the date of this notice."

Client Approval

CLIENT

Name _____

PROJECT

Job Name _____

Location _____

Job Number _____

Phase	Item	Initials	Date
Program Development			
Preliminary Color/Materials ("Mood") Boards	_____	_____	_____
Preliminary Budget/Schedule Estimates	_____	_____	_____
Revisions	_____	_____	_____
Approval to Proceed to Next Phase	_____	_____	_____
Design Development—Phase One—Schematics			
Site Plan Base Drawings	_____	_____	_____
Traffic Patterns	_____	_____	_____
Space/Layout Plans	_____	_____	_____
Preliminary Plans and Selections	_____	_____	_____
Walls	_____	_____	_____
Floors	_____	_____	_____
Ceilings	_____	_____	_____
Window Treatments	_____	_____	_____
Millwork	_____	_____	_____
Fixtures and Hardware	_____	_____	_____
Furniture	_____	_____	_____
Audio/Video	_____	_____	_____
Spa/Exercise Furnishings	_____	_____	_____
Linens, Rugs, Decorative Items	_____	_____	_____
Presentation/Sample Boards	_____	_____	_____
Budget/Schedule Estimates	_____	_____	_____
Revisions	_____	_____	_____
Approval to Proceed to Next Phase	_____	_____	_____
Design Development—Phase Two—Final			
Final Site Plan Base Drawings	_____	_____	_____
Final Traffice Patterns	_____	_____	_____
Final Space/Layout Plans	_____	_____	_____
Final Plans and Selections	_____	_____	_____
Walls	_____	_____	_____
Floors	_____	_____	_____
Ceilings	_____	_____	_____
Window Treatments	_____	_____	_____
Millwork	_____	_____	_____
Fixtures and Hardware	_____	_____	_____
Furniture	_____	_____	_____
Audio/Video	_____	_____	_____

Phase	Item	Initials	Date
Spa/Exercise Furnishings	_____	_____	_____
Linens, Rugs, Decorative Items	_____	_____	_____
Final Presentation/Sample Boards	_____	_____	_____
Final Budget/Schedule	_____	_____	_____
Revisions	_____	_____	_____
Approval to Proceed to Next Phase	_____	_____	_____
Contract Documents and Bids			
Bid Drawings and Specs	_____	_____	_____
Client Review of Bids	_____	_____	_____
Revisions	_____	_____	_____
Approval to Proceed to Next Phase	_____	_____	_____
Project Implementation			
Purchasing—Stock Items	_____	_____	_____
Wall Fabrics/Finishes	_____	_____	_____
Flooring Material	_____	_____	_____
Ceiling Materials	_____	_____	_____
Window Treatments	_____	_____	_____
Fixtures and Hardware	_____	_____	_____
Furniture	_____	_____	_____
Audio/Video	_____	_____	_____
Spa/Exercise Furnishings	_____	_____	_____
Linens, Rugs, Decorative Items	_____	_____	_____
Storage/Shipping/Handling	_____	_____	_____
Miscellaneous	_____	_____	_____
Fabrication—Custom Orders			
Wall Fabrics/Finishes	_____	_____	_____
Flooring Material	_____	_____	_____
Ceiling Materials	_____	_____	_____
Window Treatments	_____	_____	_____
Millwork	_____	_____	_____
Fixtures and Hardware	_____	_____	_____
Furniture	_____	_____	_____
Audio/Video/Security/Other Electronic	_____	_____	_____
Linens, Rugs, Decorative Items	_____	_____	_____
Storage/Shipping/Handling	_____	_____	_____
Miscellaneous	_____	_____	_____
Construction—Site Supervision			
Walls	_____	_____	_____
Floors	_____	_____	_____
Ceilings	_____	_____	_____
Miscellaneous	_____	_____	_____

Phase	Item	Initials	Date
Installation—Site Supervision			
Custom Wall Painting/Coverings			
Custom Floor Treatments			
Custom Ceiling Treatments			
Custom Window Treatments			
Millwork			
Fixtures and Hardware			
Furniture			
Audio/Video/Security/Other Electronic			
Spa/Exercise Furnishings			
Linens, Rugs, Decorative Items			
Miscellaneous			
Final Project Completion Items			
Final Client Sign-Off			

Contract with Fabricator

The interior designer frequently purchases items for the client's household or office. These may be selected from standard products lines or be specially customized for the client. In either case, the designer must be protected from the risk that the client will be dissatisfied with the item and refuse to pay. By using form 32 to document the client's approval and obtain deposits, the designer is protected to a degree from the dangers inherent in laying out money on behalf of a client. The safest approach would be for the designer to have the client contract directly with the fabricator or supplier, but this will be impractical if the fabricator or supplier will only work with designers. Also, the designer may prefer not to reveal the extent of the markup on certain items.

It is important that the specifications be clear, since quality is crucial. The materials to be used to make the product, the various stages for approval of what has been done, and a final sample or proof should all be required by the designer. In addition, the design firm should synchronize its approvals with its client's approval. If a client is going to reject custom made items, even if the items appear reasonably satisfactory based on the specifications, the designer must stop the production process and try to salvage whatever can be saved. The more closely the client is involved in the stages of approval, the greater the likelihood for a successful outcome.

The fabricator should be trustworthy enough to ensure proper production techniques and quality, but this is not always the case. Certainly the designer should review samples of the fabricator's work to see if the quality is satisfactory. If the designer feels comfortable in agreeing to take the job through the completion of fabrication, the issue of the scope of the designer's duties must be resolved. Is the designer expected to go to the fabricator's plant, handle all contacts with the fabricator, and arrange for any corrections that are necessary? The scope of duties will be a function of whether the designer or client is most competent in these areas. The client will usually rely on the expertise of the designer who must be able to monitor the performance of the fabricator and make the fabricator correct the errors that inevitably crop up in production.

What happens if, after the products are fabricated, the client refuses to pay the designer? The designer has a bill from the fabricator that must be paid. The typical scenario involves a client with (sometimes unreasonably) high standards who is unwilling to accept a product produced to less than the highest standards of quality. The fabricator expects the designer to accept the job, yet the designer finds the job is not acceptable to the client. Nor can the designer easily reject the job, since the fabricator has not made errors that would justify such a rejection. This nightmare can be avoided in several ways. Some designers simply refuse to handle money in relation to fabrication. They insist that the client contract directly with the fabricator, even if the designer is to render services during the printing process. What duties the designer performs are billed to the client on an agreed-upon basis, either as a fee, an hourly rate, or a markup. If the designer prefers to pay the fabricator, the fabricator must understand and agree to meet a quality standard consistent with the client's expectation (and the designer's agreement with the client).

The first step in dealing with a fabricator is to request a price quotation. To do this, detailed specifications must be given. It is always wise to seek more than one bid, since prices vary widely. One reason for great price variation is that fabricators have different equipment. The equipment may make the fabricator effective for one project but not another, which is reflected in the price. Asking each fabricator about what they can do most efficiently may give helpful insights into selecting the right fabricator.

Since the specifications initially given to the fabricator are always subject to change, estimates may include variable costs for different configurations of the item, differing materials, and differing quantities. When requesting quotations, always keep the specifications identical for each fabricator. Also, find out how long a quotation will hold before the fabricator will insist on rebidding the job (and may increase the price).

Once a fabricator has given an acceptable quotation, the designer wants to know that the job will be of appropriate quality and delivered on time. It is important to check the fabricator's work at various stages before allowing the job to be produced. This is usually done by seeing work in progress and a final sample or proofs. As mentioned above, this approval process allows the designer in turn to obtain approvals from the client. After approval, the fabricator is free to produce the item in conformity with the approved samples or proofs

If a large quantity of items is being produced, the designer will have to determine whether to accept more or less than the agreed-upon quantity. These "overs" or "unders" are paid for at the marginal unit cost (and thus are relatively inexpensive). In general, overs and unders will be unacceptable to the designer whose client needs an exact quantity. If the designer is ordering large quantities and will not accept either overs or unders, this should be stated in the order. A 5 or 10 percent variation in quantity might be acceptable in a situation where the item would be marketed to the public rather than delivered to a particular client.

The designer will certainly keep ownership over whatever materials he or she gives to the fabricator, such as computer files, models, or plans. If these materials are valuable, they should be insured and returned as soon as possible after fabrication. A more sensitive issue is ownership of the materials created by the fabricator in the course of the project. If, for whatever reason, the designer wishes to have a future job done by a different fabricator, the designer may want to own the production materials created by the fabricator. If the designer owns these production materials (such as molds or dyes), the designer might require the fabricator to store them without charge, and pay only for delivery charges if the designer decides to move the materials to another fabricator. Fabricators should agree to this, since the materials will never have to be moved if they satisfy the designer. At the same time, the designer should also be aware that the client may expect to own what both the designer and the fabricator create, so this must be resolved in a way consistent with the understanding between designer and fabricator.

Fabricators may seek to limit their liability to the amount paid for the job. But what if an item costs $10,000 to produce, yet the designer loses a $30,000 fee because the fabricator never delivers or delivers too late? The fabricator will also prefer to deliver "F.O.B. plant," which means that the fabricator will load the job at the plant without charge but has no responsibility after that. The designer will either arrange to pay shipping and insurance costs to the final destination or ask the fabricator to ship "C.I.F. Greenwich, Connecticut," if that is the destination. C.I.F. means that a price quotation covers the cost of the merchandise as well as insurance and freight charges to the destination. Thus, the insurance and freight charges are paid by the shipping party (in this case, the fabricator). If the fabricator does arrange this, it will no doubt want to bill an extra charge. In any case, the designer must be assured that if the job is lost or damaged in shipment, the insurance funds are available to cover the loss and, if feasible, recreation of the merchandise.

If the designer is not handling the job for the client, the client may still be very appreciative if the designer alerts the client to risks in the production process. Although form 33 is set up for the designer to contract with and pay the fabricator, it could as easily be used between the client and the fabricator.

Filling In the Form

In the Preamble fill in the date and the names and addresses of the parties. In Paragraph 1 check the appropriate box and either fill in the specifications in Paragraph 1 or add an attachment titled Schedule A. For a job with several components to produce, more than one copy of Schedule A might be used. In Paragraph 2 specify the delivery date, the place of delivery, and the terms (probably F.O.B. or C.I.F.). In Paragraph 3 restate the quantity and give the price. Then if overs and unders are acceptable, specify the price per unit for the overs and unders.

In Paragraph 4 specify when payment must be made after delivery (usually thirty days for United States fabricators, although sixty days is sometimes agreed to and, in some cases, a deposit will have to be paid). In both Paragraph 5 and Paragraph 6 indicate whether the fabricator must insure the materials and, if so, for how much. In Paragraph 6 also indicate which party will pay the expense of returning the materials.

In Paragraph 9 specify the arbitrator, the place of arbitration, and the amount beneath which claims can be brought in small claims court. In Paragraph 10 specify a term for the contract. In Paragraph 11 indicate which state's laws shall govern the contract. Have both parties sign and append a Schedule A, if necessary. The designer should either be expert enough to fill out a Schedule A or should use the assistance of a skilled production manager.

Negotiation Checklist

❏ Fill out the specifications to attain the product that the designer wants, including quantity,

materials to be used, approvals, packing, and any other specifications. (Paragraph 1 or Schedule A)

❏ Specify a delivery date. (Paragraph 2)

❏ Specify a delivery location. (Paragraph 2)

❏ Indicate the terms of delivery, such as F.O.B. or C.I.F., and be certain the job is sufficiently insured. (Paragraph 2)

❏ State that the risk of loss is borne by the fabricator until the job is delivered according to the terms of the contract. (Paragraph 2)

❏ State that time is of the essence. The fabricator will resist this, since late delivery will be an actionable breach of contract. (Paragraph 2)

❏ Do not allow the fabricator to limit damages for nondelivery or late delivery to the purchase price of the job.

❏ State the price for the quantity ordered. (Paragraph 3)

❏ Specify whether overs or unders are acceptable and, if they are, what percentages are allowed. (Paragraph 3)

❏ Determine whether any sales or other tax must be paid, and ascertain whether this tax has been included in the price or will be an additional charge.

❏ State when payment will be made after delivery, which is usually within thirty or sixty days, although the designer may have to make a deposit if credit has not been established with the fabricator. (Paragraph 4)

❏ Do not give the fabricator a security interest in the job, which the fabricator might want until full payment has been made. Such a security interest, when perfected by filing with the appropriate government agencies, would give the fabricator a right to the materials or to any sale proceeds from the materials.

❏ State that all materials supplied by the designer remain the property of the designer and must be returned when no longer needed. (Paragraph 5)

❏ Do not give the fabricator a security interest in materials supplied by the designer.

❏ Indicate that the fabricator shall pay the expense of returning the materials supplied by the designer. (Paragraph 5)

❏ State whether materials supplied by the designer shall be insured by the fabricator and, if so, for how much. (Paragraph 5)

❏ State that all materials created by the fabricator shall be the property of the designer, must be stored without charge, and must be returned when no longer needed. (Paragraph 6)

❏ Indicate who will pay for the return to the designer of materials created by the fabricator. (Paragraph 6)

❏ State whether materials created by the fabricator and owned by the designer will be insured by the fabricator and, if they are to be insured, for how much. (Paragraph 6)

❏ Decide whether the fabricator may use other companies to do part of the production process. If the designer's trust is with a particular fabricator, this practice may be ill-advised. In any case, the designer should be familiar with the true capabilities of the fabricator. Jobbing work out may cause production delays. Also, a fabricator's bid that seems too high may be the result of the fabricator marking up work to be done by others, instead of doing that work itself.

❏ If the fabricator requests a provision to extend the delivery date in the event of war, strikes, or similar situations beyond its control, the designer should specify that after some period of time the contract will terminate. This period of time might be relatively brief if the job has not yet been produced.

❏ Require approvals for all parts of the job, and hold the fabricator responsible for matching the final proofs.(Paragraph 7)

❏ Require that the fabricator meet a quality standard based on the specifications. (Paragraph 8)

❏ Do not allow the fabricator to make a blanket disclaimer of warranties, since these warranties are to protect the buyer. A warranty is a fact the buyer can rely upon, such as the fabricator's statement that a certain kind of material will be used or simply the fact that the fabricator has title to what is produced and can sell it.

❏ The designer should ascertain any extra expenses, such as charges for special work; charges for changes in the specifications after an order has been placed; charges to use materials provided by the designer on behalf of the client; charges for delays caused by the designer's tardiness in making approvals or reviewing proofs (which may be due to the client being slow); charges for having someone at the plant to approve the production as it is done; charges for samples to be air freighted; charges for storage of merchandise; charges for shipping; and any other charges.

❏ State that disputes shall be arbitrated, but do not allow the fabricator either to have the arbitration at its sole option or to specify the location as its place of business. (Paragraph 9)

❏ Specify a short contractual term, such as a period of months. (Paragraph 10)

❏ Allow the designer to terminate without charge prior to the fabricator's commencement of work or if the fabricator fails to meet the production specifications or the production schedule. (Paragraph 10)

❏ State that the contract will terminate in the event that the fabricator becomes bankrupt or insolvent. (Paragraph 10)

❏ Decide whether the death of the designer or fabricator should terminate the agreement.

❏ Specify that the designer's right to materials it supplied or materials the fabricator created will survive termination of the contract, as will the right to arbitration. (Paragraph 10)

❏ If there is to be any charge for cancellation of an order, make certain such a charge bears a reasonable relationship to expenses actually incurred by the fabricator for that order.

❏ If work beyond the original specifications is needed, define a method or standard that the fabricator will use to bill such extra work.

❏ Do not allow the fabricator to limit the time to inspect the merchandise and complain about defects, since the designer should certainly have a reasonable amount of time to do this. What is reasonable will depend on the use to which the client will put the materials. Of course, defects should be looked for and documented in writing as soon as discovered.

❏ If the fabricator uses its own form to confirm the order, review all printed terms on the form to make certain these terms are not in conflict with the designer's forms.

❏ Review the standard provisions in the introductory pages and compare them with Paragraphs 9 and 11.

Contract with Fabricator

Agreement entered into as of the _____ day of _____ 20___, between _____ _____ (hereinafter referred to as the "Designer"), located at _____ _____ and _____ (hereinafter referred to as the "Fabricator"), located at _____ , with respect to the production of certain materials (hereinafter referred to as the "Work").

Whereas, the Designer has given specifications for the Work and wishes to have the Work produced in accordance with those specifications under the terms of this Agreement; and

Whereas, the Fabricator is in the business of producing such Work and is prepared to meet the specifications and other terms of this Agreement with respect to producing the Work;

Now, therefore, in consideration of the foregoing premises and the mutual covenants hereinafter set forth and other valuable consideration, the parties hereto agree as follows:

1. Specifications. The Fabricator agrees to produce the Work in accordance with ❑ Schedule A or ❑ the following specifications:

Title _____

Description _____
_____

Quantity _____

If computer files, dyes, diagrams, models, or other guides are to be given to the fabricator, specify here
_____
_____

Materials to be used in fabrication _____
_____

Specify stages for production approvals _____
_____

Final proofs will be in the following form, prior to production of the entire quantity of the Work _____
_____

Packing _____

Other specifications _____
_____

2. Delivery and Risk of Loss. Fabricator agrees to deliver the order on or before _____, 20___ to the following location _____ and pursuant to the following terms _____ _____. The Fabricator shall be strictly liable for loss, damage, or theft of the order until delivery has been made as provided in this paragraph. Time is of the essence with respect to the delivery date.

3. Price. The price for the quantity specified in Paragraph 1 shall be $_____. Overs and unders shall not be acceptable unless specified to the contrary here _____ _____, in which case the price shall be adjusted at the rate of $_____ per _____.

4. Payment. The price shall be payable within ____ days of delivery.

5. Ownership and Return of Supplied Materials. All materials supplied by the Designer to the Fabricator shall remain the exclusive property of the Designer and be returned by the Fabricator at its expense as soon as possible upon the earlier of either the producing of the Work or the Designer's request. The Fabricator shall be liable for any loss or damage to such materials from the time of receipt until the time of return receipt by the Designer. The Fabricator ❑ shall ❑ shall not insure such materials for the benefit of the Designer in the amount of $_____.

6. Ownership and Return of Commissioned Materials. All materials created by the Fabricator for the Designer, including but not limited to sketches, mechanical art, models, type, negatives, positives, flats, dyes, or plates, shall become the exclusive property of the Designer and shall be stored without expense by the Fabricator and be returned at the Designer's request. The expense of such return of materials shall be paid by the ❑ Fabricator ❑ Designer. The Fabricator shall be liable for any loss or damage to such materials from the time of creation until the time of return receipt by the Designer. The Fabricator ❑ shall ❑ shall not insure such materials for the benefit of the Designer in the amount of $_____.

7. Proofs. If proofs are requested in the specifications, the Work shall not be produced until such proofs have been approved in writing by the Designer. The finished copies of the Work shall match the quality of the proofs.

8. Quality. The Designer shall have the right to approve the quality of the Work based on its conformity to the specifications.

9. Arbitration. All disputes arising under this Agreement shall be submitted to binding arbitration before _____ _____ at the following location: _____, and the arbitration award may be entered for judgment in any court having jurisdiction thereof. Notwithstanding the foregoing, either party may refuse to arbitrate when the dispute is for less than $_____.

10. Term and Termination. This Agreement shall have a term ending ____ months after payment pursuant to Paragraph 4. The Designer may terminate this Agreement at any time prior to the Fabricator's commencement of work and may terminate thereafter if the Fabricator fails to adhere to the specifications or production schedule for the Work. This Agreement shall also terminate in the event of the Fabricator's bankruptcy or insolvency. The rights and obligations of the parties pursuant to Paragraphs 5, 6, and 8 shall survive termination of the Agreement.

11. Miscellany. This Agreement contains the entire understanding between the parties and may not be modified, amended, or changed except by an instrument in writing signed by both parties. A waiver of any breach of any of the provisions of this Agreement shall not be construed as a continuing waiver of other breaches of the same or other provisions hereof. This Agreement shall be binding upon the parties hereto and their respective heirs, successors, assigns, and personal representatives. This Agreement shall be interpreted under the laws of the State of _____.

In Witness Whereof, the parties have signed this Agreement as of the date first set forth above.

Fabricator _____   Designer _____
            Company Name   Company Name

By _____   By _____
            Authorized Signatory, Title   Authorized Signatory, Title

Commission Contract for Art or Photography

Interior designers deal with artists in a variety of ways. A project may require the purchase of existing artworks or the commissioning of new artworks. Documentation of projects may require illustration or photography. Corporate brochures for clients may use both artworks and documentation to portray the corporate design values and culture. The design firm may also want to use artworks in its own brochures and promotions.

These artworks must satisfy not only the designer, but the client as well. While artworks occasionally may be obtained from stock libraries, it is more likely that the designer will assign a freelance artist to create the needed artworks. To ensure a greater likelihood of satisfaction, the specifications for the artworks must be as clear and detailed as possible.

Of course, there must be agreement as to the fee and what is purchased for the fee. Fine artists are primarily interested in selling physical artworks. Most illustrators and photographers seek to sell only limited, reproduction rights. If greater rights are purchased, they ask for a higher fee. If the designer (or client) is sensitive to this, the best approach may be to ask for limited rights. This should avoid paying for usage rights that are never exploited.

On the other hand, the designer must obtain all of the rights which his or her client needs. In the first instance, the designer must consider what rights will be transferred to the client. Rights can be limited in many ways, including the duration of use, geographic area of use, type of product or publication, title of the product or publication, and whether the use is exclusive or nonexclusive. Even in a transaction in which the designer is acquiring physical artworks for a client, there should be a consideration of usage rights. This is because every transfer of an artwork raises two issues: (1) Who owns the physical artwork, which may have more than one manifestation (from color printouts from a computer to glossy posters to paint on canvas); and (2) Who owns which rights of copyright (i.e., the right to make reproductions), and are these rights exclusive or nonexclusive (if they are exclusive, only the holder of the rights can exercise them).

If a fine artist sells a physical artwork, the expectation would be for the artist to retain the rights of copyright. If the designer or the client need usage rights, these would probably be nonexclusive and limited in scope.

On the other hand, the designer or the client who license illustration or photography may want all rights of copyright. This would mean the designer or client could use the work in any conceivable way. However, on closer examination, it often develops that all rights are not needed. Rather, there is a desire to prevent competitors from using the illustration or photography. Another approach would be for the artist to promise by contract that no use will be made of the artworks in certain markets without first obtaining the written consent of the designer or client. Or to agree that the client has exclusive rights in those markets where the client faces competitors, but that the client will not unreasonably withhold from the artist the right to resell the artwork in a noncompetitive way. In any case, the designer must sometimes act as an intermediary—and, perhaps, as a mediator of sorts—between the demands of the client and the desire of the artist to retain rights and earn more money for greater usage.

Expenses can be a significant aspect of the cost of illustration and, especially, photography. The designer has to know the likely range of these expenses, perhaps by setting a maximum budget to be spent. If the designer requires changes, revisions, or reshoots, this will also add to the expense. Here the designer has to be careful not to be caught in a squeeze between a client with a limited budget and an artwork cost that exceeds that budget because of changes. It would be unusual to pay for expenses when purchasing a physical artwork from a fine artist, since the expenses are usually included in the fee.

In fact, there is a fundamental issue about payment. Fees and expenses for photographers or illustrators can be substantial. Should the designer become liable for such sums at all? This same issue is present in fabrication contracts and, generally, whenever the designer becomes legally obligated to a supplier for items intended for a client. While designers often commit to pay suppliers, if the costs are very large, it may be better to have the client contract directly with the supplier and pay the supplier directly. If the designer is billing on a cost plus basis, the designer will have to have a method to charge the markup in this situation.

The artist must also work on schedule. Failure to do this should be a reason for the designer to terminate the contract.

A number of professional references will aid the designer in dealing with photographers or illustrators. These include *Pricing and Ethical Guidelines* (Graphic Artists Guild, distributed by North Light Books) and *Pricing Photography* by Michal Heron and David MacTavish (Allworth Press).

Filling In the Form

Fill in the date and the names and addresses for the artist, illustrator, or photographer as well as the designer. In Paragraph 1 give the project title and description, a description of the artworks to be created, specifications for the artworks, and any other services the artist will perform. In Paragraph 2 specify the amount of time the artist has to complete the assignment, including any procedures to review work in progress. In Paragraph 3 fill in which party will own the physical artworks as well as any preliminary or other materials (such as outtakes from a photography shoot).

If reproduction rights are being licensed, in Paragraph 4 fill in the nature of the use, the name of the product or publication, any limitations on the geographic extent or duration of the grant of rights, and whether the use is exclusive or nonexclusive. In Paragraph 5 fill in the amount of the fee, including a computation method if the fee is variable. In Paragraph 6 fill in the maximum amount which the artist is allowed to bill for expenses. In Paragraph 8 indicate how revisions or reshoots will be charged for by the artist. In Paragraph 9 indicate whether or not the artist shall receive authorship credit.

In Paragraph 13 fill in who will arbitrate, the place of arbitration, and the maximum amount that can be sued for in small claims court. State the term in Paragraph 15. In Paragraph 16 specify which state's laws will govern the contract. Both parties should then sign the contract.

Negotiation Checklist

❑ Describe the assignment in whatever detail is required, attaching another sheet to the contract if necessary. It is very important to determine exactly what the artist is agreeing to do, including any services beyond creating the artworks (such as meetings with clients or proofing). (Paragraph 1)

❑ Give specifications in detail, such as black and white or color (and number of colors, if appropriate), number of artworks, form in which the artworks are to be delivered, and whatever else is known at the time of signing the agreement. (Paragraph 1)

❑ Approve the work in progress at as many stages as possible. (Paragraph 2)

❑ Give a due date for the work to be completed, as well as due dates for each approval stage. (Paragraph 2)

❏ If the designer is to provide reference materials, the due date can be stated as a number of days after the artist's receipt of these materials. (Paragraph 2)

❏ If even a short delay would cause serious problems, make time of the essence.

❏ State that illness or other delays beyond the control of the artist will extend the due date, but only up to a limited number of days.

❏ Specify who owns the physical art in whatever form has been specified. This might be a painting, a sculpture, transparencies, negatives, PhotoShop files, and so on. (Paragraph 3)

❏ Unless there is a special reason to obtain ownership of preliminary materials used to create the artwork, the ownership of these materials would be retained by the artist. This would include the photographer's outtakes. (Paragraph 3)

❏ Be certain the grant of rights encompasses all the rights needed by the designer and, of course, by the designer's client. (Paragraph 4)

❏ State that the grant of rights extends to the client or, depending on the designer's contract with the client, gives the designer the right to assign rights to the client. (Paragraph 14)

❏ If it is likely a certain type of additional usage will be made, the amount of the re-use fee can be specified. Or the re-use fee can be expressed as a percentage of the original fee. Or the original fee can be increased and the grant of rights expanded. Another approach would be to seek all rights, but illustrators or photographers object to selling rights that may not be used and for which nothing is presumably being paid. In any case, the fact that usage fees must be paid (and permission obtained) for uses beyond the grant of rights should be kept in mind.

❏ Specify the fee. This would also cover any possible variations in the fee, such as a greater fee for the use of more artworks or for a greater media exposure than originally planned. (Paragraph 5)

❏ Determine whether sales tax must be paid. Many states provide that the license of a right of copyright does not transfer tangible property and is not taxable (assuming the physical illustrations or photographs are returned to the creator). However, the sales tax laws vary from state to state and must be checked for the particular state involved.

❏ Any expenses which the designer will reimburse to the artist should be specified to avoid misunderstandings. Some illustrators include expenses in their fee (especially if the expenses are minimal), and the designer can certainly ask that this be done, but many illustrators and virtually all photographers bill separately for expenses. (Paragraph 6)

❏ If expenses are to be reimbursed, consider putting a maximum amount on how much will be reimbursed. Any expenses beyond this amount would have to be absorbed by the artist. This makes sense if the cap is based on an estimate provided by the artist. Or, after receiving an itemized estimate of expenses from the artist, the designer may wish to attach this to the contract and state that expenses shall not exceed the estimate by more than 10 percent without the consent of the designer. (Paragraph 6)

❏ Determine whether the artist marks up expenses, such as billing 15 to 20 percent of the expenses as an additional charge. If expenses are going to be marked up, this should be stated. (Paragraph 6)

❏ If expenses will be significant, consider whether an advance against expenses is justified. If an advance against expenses is given, it should certainly have to be repaid if the expenses are never incurred.

❏ State that payment shall be made within a certain number of days after delivery of the finished art, usually within thirty days after such delivery. Obviously this should be after the date when payment will be received from the client, unless the designer is willing to bear the negative cash flow. (Paragraph 7)

❏ Deal with the issue of payment for work-in-progress that is postponed but not cancelled. A pro rata billing might be appropriate to handle this. (Paragraph 7)

❏ The fee for cancellation of the assignment should be specified. The designer should have the right to stop work on the project without being liable for more than the work done to date by the artist, unless special circumstances have caused the artist to have other losses. Such losses might, for example, be caused by cancellation on such short notice that a photographer is unable to schedule other work. (Paragraph 7)

❏ Specify any advances to be paid against the fee. A schedule of payments might be necessary for an extensive job, in which case the designer might also want advances from the client.

❏ Revisions or reshoots can be a problem. The artist should be given the first opportunity to make revisions or do reshoots, after which the designer should be able to change to another artist. (Paragraph 8)

❏ If revisions or reshoots are the fault of the artist, no additional fee should be charged. However, if the designer changes the nature of the assignment, additional fees will be payable. Again, if the designer is making changes because of changes by the client, the

designer's contract with the client will have to provide for additional payments. (Paragraph 8)

❏ If the artist is to receive authorship credit, the designer may allow the artist to remove his or her name if changes are done by someone else. (Paragraph 8)

❏ With respect to revisions or the assignment itself, the designer should seek to avoid forcing the artist to rush or work unusual hours since the fees for work under such stress may be higher.

❏ Document any changes in the assignment in writing, since there may later be a question as to whether the changes were executed accurately and whether they came within the initial description of the project. Paragraph 16 requires that all modifications to the agreement be written. Form 20, the Work Change Order Form, can be used as necessary to document changes.

❏ State whether the artist will receive name credit with the image. (Paragraph 9)

❏ State if copyright notice for the photographs or illustrations will appear in the name of the photographer or illustrator when the design is published. (Paragraph 10)

❏ The artist must obtain releases with respect both to using copyrighted work or, in some cases, using art created by other artists. Releases for models may also be necessary. Such releases should protect both the designer and the designer's client. (Paragraph 11)

❏ The designer may want a warranty and indemnity provision, in which the artist states the work is not a copyright infringement and not libelous and agrees to pay for the designer's damages and attorney's fees if this is not true. Such a warranty should not extend to materials provided by the designer or client for use in the artwork. (Paragraph 12)

❏ Include a provision for arbitration, except as to amounts that can be sued for in small claims court. (Paragraph 13)

❏ Allow the artist the right to assign money payable under the contract, unless there is a particular reason not to do so. (Paragraph 14)

❏ Give the designer the right to assign the contract or rights under the contract. The designer will want to assign rights to the client. (Paragraph 14)

❏ Specify a short term for the agreement. (Paragraph 15)

❏ Allow the designer to terminate if the artist does not meet the project's specifications, falls behind schedule, or becomes insolvent. (Paragraph 15)

❏ Compare the standard provisions in the introductory pages with Paragraph 16.

Other Provisions That Can Be Added to Form 34

❏ Noncompetition. If a client is concerned about competitors using the same art or having a similar look, one solution is to insist on an all rights contract. The artist would have no right to re-use the work at all. A less extreme solution is to have a noncompetition provision, although even this can be objectionable since the artist cannot risk his or her livelihood by agreeing not to work in a particular style. In any case, a noncompetition provision might read as follows:

Noncompetition. The Artist agrees not to make or permit any use of the Artworks or similar artworks that would compete with or impair the use of the Image by the Designer or its client. The Artist shall submit any proposed uses of the Artworks or similar artworks to the Designer for approval, which approval shall not be unreasonably withheld.

Commission Contract for Art or Photography

Agreement entered into as of the _____ day of _____, 20 _____, between _____ (hereinafter referred to as the "Artist"), located at _____ and _____ (hereinafter referred to as the "Designer"), located at _____, with respect to the creation of certain artworks (hereinafter referred to as the "Artworks").

Whereas, Artist is a professional artist, illustrator, or photographer of good standing;

Whereas, Designer wishes the Artist to create the Artworks described more fully herein; and

Whereas, Artist wishes to create such Artworks pursuant to this Agreement;

Now, Therefore, in consideration of the foregoing premises and the mutual covenants hereinafter set forth and other valuable considerations, the parties hereto agree as follows:

1.   **Description.** The Artist agrees to create the Artworks in accordance with the following specifications:

Project title and description of Artworks _____
_____
_____
_____

Other specifications _____
_____
_____

Other services to be rendered by Artist _____
_____
_____

2. Due Date. The Artist agrees to deliver the Artworks within ____ days after the later of the signing of this Agreement or, if the Designer is to provide reference, layouts, or specifications, after the Designer has provided same to the Artist. If the Designer is to review and approve the work in progress, specify the details here
_____
_____
_____

3.   **Ownership of Physical Artworks.** The ownership of the physical Artworks as specified in Paragraph 1 shall be the property of _____. Sketches and any other materials created in the process of making the finished Artworks shall remain the property of the Artist, unless indicated to the contrary here _____.

4.   **Grant of Rights.** Artist grants to the Designer the right to display the Artworks to the public as well as the following additional usage rights:

For use as _____

For the product or publication named _____

These rights shall be worldwide and for the full life of the copyright and any renewals thereof unless specified to the contrary here _____

These rights are ❑ exclusive ❑ nonexclusive

5. Fee. Designer agrees to pay the following price: $_____ . If usage rights are granted and the fee varies with the amount or nature of usage, the fee shall be computed as follows:

_____
_____
_____

6. Expenses. Designer agrees to reimburse the Artist for expenses incurred in creating the Artworks, provided that such expenses shall be itemized and supported by invoices, shall not be marked up, and shall not exceed $_____ in total.

7. Payment. Designer agrees to pay the Artist within thirty days of the date of Artist's billing, which shall be dated as of the date of delivery of the Artworks. In the event that work is postponed or cancelled at the request of the Designer, the Artist shall have the right to bill and be paid pro rata for work completed through the date of that request, but the Designer shall have no further liability hereunder.

8. Revisions or Reshoots. The Artist shall be given the first opportunity to make any revisions or reshoots requested by the Designer. If the revisions or reshoots are not due to any fault on the part of the Artist, an additional fee shall be charged as follows _____

_____

If the Artist objects to any revisions to be made by the Designer, the Artist shall have the right to have any authorship credit and copyright notice in his or her name removed from the Artworks.

9. Authorship Credit. Authorship credit in the name of the Artist ❑ shall ❑ shall not accompany the Artworks when reproduced.

10. Copyright Notice. Copyright notice in the name of the Artist ❑ shall ❑ shall not accompany the Artworks when reproduced.

11. Releases. The Artist agrees to obtain releases for any art, photography, or other copyrighted materials to be incorporated by the Artist into the Artworks, as well as for any models who will be portrayed in the Artworks.

12. Warranty and Indemnity. The Artist warrants and represents that he or she is the sole creator of the Artworks and owns all rights granted under this Agreement, that the Artworks are an original creation (except for materials obtained with the written permission of others or materials from the public domain), that the Artworks do not infringe any other person's copyrights or rights of literary property, nor do they violate the rights of privacy of, or libel, other persons. The Artist agrees to indemnify and hold harmless the Designer against any claims, judgments, court costs, attorney's fees, and other expenses arising from any alleged or actual breach of this warranty.

13. Arbitration. All disputes arising under this Agreement shall be submitted to binding arbitration before _____ in the following location _____ and settled in accordance with the rules of the American Arbitration Association. Judgment upon the arbitration award may be entered in any court having jurisdiction thereof. Disputes in which the amount at issue is less than $＿＿＿＿＿ shall not be subject to this arbitration provision.

14. Assignment. The Designer shall have the right to assign any or all of its rights and obligations pursuant to this Agreement. The Artist shall have the right to assign monies due to him or her under the terms of this Agreement, but shall not make any other assignments hereunder.

15. Term and Termination. This Agreement shall have a term ending ＿＿＿ months after payment pursuant to Paragraph 7. The Designer may terminate this Agreement at any time prior to the Artist's commencement of work and may terminate thereafter if the Artist fails to adhere to the specifications or schedule for the Artworks. This Agreement shall also terminate in the event of the Artist's bankruptcy or insolvency. The rights and obligations of the parties pursuant to Paragraphs 3, 4, 9, 10, 11, 12, 13, and 14 shall survive termination of this Agreement.

16. Miscellany. This Agreement constitutes the entire understanding between the parties. Its terms can be modified only by an instrument in writing signed by both parties. A waiver of a breach of any of the provisions of this Agreement shall not be construed as a continuing waiver of other breaches of the same or other provisions hereof. This Agreement shall be binding upon the parties hereto and their respective heirs, successors, assigns, and personal representatives. This Agreement shall be governed by the laws of the State of ＿＿＿＿＿.

In Witness Whereof, the parties hereto have signed this Agreement as of the date first set forth above.

Artist ＿＿＿＿＿＿＿＿＿＿＿＿＿＿＿   Designer ＿＿＿＿＿＿＿＿＿＿＿＿＿＿
                                              Company Name

                                              By ＿＿＿＿＿＿＿＿＿＿＿＿＿＿＿＿
                                                  Authorized Signatory, Title

Designer-Sales Agent Contract

If the interior designer or design firm hires a sales agent to generate business, form 35 is the appropriate contract to use. Designers may legitimately wonder why the practice of having a sales agent does not play a greater role in the field of design. Most designers, when questioned, will say that they obtain work by word of mouth. They do not advertise, do direct mail, or make cold calls to potential clients. This is because many designers feel that appearing to seek work is undignified. Whether such an attitude can survive in the increasingly competitive global marketplace, especially for new designers seeking to establish their businesses, is an issue that each designer will have to face.

Larger design firms may use an employee to develop business through a combination of overtures to potential clients, promotional pieces, sophisticated use of press releases and other types of publicity (such as articles written by or about principals of the firm), and participation in organizations where a designer might meet either clients or peers. Many owners of firms feel that they must be solely responsible for generating business. If an agent is retained for the sale of design, form 35 provides a contractual framework. Of course, each provision would have to be carefully examined. For example, the designer is used to doing billing and servicing accounts. So there would be little reason to give the agent any commission on accounts not obtained directly by the agent. The mix of fees, expenses, and overhead costs would have to be carefully analyzed to make certain that the work obtained would be profitable. Whether such arrangements will come into existence depends in part on the willingness of clients to deal, at least initially, with someone other than the designer.

In any case, an agent who obtains clients could be of great value to a designer. Instead of seeking work, the designer can devote more time to his or her creativity. The cost to the designer is the agent's commission, which would have to be carefully negotiated, but the hope is that the agent will enable the designer to earn more. The agent may have better contacts and be able to secure a better quality of client and more remunerative assignments.

The agent should not be given markets in which the agent cannot effectively sell. For example, an agent in New York may not be able to sell in Los Angeles or London. Nor should the agent be given exclusivity in markets in which the designer may want to sell or want to have other agents sell.

The length of the contract should not be overly long, or should be subject to a right of termination on notice, because, if the agent fails to sell, the designer must take over sales or find another agent. The agent's promise to use best efforts is almost impossible to enforce.

Promotion is an important aspect of the agent's work for the designer. The designer will have to provide sufficient samples for the agent to work effectively. Beyond this, direct mail campaigns and paid advertising may gain clients. If the designer is willing to undertake such campaigns, the sharing of these promotional expenses must be agreed to between the designer and agent.

One sticky issue can be house accounts, which are clients of the designer not obtained by the agent. Both the definition of house accounts and the commission paid to the agent on such accounts must be negotiated. In all likelihood, the designer will not have an exclusive relationship with a sales agent and, therefore, commissions will not be paid on house accounts.

Termination raises another difficult issue, since the agent may feel that commissions should continue to be paid for assignments obtained by the designer after termination from clients originally contacted by the agent. There are several approaches to resolve this. The agent may be given a continuing right to commissions for a limited time depending on how long the representation lasted. Or the designer may make a payout to the agent, either in a lump sum or in installments over several years. If the relationship was brief and unsuccessful, of course, the agent should have no rights at termination except to collect commissions for assignments obtained prior to termination.

In the unusual circumstance in which the agent would handle billings and provide accountings, the designer would want to be able to review the books and records of the agent. It is far more likely that the designer will bill, collect, and remit to the agent whatever commissions are due. Since both the designer and agent provide personal services, the contract should not be assignable.

Filling In the Form

In the Preamble fill in the date and the names and addresses of the designer and agent. In Paragraph 1 indicate the geographical area and markets in which the agent will represent the designer, and whether the representation will be exclusive or nonexclusive. In Paragraph 4 fill in the length of the term. In Paragraph 5 fill in the commission rate. In Paragraph 7 state when the agent will be paid.

In Paragraph 8 indicate how promotional expenses will be shared. In Paragraph 11 state when and for how long the agent shall have a right to commissions after termination. In Paragraph 13 give the names of the arbitrator and the place for arbitration, as well as filling in the maximum amount that can be sued for in small claims court. In Paragraph 17 fill in which state's laws will govern the contract. Both parties should then sign the contract.

Negotiation Checklist

❏ Limit the scope of the agent's representation by geography and types of markets. (Paragraph 1)

❏ State whether the representation is exclusive or nonexclusive. (Paragraph 1) In the unusual case of exclusive representation, the agent will have a right to commissions on assignments obtained by other agents. Assignments obtained by the designer would then fall under the House Account provision discussed under Other Provisions.

❏ If the agent uses other agents for certain markets, review the impact of this on the amount of commissions.

❏ Any rights not granted to the agent should be reserved to the designer. (Paragraph 1)

❏ Require that the agent use best efforts to sell the work of the designer. (Paragraph 2)

❏ Require that the agent shall keep the designer promptly and regularly informed with respect to negotiations and other matters, and shall submit all offers to the designer.

❏ State that any contract negotiated by the agent is not binding unless signed by the designer.

❏ If the designer is willing to give the agent a power of attorney so the agent can sign on behalf of the designer, the power of attorney should be very specific as to what rights the agent can exercise.

❏ Require that the agent keep confidential all matters handled for the designer.

❏ Give the designer the right to accept or reject any assignment that is obtained by the agent. (Paragraph 2)

❏ Specify that portfolios be supplied to the agent by the designer. (Paragraph 3)

❏ If the portfolios are valuable, specify the value.

❏ Require the agent to insure the portfolios at the value agreed to.

❏ Raise the agent's responsibility for the samples to strict liability for any loss or damage.

❏ Provide for a short term, such as one year. (Paragraph 4) This interplays with the termination provision. Since termination is permitted on thirty days notice in Paragraph 11, the length of the term is of less importance in this contract.

❏ If the contract has a relatively long term and cannot be terminated on notice at any time, allow termination if the agent fails to generate a certain level of sales on a quarterly, semiannual, or annual basis.

❏ If the contract has a relatively long term and cannot be terminated on notice at any time, allow for termination if a certain agent dies or leaves the agency.

❏ Specify the commission percentage for assignments obtained by the agent during the term of the contract. (Paragraph 5)

❏ State that the commission shall be computed on the billing less any expenses incurred by the designer, especially if expenses are substantial. (Paragraph 5)

❏ State that commissions are not payable on billings that have not been collected. (Paragraph 5)

❏ Confirm that the agent will not collect a commission for the designer's speaking fees, grants, or prizes.

❏ Determine who will bill and collect from the client. The contract provides for the designer to do this, since keeping control over the accounts receivable is usually desirable. (Paragraph 6)

❏ If the agent is collecting billings, give the designer the right to collect his or her share directly from clients. This might provide some protection against the agent's insolvency or holding of money in the event of a dispute.

❏ Require payments to be made quickly after billings are collected. (Paragraph 7)

❏ If the designer agrees to pay interest on late payments, specify a reasonable interest rate.

❏ If the agent is collecting the billings, require the agent to treat money due the designer as trust funds and hold it in an account separate from accounts for the funds of the agency.

❏ Share promotional expenses, such as direct mail campaigns or advertising. (Paragraph 8)

❏ State that both parties must agree before promotional expenses may be incurred by the agent. (Paragraph 8)

❏ Require the agent to pay for a specified minimum amount of promotional expenses, perhaps without any sharing on the part of the designer.

❏ If expenses incurred by the agent benefit several designers, be certain there is a fair allocation of expenses.

❏ Require the agent to bear miscellaneous marketing expenses, such as messengers, shipping, and the like. (Paragraph 8)

❏ If the agent insists that the designer bear certain expenses, require the designer's approval for expenses in excess of a minimum amount.

❏ If the designer is billing, state that the agent shall receive a copy of the invoice given to the client, and vice versa if the agent is billing. (Paragraph 9)

❏ Provide for full accountings on a regular basis, such as every six months, if requested. (Paragraph 9)

❏ Give a right to inspect books and records on reasonable notice. (Paragraph 10)

❏ Allow for termination on thirty days notice to the other party. (Paragraph 11)

❏ State that the agreement will terminate in the event of the agent's bankruptcy or insolvency. (Paragraph 11)

❏ Specify for how long, if at all, the agent will receive commissions from assignments obtained by the designer from clients developed by the agent during the time the contract was in effect. (Paragraph 11) For example, if the agency contract lasted for less than a year, the agent might have such a right for 3 months after termination. If the agency contract lasted more than a year but less than two years, the right might continue for 6 months after termination. If the agent has a right to commissions after termination for too long a period, the designer may find it difficult to find another agent.

❏ Do not give the agent any rights to commissions from house accounts after termination.

❏ Instead of allowing the agent to collect commissions for some period of time after termination, a fixed amount might be stated in the original contract. For example, a percentage of the average annual billings generated by the agent for the prior three years might be payable in 3 installments over a year. The percentages and payment schedule are negotiable, but the designer must avoid any agreement that would make it difficult either to earn a living or find another agent. The percentage to be paid might increase if the agent has represented the designer for a longer period (or decrease for a shorter period), but should be subject to a cap or maximum amount.

❏ Do not allow assignment of the contract, since both the agent and the designer are rendering personal services. (Paragraph 12)

❏ If the agent is billing and paying the designer, allow the designer to assign payments due to him or her under the contract. (Paragraph 12)

❏ If the agent represents designers who may be competitive with one another, decide what precautions might be taken against favoritism. Whether it is advantageous or disadvantageous to have an agent represent competing talent would depend on the unique circumstances of each case.

❏ Provide for arbitration of disputes in excess of the amount that can be sued for in small claims court. (Paragraph 13)

❏ Compare the standard provisions in the introductory pages with Paragraphs 14-17.

Other Provisions That Can Be Added to Form 35

❏ House accounts. In the unusual case in which a designer retains an agent on an exclusive basis, it would be necessary to define and deal with house accounts. A house account is usually an account obtained by other agents prior to the contract or obtained by the designer at any time. If the agent is to benefit from these accounts, a commission must be specified (presumably less than the commission for accounts obtained by the agent). The designer may not want to pay any commission on these accounts, while the agent may want the full commission specified in Paragraph 5. If commissions are to be paid on house accounts, there should be a Schedule of House Accounts attached to the contract. This can be supplemented if house accounts are developed after the contract is signed. The Schedule of House Accounts is dated and then the names and addresses of the clients to be treated as house accounts are filled in.

❏ House accounts, _____ percent of the billing. For purposes of this Agreement, house accounts are defined as accounts obtained by the Designer at any time or obtained by another agent representing the Designer prior to the commencement of this Agreement and are listed in the Schedule of House Accounts attached to this Agreement.

Schedule of House Accounts

Date _____

1. _____
   (Name and address of client)

2. _____
   (Name and address of client)

3. (etc.)

Designer-Sales Agent Contract

Agreement, entered into as of this _____ day of _____, 20____, between _____ (hereinafter referred to as the "Designer"), located at _____, and

(hereinafter referred to as the "Agent"), located at _____

_____;

Whereas, the Designer is an established designer of proven talents; and

Whereas, the Designer wishes to have an agent represent him or her in marketing the designer's services; and

Whereas, the Agent is capable of marketing the services of the Designer; and

Whereas, the Agent wishes to represent the Designer;

Now, Therefore, in consideration of the foregoing premises and the mutual covenants hereinafter set forth and other valuable consideration, the parties hereto agree as follows:

1. **Agency.** The Designer appoints the Agent to act as his or her representative:

   (A) in the following geographical area _____

   (B) for the following interior design markets:
   ❏ Residential   ❏ Commercial   ❏ Other, specified as _____

   (C) to be the Designer's   ❏ exclusive   ❏ nonexclusive agent for the area and markets indicated.

Any rights not granted to the Agent are reserved to the Designer.

2. **Best Efforts.** The Agent agrees to use his or her best efforts in promoting the Designer's work for the purpose of securing clients for the Designer. The Agent shall negotiate the terms of any assignment that is offered, but the Designer may reject any assignment if he or she finds the terms thereof unacceptable.

3. **Portfolio.** The Designer shall provide the Agent with such portfolios of work as are from time to time necessary for the purpose of securing assignments. These portfolios shall remain the property of the Designer and be returned on termination of this Agreement. The Agent shall take reasonable efforts to protect the portfolios from loss or damage, but shall be liable for such loss or damage only if caused by the Agent's negligence.

4. **Term.** This Agreement shall take effect as of the date first set forth above, and remain in full force and effect for a term of _____, unless terminated as provided in Paragraph 11.

5. **Commissions.** The Agent shall be entitled to the following commissions on assignments obtained by the Agent during the term of this Agreement: _____ percent of the billing.

It is understood by both parties that no commissions shall be paid on assignments rejected by the Designer or for which the Designer fails to receive payment, regardless of the reason payment is not made. Further, no commissions shall be payable for any part of the billing that is due to expenses (other than normal overhead expenses) incurred by the Designer in performing the assignment, whether or not such expenses are reimbursed by the client. In the event that a flat fee is paid by the client, it shall be reduced by the amount of expenses (other than normal overhead expenses) incurred by the Designer in performing the assignment, and the Agent's commission shall be payable only on the fee as reduced for expenses.

Commissions payable after termination of this Agreement are covered in Paragraph 11.

6. Billing. The Designer shall be responsible for all billings.

7. Payments. The Designer shall make all payments due within _____ days of receipt of any fees covered by this Agreement.

8. Promotional Expenses. Promotional expenses, including but not limited to promotional mailings and paid advertising, shall be mutually agreed to by the parties and paid _____ percent by the Agent and _____ percent by the Designer. The Agent shall bear the expenses of shipping, messengers, telephone, and similar marketing expenses.

9. Accountings. The Designer shall send copies of invoices to the Agent when rendered. If requested, the Designer shall also provide the Agent with semiannual accountings showing all assignments for the period, the clients' names and addresses, the fees paid, expenses incurred by the Designer, the dates of payment, the amounts on which the Agent's commissions are calculated, and the sums due less those amounts already paid.

10. Inspection of the Books and Records. The Designer shall keep the books and records with respect to payments due each party at his or her place of business and permit the other party to inspect these books and records during normal business hours on the giving of reasonable notice.

11. Termination. This Agreement may be terminated by either party by giving thirty (30) days written notice to the other party. If the Designer receives assignments after the termination date from clients originally obtained by the Agent during the term of this Agreement, the commission specified in Paragraph 5 shall be payable to the Agent under the following circumstances. If the Agent has represented the Designer for _____ months or less, the Agent shall receive a commission on such assignments received by the Designer within _____ days of the date of termination. This period shall increase by thirty (30) days for each additional _____ months that the Agent has represented the Designer, but in no event shall such period exceed _____ days. In the event of the bankruptcy or insolvency of the Agent, this Agreement shall also terminate. The rights and obligations under Paragraphs 3, 6, 7, 8, 9, and 10 shall survive termination.

12. Assignment. This Agreement shall not be assigned by either of the parties hereto.

13. Arbitration. Any disputes arising under this Agreement shall be settled by arbitration before _____ under the rules of the American Arbitration Association in the City of _____, except that the parties shall have the right to go to court for claims of $_____ or less. Any award rendered by the arbitrator may be entered in any court having jurisdiction thereof.

14. Notices. All notices shall be given to the parties at their respective addresses set forth above.

15. Independent Contractor Status. Both parties agree that the Agent is acting as an independent contractor. This Agreement is not an employment agreement, nor does it constitute a joint venture or partnership between the Designer and Agent.

16. Amendments, Mergers, Successors, and Assigns. All amendments to this Agreement must be written. This Agreement incorporates the entire understanding of the parties. It shall be binding on and inure to the benefit of the successors, administrators, executors, or heirs of the Agent and Designer.

17. Governing Law. This Agreement shall be governed by the laws of the State of _____.

In Witness Whereof, the parties have signed this Agreement as of the date set forth above.

Designer _____   Agent _____
          Company name   Company name

By _____   By _____
    Authorized Signatory, Title   Authorized Signatory, Title

Designer's Lecture Contract

Many interior designers find lecturing to be both a source of income and a rewarding opportunity to express their feelings about their work and their profession of design. High schools, colleges, conferences, professional societies, and other institutions often invite designers to lecture. Slides of the designs may be used during these lectures and, in some cases, an exhibition may be mounted during the designer's visit.

A contract ensures that everything goes smoothly. For example, who should pay for slides that the designer has to make for that particular lecture? Who will pay for transportation to and from the lecture? Who will supply materials for a demonstration of technique? Will the designer have to give one lecture in a day or, as the institution might prefer, many more? Will the designer have to review portfolios of students? Resolving these kinds of questions, as well as the amount of and time to pay the fee, will make any lecture a more rewarding experience.

Filling In the Form

In the Preamble give the date and the names and addresses of the parties. In Paragraph 1 give the dates when the designer will lecture, the nature and extent of the services the designer will perform, and the form in which the designer is to bring examples of his or her work. In Paragraph 2 specify the fee to be paid to the designer and when it will be paid during the designer's visit.

In Paragraph 3 give the amounts of expenses to be paid (or state that none or all of these expenses are to be paid), specify which expenses other than travel and food and lodging are covered, and show what will be provided by the sponsor (such as food or lodging). In Paragraph 10 indicate which state's law will govern the contract. Then have both parties sign the contract. On the Schedule of Designs, list the works (such as computer assisted renderings, photographs, furnishings, and the like) to be used for illustration and their insurance value.

Negotiation Checklist

❏ How long will the designer be required to stay at the sponsoring institution in order to perform the required services? (Paragraph 1)

❏ What are the nature and extent of the services the designer will be required to perform? (Paragraph 1)

❏ What slides, original designs, or other materials must the designer bring? (Paragraph 1)

❏ Specify the work facilities that the sponsor will provide the designer. (Paragraph 2)

❏ Specify the fee to be paid to the designer. (Paragraph 2)

❏ Give the time the fee is to be paid. (Paragraph 2)

❏ Require that part of the fee be paid in advance.

❏ Specify the expenses that will be paid by the sponsor, including the time for payment of these expenses. (Paragraph 3)

❏ Indicate what the sponsor may provide in place of paying expenses, such as giving lodging, meals, or a car. (Paragraph 3)

❏ If illness prevents the designer from coming to lecture, state that an effort will be made to find another date. (Paragraph 4)

❏ If the sponsor must cancel for a reason beyond its control, indicate that the expenses incurred by the designer must be paid and there will be an attempt to reschedule. (Paragraph 4)

❏ If the sponsor cancels within 48 hours of the time designer is to arrive, consider requiring that the full fee as well as expenses be paid.

❏ Provide for the payment of interest on late payments by the sponsor. (Paragraph 5)

❏ Retain for the designer all rights, including copyrights, in any recordings of any kind which may be made of the designer's visit. (Paragraph 6)

❏ If the sponsor wishes to use a recording of the designer's visit, such as a video, require that the sponsor obtain the designer's written permission and that, if appropriate, a fee be negotiated for this use. (Paragraph 6)

❏ Provide that the sponsor is strictly responsible for loss or damage to any designs from the time they leave the designer's studio until they are returned there. (Paragraph 7)

❏ Require the sponsor to insure the designs and specify insurance values. (Paragraph 7)

❏ Consider which risks may be excluded from the insurance coverage.

❏ Consider whether the designer should be the named beneficiary of the insurance coverage for his or her works.

❏ Provide who will pay the cost of packing and shipping the works to and from the sponsor. (Paragraph 8)

❏ Provide who will take the responsibility to pack and ship the works to and from the sponsor.

❏ Compare the standard provisions in the introductory pages with Paragraphs 9–10.

Designer's Lecture Contract

Agreement, dated the _____ day of _____, 20____, between _____ (hereinafter referred to as the "Designer"), located at _____ and
_____ (hereinafter referred to as the "Sponsor"), located at
_____ .

Whereas, the Sponsor is familiar with and admires the work of the Designer; and

Whereas, the Sponsor wishes the Designer to visit the Sponsor to enhance the opportunities for its students to have contact with a working professional designer; and

Whereas, the Designer wishes to lecture with respect to his or her work and perform such other services as this contract may call for;

Now, Therefore, in consideration of the foregoing premises and the mutual covenants hereinafter set forth and other valuable considerations, the parties hereto agree as follows:

1.   Designer to Lecture. The Designer hereby agrees to come to the Sponsor on the following date(s): _____ and perform the following services: _____ .
The Designer shall use best efforts to make his or her services as productive as possible to the Sponsor. The Designer further agrees to bring examples of his or her own work in the form of _____ .

2.   Payment. The Sponsor agrees to pay as full compensation for the Designer's services rendered under Paragraph 1 the sum of $_____. This sum shall be payable to the Designer on completion of the _____ day of the Designer's residence with the Sponsor.

3.   Expenses. In addition to the payments provided under Paragraph 2, the Sponsor agrees to reimburse the Designer for the following expenses:

   (A) Travel expenses in the amount of $_____.
   (B) Food and lodging expenses in the amount of $_____.
   (C) Other expenses listed here: _____ in the amount of $_____.

The reimbursement for travel expenses shall be made fourteen (14) days prior to the earliest date specified in Paragraph 1.

The reimbursement for food, lodging, and other expenses shall be made at the date of payment specified in Paragraph 2, unless a contrary date is specified here: _____ .

In addition, the Sponsor shall provide the Designer with the following:

(A) Tickets for travel, rental car, or other modes of transportation as follows:

_____

_____

(B) Food and lodging as follows:

_____

_____

(C) Other hospitality as follows:

_____

_____

4. Inability to Perform. If the Designer is unable to appear on the dates scheduled in Paragraph 1 due to illness, the Sponsor shall have no obligation to make any payments under Paragraphs 2 and 3, but shall attempt to reschedule the Designer's appearance at a mutually acceptable future date. If the Sponsor is prevented from having the Designer appear by Acts of God, hurricane, flood, governmental order, or other cause beyond its control, the Sponsor shall be responsible only for the payment of such expenses under Paragraph 3 as the Designer shall have actually incurred. The Sponsor agrees in such a case to attempt to reschedule the Designer's appearance at a mutually acceptable future date.

5. Late Payment. The Sponsor agrees that, in the event it is late in making payment of amounts due to the Designer under Paragraphs 2,3, or 8, it will pay as additional liquidated damages _____ percent in interest on the amounts it is owing to the Designer, said interest to run from the date stipulated for payment in Paragraphs 2, 3, or 8 until such time as payment is made.

6. Copyrights and Recordings. Both parties agree that the Designer shall retain all rights, including copyrights, in relation to recordings of any kind made of the appearance or any works shown in the course thereof. The term "recording" as used herein shall include any recording made by electronic transcription, tape recording, wire recording, film, videotape, or other similar or dissimilar methods of recording, whether now known or hereinafter developed. No use of any such recording shall be made by the Sponsor without the written consent of the Designer and, if stipulated therein, additional compensation for such use.

7. Insurance and Loss or Damage. The Sponsor agrees that it shall provide wall-to-wall insurance for the works listed on the Schedule of Designs for the values specified therein. The Sponsor agrees that it shall be fully responsible and have strict liability for any loss or damage to the designs from the time said designs leave the Designer's residence or studio until such time as it is returned there.

8. Packing and Shipping. The Sponsor agrees that it shall fully bear any costs of packing and shipping necessary to deliver the works specified in Paragraph 7 to the Sponsor and return them to the Designer's residence or studio.

9. Modification. This contract contains the full understanding between the parties hereto and may only be modified in a written instrument signed by both parties.

10. Governing Law. This contract shall be governed by the laws of the State of _____.

In Witness Whereof, the parties hereto have signed this Agreement as of the date first set forth above.

Designer _____   Sponsor _____
                                              Company Name

                                    By _____
                                           Authorized Signatory, Title

Schedule of Designs

Title	Description	Size	Value
1.			
2.			
3.			
4.			

Licensing Contract to Merchandise Designs

Licensing is the granting of rights to use designs created by the designer to manufacture furnishings, fabrics, wall paper, and related applications. Needless to say, this can be very lucrative for the designer. So many of the products used in everyday life depend on design qualities to make them attractive to purchasers. For the designer to enter the world of manufactured, mass-produced goods offers the opportunity for new audiences and new modes of production and distribution. An excellent guide to the subject of licensing is *Licensing Art & Design* by Caryn Leland (Allworth Press). The potentially large sums of money involved, as well as the possible complexity of licensing agreements, make *Licensing Art & Design* a valuable resource for designers who either are licensing designs or would like to enter the field of licensing. Form 37, the Licensing Contract to Merchandise Designs, is adapted from a short-form licensing agreement contained in *Licensing Art & Design*, which also offers a long-form licensing agreement

Filling In the Form

In the Preamble fill in the date and the names and addresses of the parties. In Paragraph 1 indicate whether the rights are exclusive or nonexclusive, give the name and description of the design, state what types of merchandise the design can be used for, specify the geographical area for distribution, and limit the term of the distribution.

In Paragraph 3 specify the advance, if any, and the royalty percentage. State the date on which payments and statements of account are to begin in Paragraph 4. Indicate the number of samples to be given to the designer in Paragraph 6. In Paragraph 14 specify which state's laws will govern the contract. Give addresses for correspondence relating to the contract in Paragraph 15. Have both parties sign the contract.

Negotiation Checklist

❏ Carefully describe the design to be licensed. (Paragraph 1)

❏ State whether the rights given to the licensee are exclusive or nonexclusive. (Paragraph 1)

❏ Indicate which kinds of merchandise the design is being licensed for. (Paragraph 1)

❏ State the area in which the licensee may sell the licensed products. (Paragraph 1)

❏ Give a term for the licensing contract. (Paragraph 1)

❏ Consider specifying a price range within which the product must sell.

❏ Consider limiting the outlets that may carry the product, such as allowing sales only through showrooms or only through retail outlets such as department stores and similar retailers.

❏ Reserve all copyrights in the design to the designer. (Paragraph 2)

❏ Require that credit and copyright notice (if the design is copyrightable) appear in the designer's name on all licensed products. (Paragraph 2)

❏ Require that credit and copyright notice in the designer's name appear on packaging, advertising, displays, and all publicity.

❏ Have the right to approve packaging, advertising, displays, and publicity.

❏ Give the licensee the right to use the designer's name and, in an appropriate case, picture, provided that any use must be to promote the product using the design and must be in dignified taste.

❏ Determine whether the royalty should be based on retail price or, as is more commonly the case, on net price, which is what the manufacturer actually receives. (Paragraph 3)

❏ If any expenses are to reduce the amount on which royalties are calculated, these expenses must be specified.

❏ Specify the royalty percentage. (Paragraph 3)

❏ Require the licensee to pay an advance against royalties to be earned. (Paragraph 3)

❏ Indicate that any advance is nonrefundable. (Paragraph 3)

❏ Require minimum royalty payments for the term of the contract, regardless of sales.

❏ Require monthly or quarterly statements of account accompanied by any payments that are due. (Paragraph 4)

❏ Specify the information to be contained in the statement of account, such as units sold, total revenues received, special discounts, and the like. (Paragraph 4)

❏ Give the designer a right to inspect the books and records of the licensee. (Paragraph 5)

❏ Provide that if an inspection of the books and records uncovers an error to the disadvantage of the designer and that error is more than 5 percent of the amount owed designer, then the licensee shall pay for the cost of the inspection and any related costs.

❏ Provide for a certain number of samples to be given to the designer by the manufacturer. (Paragraph 6)

❏ Give the designer a right to purchase additional samples at manufacturing cost or, at least, at no more than the price paid by wholesalers. (Paragraph 6)

❏ Consider whether the designer will want the right to sell the products at retail price, rather than being restricted to using the samples and other units purchased for personal use.

❏ Give the designer a right of approval over the quality of the reproductions to protect the designer's reputation. (Paragraph 7)

❏ Require that the licensee give best efforts to promoting the licensed products. (Paragraph 8)

❏ Specify an amount of money that the licensee must spend on promotion.

❏ Specify the type of promotion that the licensee will provide.

❏ Reserve to the designer any trademarks or other rights growing out of the licensee's use of the design. (Paragraph 9)

❏ If the licensee's usage may create trademarks or other rights in the product, it is important that these rights be owned by the designer after termination of the license.

❏ Reserve all rights to the designer that are not expressly transferred. (Paragraph 10)

❏ Require the licensee to indemnify the designer for any costs arising out of the use of the design on the licensed products. (Paragraph 11)

❏ Have the licensee provide liability insurance with the designer as a named beneficiary to protect against defects in the products.

❏ Forbid assignment by the licensee, but let the designer assign royalties. (Paragraph 12)

❏ Specify the grounds for terminating the contract, such as the bankruptcy or insolvency of the licensee, failure of the licensee to obey the terms of the contract, cessation of manufacture of the product, or insufficient sales of the licensed products. (This partially covered in Paragraph 4.)

❏ Decide whether the death of the designer or licensee should terminate the agreement.

❏ Compare the standard provisions in the introductory pages with Paragraphs 13–16.

Licensing Contract to Mechandise Designs

Agreement made this _____ day of _____, 20_____, between _____ (hereinafter referred to as the "Designer"), located at _____ and _____ (hereinafter referred to as the "Licensee"), located at _____ with respect to the use of a certain design created by the Designer (hereinafter referred to as the "Design") for manufactured products (hereinafter referred to as the "Licensed Products").

Whereas, the Designer is a professional designer of good standing; and

Whereas, the Designer has created the Design which the Designer wishes to license for purposes of manufacture and sale; and

Whereas, the Licensee wishes to use the Design to create a certain product or products for manufacture and sale; and

Whereas, both parties want to achieve the best possible quality to generate maximum sales;

Now, Therefore, in consideration of the foregoing premises and the mutual covenants hereinafter set forth and other valuable consideration, the parties hereto agree as follows:

1. Grant of Merchandising Rights. The Designer grants to the Licensee the ❏ exclusive ❏ nonexclusive right to use the Design, titled _____ and described as _____, which was created and is owned by the Designer, as or as part of the following type(s) of merchandise _____ _____ for manufacture, distribution, and sale by the Licensee in the following geographical area _____ _____ and for the following period of time _____.

2. Ownership of Copyright. The Designer shall retain all copyrights in and to the Design. The Licensee shall identify the Designer as the creator of the Design on the Licensed Products and shall, if the Design is copyrightable, reproduce thereon a copyright notice for the Designer which shall include the word "Copyright" or the symbol for copyright, the Designer's name, and the year of first publication.

3. Advance and Royalties. Licensee agrees to pay Designer a nonrefundable advance in the amount of $_____ upon signing this Agreement, which advance shall be recouped from first royalties due hereunder. Licensee further agrees to pay Designer a royalty of _____ percent (_____%) of the net sales of the Licensed Products. "Net Sales" as used herein shall mean sales to customers less prepaid freight and credits for lawful and customary volume rebates, actual returns, and allowances. Royalties shall be deemed to accrue when the Licensed Products are sold, shipped, or invoiced, whichever first occurs.

4. Payments and Statements of Account. Royalty payments shall be paid monthly on the first day of each month commencing _____, 20 _____, and Licensee shall with each payment furnish Designer with a monthly statement of account showing the kinds and quantities of all Licensed Products sold, the prices received therefor, and all deductions for freight, volume rebates, returns, and allowances. The Designer shall have the right to terminate this Agreement upon thirty (30) days notice if Licensee fails to make any payment required of it and does not cure this default within said thirty (30) days, whereupon all rights granted herein shall revert immediately to the Designer.

5. Inspection of Books and Records. Upon prior written notice, Designer shall have the right to inspect Licensee's books and records concerning sales of the Licensed Products.

6. Samples. Licensee shall give the Designer _____ samples of the Licensed Products for the Designer's personal use. The Designer shall have the right to purchase additional samples of the Licensed Products at the Licensee's manufacturing cost.

7. Quality of Reproductions. The Designer shall have the right to approve the quality of the reproduction of the Design on the Licensed Products, and the Designer agrees not to withhold approval unreasonably.

8. Promotion. Licensee shall use its best efforts to promote, distribute, and sell the Licensed Products.

9. Trademarks and Other Rights. The Licensee's use of the Design shall inure to the benefit of the Designer if the Licensee acquires any trademarks, trade rights, equities, titles, or other rights in and to the Design whether by operation of law, usage, or otherwise during the term of this Agreement or any extension thereof. Upon the expiration of this Agreement or any extension thereof or sooner termination, Licensee shall assign and transfer the said trademarks, trade rights, equities, titles, or other rights to the Designer without any consideration other than the consideration of this Agreement.

10. Reservation of Rights. All rights not specifically transferred by this Agreement are reserved to the Designer.

11. Indemnification. The Licensee shall hold the Designer harmless from and against any loss, expense, or damage occasioned by any claim, demand, suit, or recovery against the Designer arising out of the use of the Design for the Licensed Products.

12. Assignment. Neither party shall assign rights or obligations under this Agreement, except that the Designer may assign the right to receive money due hereunder.

13. Nature of Contract. Nothing herein shall be construed to constitute the parties hereto as joint venturers, nor shall any similar relationship be deemed to exist between them.

14. Governing Law. This Agreement shall be construed in accordance with the laws of the state of _____; Licensee consents to the jurisdiction of the courts of the state of _____.

15. Addresses. All notices, demands, payments, royalty payments, and statements shall be sent to the Designer at the following address _____ and to the Licensee at _____.

16. Modifications in Writing. This Agreement constitutes the entire agreement between the parties hereto and shall not be modified, amended, or changed in any way except by a written agreement signed by both parties hereto.

In Witness Whereof, the parties have signed this Agreement as of the date first set forth above.

Designer _____   Licensee _____
         Company Name   Company Name

By _____   By _____
   Authorized Signatory, Title   Authorized Signatory, Title

Nondisclosure Agreement for Submitting Ideas

What can be more frustrating than having a great idea and not being able to share it with anyone? Especially if the idea has commercial value, sharing it is often the first step on the way to realizing the remunerative potential of the concept. The designer wants to show the idea to a manufacturer, distributor, or client. But how can the idea be protected?

Ideas are not protected by copyright, because copyright only protects the expression of an idea. Also, copyright does not protect useful objects. The idea to create a design for a unique chair is not copyrightable, both because it is only an idea and a chair is a useful object. On the other hand, if the chair incorporated visual imagery such as an artwork, the artwork would be copyrightable once it had actually been created (i.e., expressed). Of course, copyright is not the only form of legal protection.

An idea might be patentable or lead to the creation of a trademark. For example, a design patent can be granted to someone who invents any new and nonobvious ornamental design for a product to be placed in commerce. The design patent protects the appearance of the product, but not its functional or structural aspects. The design patent has a term of fourteen years and does not require the payment of fees to keep it in force. Since obtaining a design patent that truly gives protection requires expert legal advice, the U. S. Patent and Trademark Office advises that "It would be prudent to seek the services of a registered patent attorney or agent." Additional information is available from the United States Patent and Trademark Office Web site at *www.uspto.gov/*. Click on "Patents" and "Index," until you find the listings for "Design Patents" and "Design Patent Application, Guide to Filing a." Obtaining a trademark is discussed more thoroughly under form 45, but, briefly, a trademark identifies the source of goods or services to prevent confusion among the public.

Neither a design patent nor a trademark are ideal for protecting the disclosure of an idea that is not yet an actual product being sold in commerce. Then how does a designer disclose an idea for a product or other creation without risking that the other party will simply steal the idea?

This can be done by the creation of an express contract, an implied contract (revealed by the course of dealing between the parties), or a fiduciary relationship (in which one party owes a duty of trust to the other party). Form 38, the Nondisclosure Agreement, creates an express contract between the party disclosing the idea and the party receiving it who agrees to negotiate in good faith if the idea is used. Form 38 is adapted from a letter agreement in *Licensing Art & Design* by Caryn Leland (Allworth Press).

What should be done if a company refuses to sign a nondisclosure agreement or, even worse, has its own agreement for the designer to sign? Such an agreement might say that the company will not be liable for using a similar idea and will probably place a maximum value on the idea (such as a few hundred dollars). At this point, the designer has to evaluate the risk. Does the company have a good reputation or is it notorious for appropriating ideas? Are there other companies willing to sign a nondisclosure agreement that could be approached with the idea? If not, taking the risk may make more sense than never exploiting the idea at all. A number of steps, set out in the negotiation checklist, should then be taken to try and gain some protection. The designer will have to make these evaluations on a case-by-case basis.

Filling In the Form

In the Preamble fill in the date and the names and addresses of the parties. In Paragraph 1 describe the information to be disclosed without giving away what it is. Have both parties sign the agreement.

Negotiation Checklist

❏ Disclose what the information concerns without giving away what is new or innovative. For example, "an idea for a unique design for a chair" might interest a manufacturer but would not give away the appearance or specifications. (Paragraph 1)

❏ State that the recipient is reviewing the information to decide whether to embark on commercial exploitation. (Paragraph 2)

❏ Require the recipient to agree not to use or transfer the information. (Paragraph 3)

❏ State that the recipient receives no rights in the information. (Paragraph 3)

❏ Require the recipient to keep the information confidential. (Paragraph 4)

❏ State that the recipient acknowledges that disclosure of the information would cause irreparable harm to the designer. (Paragraph 4)

❏ Require good faith negotiations if the recipient wishes to use the information after disclosure. (Paragraph 5)

❏ Allow no use of the information unless agreement is reached after such negotiations. (Paragraph 5)

If the designer wishes to disclose the information despite the other party's refusal to sign the designer's nondisclosure form, the designer should take a number of steps:

❏ First, before submission, the idea should be sent to a neutral third party (such as a notary public or professional design society) to be held in confidence.

❏ Anything submitted should be marked with copyright and trademark notices, when appropriate. For example, the idea may not be copyrightable, but the written explanation of the idea certainly is. The copyright notice could be for that explanation, but might make the recipient more hesitant to steal the idea.

❏ If an appointment is made, confirm it by letter in advance and sign any log for visitors.

❏ After any meeting, send a letter that covers what happened at the meeting (including any disclosure of confidential information and any assurances that information will be kept confidential) and, if at all possible, have any proposal or follow-up from the recipient be in writing.

Nondisclosure Agreement for Submitting Ideas

Agreement, entered into as of this ＿＿＿ day of ＿＿＿＿＿＿, 20＿＿, between ＿＿＿＿＿＿＿＿＿＿＿＿ (hereinafter referred to as the "Designer"), located at ＿＿＿＿＿＿＿＿＿＿＿＿＿＿＿＿＿＿＿＿＿, and ＿＿＿＿＿＿＿＿＿＿＿＿＿＿＿＿＿ (hereinafter referred to as the "Recipient"), located at ＿＿.

Whereas, the Designer has developed certain valuable information, concepts, ideas, designs, or products, which the Designer deems confidential (hereinafter referred to as the "Information"); and

Whereas, the Recipient is in the business of using such Information for its projects and wishes to review the Information; and

Whereas, the Designer wishes to disclose this Information to the Recipient; and

Whereas, the Recipient is willing not to disclose this Information, as provided in this Agreement.

Now, Therefore, in consideration of the foregoing premises and the mutual covenants hereinafter set forth and other valuable considerations, the parties hereto agree as follows:

1. **Disclosure.** Designer shall disclose to the Recipient the Information, which concerns:

＿＿＿

2. **Purpose.** Recipient agrees that this disclosure is only for the purpose of the Recipient's evaluation to determine its interest in the commercial exploitation of the Information.

3. **Limitation on Use.** Recipient agrees not to manufacture, sell, deal in, or otherwise use or appropriate the disclosed Information in any way whatsoever, including but not limited to adaptation, imitation, redesign, or modification. Nothing contained in this Agreement shall be deemed to give Recipient any rights whatsoever in and to the Information.

4. **Confidentiality.** Recipient understands and agrees that the unauthorized disclosure of the Information by the Recipient to others would irreparably damage the Designer. As consideration and in return for the disclosure of this Information, the Recipient shall keep secret and hold in confidence all such Information and treat the Information as if it were the Recipient's own proprietary property by not disclosing it to any person or entity.

5. **Good Faith Negotiations.** If, on the basis of the evaluation of the Information, Recipient wishes to pursue the exploitation thereof, Recipient agrees to enter into good faith negotiations to arrive at a mutually satisfactory agreement for these purposes. Until and unless such an agreement is entered into, this nondisclosure Agreement shall remain in force.

6. **Miscellany.** This Agreement shall be binding upon and shall inure to the benefit of the parties and their respective legal representatives, successors, and assigns.

In Witness Whereof, the parties have signed this Agreement as of the date first set forth above.

Designer ＿＿＿＿＿＿＿＿＿＿＿＿＿＿＿ Recipient ＿＿＿＿＿＿＿＿＿＿＿＿＿＿
              Company Name

By ＿＿＿＿＿＿＿＿＿＿＿＿＿＿＿＿＿ By ＿＿＿＿＿＿＿＿＿＿＿＿＿＿＿＿
       Authorized Signatory, Title   Authorized Signatory, Title

Contract with an Independent Contractor

FORM 39

Designers (and their clients) often hire independent contractors, such as carpenters, furniture restorers, painters, and other skilled artisans. Form 39 can be used by the designer, or by the designer's client, to contract with an independent contractor. The advantage of having the client contract directly is that the designer is not in an intermediary position with its attendant risks. However, the designer should advise the client to consult with the client's attorney for contract forms and advice when contracting with an independent contractor, since the designer should never give or appear to give legal advice. Also, while the designer may suggest contractors to the client, it is wise to have the client make the final selection of the contractor. If the designer likes to work with particular contractors and insists the client hires among them, the designer should be prepared to be blamed by the client if anything goes wrong—even if the client has contracted directly with the contractor and the designer has no legal liability.

Independent contractors run their own businesses and hire out on a job by job basis. They are not employees, which saves the designer in terms of employee benefits, payroll taxes, and paperwork. By not being an employee, the independent contractor does not have to have taxes withheld and is able to deduct all business expenses directly against income.

A contract with an independent contractor serves two purposes. First, it shows the intention of the parties to have the services performed by an independent contractor. Second, it shows the terms on which the parties will do business.

As to the first purpose of the contract—showing the intention to hire an independent contractor, not an employee, the contract can be helpful if the Internal Revenue Service (IRS) decides to argue that the independent contractor was an employee. The tax law automatically classifies as independent contractors physicians, lawyers, general building contractors, and others who follow an independent trade, business, or profession, in which they offer their services to the public on a regular basis. However, many people do not fall clearly into this group. IRS guidelines as to the employee-independent contractor distinction are discussed in relation to form 43.

The second purpose of the contract is to specify the terms agreed to between the parties. What services will the contractor provide and when will the services be performed? On what basis and when will payment be made by the designer? If a project fee is to be paid, will it be paid in installments so that the payment of fees is closely matched to the progression of work? Will there be an advance, perhaps to help defray expenses? Will the designer demand a provision for retainage, so that 10–15 percent of all payments are withheld until satisfactory completion of the work, and will the contractor agree to this?

There should be agreement about a schedule, which would include start and completion dates. Whether time is of the essence, which would require that time deadlines be strictly met, should also be indicated in the contract. It may be that after the date of substantial completion, when space can be occupied without risk, time will be made of the essence to encourage promptly moving ahead to final completion when everything is finished, any necessary inspections have been made, and, if need, a certificate of occupancy has been obtained.

The designer should consult with his or her insurance agent with respect to the insurance the designer should carry when dealing with independent contractors. Certainly the designer should make sure there is adequate coverage for property damage or liability arising from lawsuits for injuries. The contractor should definitely have its own liability policy as well as workers' compensation and any state disability coverage. The designer may require the independent contractor to maintain a certain level of insurance in force and include the designer as an additional named beneficiary of that policy.

Independent contractors can perform large jobs or render a day's services. Form 39 is designed to help designers deal with small independent contractors who are performing a limited amount of work. The negotiation checklist is also directed toward this situation. However, some further discussion is necessary to cover the issues arising when the designer has a larger project to complete.

If the designer were dealing with a substantial renovation or other construction, the contract would have to be more complex. First, it is always wise to have references for a contractor who is new to the designer. Keep deposits small, since it can be hard to get a deposit back if the contractor does not perform. There should also be clarity as to the quality and perhaps even the brands of any materials to be used. The contractor can be asked to post a surety bond, which is a bond to guarantee full performance. However, many small contractors may have difficulty obtaining such a bond, since the insurance company may require the posting of collateral. In any event, the designer might explore with his or her own insurance agent the feasibility of demanding this from the contractor. A point to keep in mind is that the contractor's failure to pay subcontractors or suppliers of material can result in a lien against the property where the work has been done. A lien is like a mortgage on a building; it must be satisfied or removed before the property can be sold. A surety bond would avoid problems with liens. Another approach is to require the contractor and any subcontractors to provide the designer with waiver of liens when the work is finished.

A contractor should be required to give a bid. That bid will be the basis for the terms of the contract. The contractor may want to wait until after completing the work to determine a fee. Obviously this is unacceptable. The contractor may want to charge a fee for labor, but charge cost plus a markup for materials. This is probably also unacceptable, since the designer has a budget and needs to know that budget can be met. Another variation is for the contractor to allow for a 10 percent variation in the bid or the costs of materials based on what actually happens. This should be carefully evaluated by the designer, but is less desirable than a firm fee. The fee and the job description should be modified only by a written amendment to the contract. If this isn't required, disputes are likely to result.

The designer should, if possible, require the contractor to warrant a number of facts, such as the contractor being licensed if necessary, the materials being new and of good quality, the contractor being responsible for any damages arising from its work, and any construction being guaranteed for some period of time. The contractor would agree to protect the designer (by paying losses, damages, and any attorney's fees) in the event any of these warranties were breached. If permits are necessary to do the work, the contract should specify who will obtain the permit.

Keep in mind that form 39 is designed for projects of limited scale, not the hiring of builders for major renovations that would usually require the guidance of an architectural firm.

Filling In the Form

In the Preamble fill in the date and the names and addresses of the parties. In Paragraph 1 show in detail what services are to be performed. Attach another sheet of description or a list of procedures, phases, specifications, diagrams, or plans to the contract, if needed. If the designer is to obtain or pay for permits, fill in that information. Indicate if the contractor is to obtain a payment bond or a performance bond. In Paragraph 2 give a schedule. In Paragraph 3 deal with the fee and expenses. In Paragraph 4 specify a time for payment.

In Paragraph 5 indicate how cancellations will be handled. In Paragraph 6[E] fill in any special criteria that the contractor should warrant as true. In Paragraph 7 fill in the information with respect to insurance the contractor must carry. In Paragraph 10 specify who will arbitrate, where the arbitration will take place, and, if local small claims court would be better than arbitration, give amounts under the small claims court dollar limit as an exclusion from arbitration. In Paragraph 11 give the state whose laws will govern the contract. Have both parties sign the contract.

Negotiation Checklist

❏ Carefully detail the services to be performed. If necessary, attach an additional sheet of description, a list of procedures, phases, specifications, diagrams, or plans. (Paragraph 1)

❏ Require the contractor to obtain and pay for any needed permits. (Paragraph 1)

❏ Indicate that the contractor has taken into account when setting fees any special circumstances regarding access, location, existing conditions, and the like. (Paragraph 1)

❏ Require that when the project is completed, the contractor and any subcontractors will provide the designer with waivers of liens. (Paragraph 1)

❏ Especially for commercial projects, require the contractor to obtain a performance bond and a payment bond. (Paragraph 1)

❏ Set the standard the contractor must meet, such as work of the highest quality. (Paragraph 1)

❏ Set the standard by which the work will be judged, such as that the work must be satisfactory to the designer. (Paragraph 1)

❏ Determine whether a certain number of workers should always have to be present for the project.

❏ Clarify that the contractor must supervise any workers. (Paragraph 1)

❏ Consider having the contractor give a general release to the designer after payment has been made so no question can arise about money being owed to the contractor.

❏ Give a schedule for performance. (Paragraph 2)

❏ With respect to the schedule, consider making time of the essence, so that lateness will be a breach of the contract. (Paragraph 2)

❏ State the method for computing the fee. (Paragraph 3)

❏ If a project fee is used, pay in installments so the contractor does not get paid ahead of the work. (Paragraph 3)

❏ If the contractor is to bill for expenses, limit which expenses may be charged. (Paragraph 3)

❏ Require full documentation of expenses in the form of receipts and invoices. (Paragraph 3)

❏ Place a maximum amount on the expenses that can be incurred. (Paragraph 3)

❏ Pay an advance against expenses, if the amount of the expenses are too much for the contractor to wait to receive back at the time of payment for the entire job. (Paragraph 3)

❏ State a time for payment. (Paragraph 4)

❏ Provide that notice will be given before termination for cause so the delay or other problem can be cured. (Paragraph 5)

❏ Indicate whether the bankruptcy or insolvency of the contractor should terminate the contract. (Paragraph 5)

❏ Decide whether the death of the designer or contractor should terminate the agreement.

❏ Consider setting a reasonable amount for "liquidated damages," such as a daily dollar amount the contractor must pay the designer if the completion deadline isn't met. (Paragraph 5)

❏ Consider offering a bonus for early completion, if there is a damages provision for late completion.

❏ Even if liquidated damages are paid, reserve the right to sue for damages. After termination, for example, the designer may have to hire a different contractor to finish the job and may end up paying the new contractor far more than the liquidated damages received from the old contractor. (Paragraph 5)

❏ If expenses are billed for, consider whether any markup should be allowed.

❏ Require warranties that the contractor is legally able to perform the contract (including being licensed, if that is necessary), that all services will be done in a professional manner, that any subcontractor or employee hired by the contractor will be professional, that the contractor will pay all taxes for the contractor and his or her employees, and any other criteria for the proper performance of the services. (Paragraph 6)

❏ Review insurance coverage with the designer's insurance agent.

❏ Specify what insurance coverage the contractor must have. (Paragraph 7)

❏ Require that the contract cover the designer as an additional named insured. (Paragraph 7)

❏ Make certain the contractor actually obtains the insurance coverage and follows through in naming the designer as an additional named insured.

❏ State that the parties are independent contractors and not employer-employee. (Paragraph 8)

❏ Do not allow assignment of rights or obligations under the contract. (Paragraph 9)

❏ The designer should check with his or her attorney as to whether arbitration is better than suing in the local courts, and whether small claims court might be better than arbitration. (Paragraph 10)

❏ If the designer has not appointed a project representative and the contractor requests this, comply with the request.

❏ Require that changes to the contract be written and signed by both parties, including work change orders.(Paragraph 11)

❏ If a work change order affects the fee, as will frequently be the case, the work change order should detail the impact on the fee. (Paragraph 11)

❏ Compare Paragraph 11 with the standard provisions in the introduction.

Contract with an Independent Contractor

Agreement entered into as of the _____ day of _____, 20___, between _____ (hereinafter referred to as the "Designer"), located at _____, and _____, (hereinafter referred to as the "Contractor"), located at _____.

The Parties hereto agree as follows:

1. Services to be Rendered. The Contractor agrees to perform the following services for the Designer:

_____

_____

_____

_____

_____

The Contractor has reviewed special aspects of the project, such as location, existing features, access, and the like, and has incorporated all such considerations into the fee specified in Paragraph 3.

If any permits are necessary to perform these services, the Contractor shall obtain these permits at its expense unless provided to the contrary here _____

The Contractor shall obtain payment and performance bonds as follows:

_____

_____

_____

The Contractor shall provide work of the highest quality, which shall be completed to the satisfaction of the Designer. The Contractor shall be responsible for supervision of the work in progress. Upon completion, the Contractor shall provide the Designer with waivers of liens both for the Contractor and any subcontractors used by the Contractor.

If needed, a list of procedures, phases, specifications, diagrams, or plans for the services shall be attached to and made part of this Agreement.

2. Schedule. The Contractor shall complete the services pursuant to the following schedule:

_____

_____

_____

Time shall be of the essence for performance under this contract.

3. Fee and Expenses. The Designer shall pay the Contractor as follows:

❏ Project rate $_____, in installments as follows _____

_____

❏ Day rate $_____ / day

❏ Hourly rate $_____ / hour

❏ Other _____ $_____

The Designer shall reimburse the Contractor only for the expenses listed here:

_____
_____
_____

Expenses shall not exceed $_____. The Contractor shall provide full documentation for any expenses to be reimbursed, including receipts and invoices. An advance of $_____ against expenses shall be paid to the Contractor and recouped when Payment is made pursuant to Paragraph 4.

4.   Payment. Payment shall be made: ❏ at the end of each day ❏ upon completion of the project ❏ within thirty (30) days of Designer's receipt of Contractor's invoice ❏ Other _____

5.   Termination. This Agreement may be terminated at any time for cause by either party notifying the other party in writing of that party's breach of the Agreement and giving five (5) business days for a cure, after which the notifying party may terminate if there has been no cure of the breach. Causes for termination shall include, but not be limited to, failure to perform any duty pursuant to this Agreement in a timely manner, postponements of the Project for more than ____ business days in total, and the bankruptcy or insolvency of a party hereto. While reserving all other rights under this Agreement, including the right to sue for damages, in the event that the Project is terminated, the Designer shall have the right to be paid $____ for each day that the Contractor has fallen behind the schedule.

6.   Warranties. The Contractor warrants as follows:
   (A) Contractor is fully able to enter into and perform its obligations pursuant to this Agreement, including but not limited to having any licenses that may be necessary to perform the services required hereunder.
   (B) All services shall be performed in a professional manner.
   (C) If employees or subcontractors are to be hired by Contractor, they shall be competent professionals.
   (D) Contractor shall pay all necessary local, state, or federal taxes, including but not limited to withholding taxes, workers' compensation, F.I.C.A., and unemployment taxes, for Contractor and its employees.
   (E) Any other criteria for performance are as follows _____
      _____
      _____

7.   Insurance. The Contractor agrees to carry liability insurance and name Designer as an additional named insured under its policy and furnish to Designer certificates showing liability coverage of not less than $_____ applicable to the services to be performed hereunder. The insurer must be a company recognized to do business in the State of _____. Such company shall be required to give the Designer ten (10) days notice prior to cancellation of any such policy. Failure to obtain or keep in force such liability insurance shall allow the Designer to obtain such coverage and charge the amount of premiums as an offset against fees payable hereunder to the Contractor. In addition, the Contractor shall maintain in force the following other types of insurance

_____
_____
_____

8.   Relationship of Parties. Both parties agree that the Contractor is an independent contractor. This Agreement is not an employment agreement, nor does it constitute a joint venture or partnership between the Designer and Contractor. Nothing contained herein shall be construed to be inconsistent with this independent contractor relationship.

9.   Assignment. This Agreement may not be assigned by either party without the written consent of the other party hereto.

10. Arbitration. All disputes shall be submitted to binding arbitration before _____ in the following location _____ and settled in accordance with the rules of the American Arbitration Association. Judgment upon the arbitration award may be entered in any court having jurisdiction thereof. Disputes in which the amount at issue is less than $_____ shall not be subject to this arbitration provision.

11. Miscellany. This Agreement constitutes the entire agreement between the parties. Its terms can be modified only by an instrument in writing signed by both parties, including but not limited to work change orders. This Agreement shall be binding on the parties, their heirs, successors, assigns, and personal representatives. A waiver of a breach of any of the provisions of this Agreement shall not be construed as a continuing waiver of other breaches of the same or other provisions hereof. This Agreement shall be governed by the laws of the State of _____.

In Witness Whereof, the parties hereto have signed this as of the date first set forth above.

Designer _____   Contractor _____
                Company Name

By _____
          Authorized Signatory

Employment Application
Employment Agreement
Restrictive Covenant for Employment

FORM 40 **FORM 41** **FORM 42**

Hiring new employees should invigorate and strengthen the interior design firm. However, proper management practices have to be followed or the results can be disappointing and, potentially, open the firm to the danger of litigation. The process of advertising a position, interviewing, and selecting a candidate should be shaped in such a way that the firm maintains clarity of purpose and fortifies its legal position.

The hiring process should avoid violating any state or federal law prohibiting discrimination, including discrimination on the basis of race, religion, age, sex, or disability. Help-wanted advertising, listings of a position with an employment agency, application forms to be filled in, questions asked during an interview, statements in the employee handbook or office manual, and office forms should all comply with these anti-discrimination laws.

The firm should designate an administrator to handle human resources. That person should develop familiarity with the legal requirements and review the overall process to protect the firm and ensure the best candidates are hired. All employment matters—from résumés, applications, interview reports, documentation as to employment decisions to personnel files, and employee benefit information—should channel through this person.

The human resources administrator should train interviewers with respect both to legalities and the goals of the firm. Firms that lack job descriptions may not realize that this is detrimental to the firm as well as the potential employee. Not only will the employee have a more difficult time understanding the nature of the position, but the interviewer will have a harder task of developing a checklist of desirable characteristics to look for in the interview and use as a basis of comparison among candidates. This vagueness may encompass not only the duties required in the position, but also the salary, bonuses, benefits, duration, and grounds for discharge with respect to the position. Such ambiguity is likely to lead to dissatisfaction on both sides, which is inimical to a harmonious relationship and productive work environment.

The design firm should keep in mind that employment relationships are terminable at will by either the employee or the firm, unless the firm has promised that the employment will have a definite duration. Unless the firm intends to create a different relationship, it should take steps throughout the hiring process to make clear that the employment is terminable at will. So, for example, form 40 indicates this in the declaration signed by the applicant. The administrator should make certain that nothing in the advertisements, application, job description, interview, employee handbook, office manual, or related documents give an impression of long-term or permanent employment. Interviewers, who may be seeking to impress the applicant with the pleasant ambience and creative culture of the firm, should not make statements such as, "Working here is a lifetime career."

The application also offers the opportunity to inform the applicant that false statements are grounds for discharge. In addition, the applicant gives permission to contact the various employers, educational institutions, and references listed in the application.

Because the employment application presents the design firm with an opportunity to bolster various goals in the employment process, the application is used in addition to the résumé that the employee would also be expected to make available. The application, of course, is only the beginning of the relationship between employer and employee, but it starts the relationship in a proper way that can be bolstered by the interview, the employee handbook, and related policies that ensure clarity with respect to the employee's duties and conditions of employment.

The employment agreement evolves from the process of application and interviews. It allows the design firm to reiterate that the employment is terminable at will. It also clarifies for both parties the terms of the employment, such as the duties, salary, benefits, and reviews. By clarifying the terms, it minimizes the likelihood of misunderstandings or disputes. It can also provide for arbitration in the event that disputes do arise.

The design firm may want to protect itself against the possibility that an employee will leave and go into competition with or harm the firm. For example, the employee might start his or her own business and try to take away clients, work for a competitor, or sell confidential information. The design firm can protect against this by the use of a restrictive covenant, which can either be part of the employment agreement or a separate agreement. The restriction must be reasonable in terms of duration and geographic scope. It would be against public policy to allow a firm to ban an employee from ever again pursuing a career in interior design. However, a restriction that for six months or a year after leaving the firm the employee will neither work for competitors nor start a competing firm in the same city would have a likelihood of being enforceable. Laws vary from state to state. It is wise to provide separate or additional consideration for the restrictive covenant to lessen the risk of its being struck down by a court (such as allocating a portion of wages to the restrictive covenant). This is best done at the time of first employment, since asking someone who is currently employed to sign a restrictive covenant may raise a red flag about relative bargaining positions and the validity of the consideration.

Certainly these agreements may be done as letter agreements, which have a less formal feeling and may appear more inviting for an employee to sign. For that reason, form 41 and form 42 take the form of letters to the employee. Regardless of whether letters countersigned by the employee or more formal agreements are used, the employment agreement and the restrictive covenant should be reviewed by an attorney with an expertise in employment law.

Two helpful books for developing successful programs with respect to employment are *From Hiring to Firing* and *The Complete Collection of Legal Forms for Employers*, both written by Steven Mitchell Sack (Legal Strategies Publications).

Filling In Form 40
This is filled in by the employee and is self-explanatory.

Filling In Form 41
Using the design firm's stationery, give the date and name and address of the prospective employee. In the opening paragraph fill in the name of the design firm. In Paragraph 1 give the position for which the person is being hired and the start date. In Paragraph 2 indicate the duties of the position. In Paragraph 3 give the annual compensation. In Paragraph 4 fill in the various benefits.

In Paragraph 8 indicate who would arbitrate, where arbitration would take place, and consider inserting the local small claims court limit so small amounts can be sued for in that forum (assuming the design firm is eligible to sue in the local small claims court). In Paragraph 9 fill in the state whose laws will govern the agreement. The design firm should sign two copies, the employee should countersign, and each party should keep one copy of the letter.

Filling In Form 42
Using the design firm's stationery, give the date and name and address of the prospective

employee. In the opening paragraph fill in the date of the Employment Agreement (which is likely to be the same date as this letter) and the name of design firm. In Paragraph 1 enter a number of months. In Paragraph 3 give the additional compensation that the design firm will pay. In Paragraph 6 fill in the state whose laws will govern the agreement. The design firm should sign two copies, the employee should countersign, and each party should keep one copy of the letter.

Checklist

❏ Appoint a human resources administrator for the firm.

❏ Avoid anything that may be discrimination in advertising the position, in the application form, in the interview, and in the employee handbook and other employment-related documents.

❏ Retain copies of all advertisements, including records on how many people responded and how many were hired.

❏ In advertisements or job descriptions refer to the position as "full-time" or "regular," rather than using words that imply the position may be long-term or permanent.

❏ Do not suggest that the position is secure (such as "career path" or "long-term growth").

❏ Never make claims about guaranteed earnings that will not, in fact, be met.

❏ Don't require qualifications beyond what are necessary for the position, since doing so may discriminate against people with lesser qualifications who could have done the job.

❏ Make certain the qualifications do not discriminate against people with disabilities who might nonetheless be able to perform the work.

❏ Carefully craft job descriptions to aid both applicants and interviewers.

❏ Train interviewers and monitor their statements and questions to be certain the firm is in compliance with anti-discrimination laws.

❏ Be precise in setting forth the salary, bonuses, benefits, duration, and grounds for discharge with respect to the position.

❏ Make certain the candidates have the immigration status to work legally in the United States.

❏ Do not ask for church references while in the hiring process.

❏ Avoid asking for photographs of candidates for a position.

❏ Never allow interviewers to ask questions of women they would not ask of men.

❏ Never say to an older candidate that he or she is "overqualified".

❏ Instruct interviewers never to speak of "lifetime employment" or use similar phrases.

❏ Have the candidate give permission for the firm to contact references, prior employers, and educational institutions listed in the application.

❏ When contacting references and others listed in the application, make certain not to slander or invade the privacy of the applicant.

❏ Have the candidate acknowledge his or her understanding that the employment is terminable at will.

❏ Stress the importance of truthful responses and have the candidate confirm his or her knowledge that false responses will be grounds for dismissal.

❏ Always get back to applicants who are not hired and give a reason for not hiring them.

The reason should be based on the job description, such as, "We interviewed many candidates and hired another individual whose background and skills should make the best match for the position."

❏ Consult with an attorney with expertise in the employment field before inquiring into arrests, asking for polygraph tests, requesting pre-employment physicals, requiring psychological or honesty tests, investigating prior medical history, or using credit reports, since this behavior may be illegal.

❏ Create an employee handbook that sets forth all matters of concern to employees, from benefits to standards for behavior in the workplace to evaluative guidelines with respect to performance.

❏ Consider whether the firm wants to have a restrictive covenant with the employee.

❏ If a restrictive covenant is to be used, decide what behavior would ideally be preventable—working for a competitor, creating a competitive business, contacting the design firm's clients, inducing other employees to leave, or using confidential information (such as customer lists or trade secrets).

❏ Give a short duration for the covenant, such as six months or one year.

❏ Make clear that additional consideration was paid to the employee for agreeing to the restrictive covenant.

❏ If there is a breach of the restrictive covenant, consult an attorney and immediately put the employee on notice of the violation.

❏ Consider whether the firm wants an arbitration clause with the employee, since such a clause allows the firm to determine where and before which arbitrators the arbitration will take place.

❏ Make certain that any contract confirming the employment specifies that the employment is terminable at will (unless the designer wishes to enter into a different arrangement). It should also clarify the duties of the employee, set forth the salary, benefits, and related information, provide for arbitration if desired, and delineate any restrictive covenant (unless that is to be in a separate document entered into at the same time).

Employment Application

Date _____

Applicant's Name _____

Address _____

_____

Daytime telephone _____ E-mail address _____

Social Security Number _____

Position for which you are applying _____

How did you learn about this position? _____

Are you 18 years of age or older?   ❏ Yes   ❏ No

If you are hired for this position, can you provide written proof that you may legally work in the United States?
❏ Yes   ❏ No

On what date are you able to commence work? _____

Employment History

Are you currently employed?   ❏ Yes   ❏ No

Starting with your current or most recent position, give the requested information:

1. Employer _____

Address _____

Supervisor _____

Telephone Number _____ E-mail Address _____

Dates of Employment _____ Salary _____

Description of your job title and duties _____

_____

Reason for leaving position _____

May we contact this employer for a reference?   ❏ Yes   ❏ No

2. Employer _____

Address _____

Supervisor _____

Telephone Number _____ E-mail Address _____

Dates of Employment _____ Salary _____

Description of your job title and duties _____

_____

Reason for leaving position _____

May we contact this employer for a reference?   ❏ Yes   ❏ No

3. Employer _____

Address _____

Supervisor _____

Telephone Number _____ E-mail Address _____

Dates of Employment _____ Salary _____

Description of your job title and duties _____

_____

Reason for leaving position _____

May we contact this employer for a reference?   ❏ Yes   ❏ No

List and explain any special skills relevant for the position for which you are applying that you have acquired from your employment or other activities (include computer software in which you are proficient).

_____
_____
_____
_____
_____
_____
_____
_____
_____
_____

Educational History

	Name and Address of School	Study Specialty	Number of Years Completed	Degree or Diploma
High School				
College				
Graduate School				
Other Education				

Describe any internships, other specialized training (including job-related experience in the United States military), extracurricular activities, licenses, or degrees that would be particularly helpful in performing this position.

_____

_____

_____

_____

_____

_____

To make inquiries about your work record, do we need any information about your name or your use of another? ❏ Yes ❏ No If you answer yes, please explain _____

_____

References

1. Name _____ Telephone _____
   Address _____ E-mail address _____
   How long and in what context have you known this reference? _____

   _____

2. Name _____ Telephone _____
   Address _____ E-mail address _____
   How long and in what context have you known this reference? _____

   _____

3. Name _____ Telephone _____
   Address _____ E-mail address _____
   How long and in what context have you known this reference? _____

   _____

Applicant's Declaration

I understand that the information given in this employment application will be used in determining whether or not I will be hired for this position. I have made certain to give only true answers and understand that any falsification or willful omission will be grounds for refusal of employment or dismissal.

I understand that the employer hires on an employment-at-will basis, which employment may be terminated either by me or the employer at any time, with or without cause, for any reason consistent with applicable state and federal law. If I am offered the position for which I am applying, it will be employment-at-will, unless a written instrument signed by an authorized executive of the employer changes this.

I know that this application is not a contract of employment. I am lawfully authorized to work in the United States and, if offered the position, will give whatever documentary proof of this as the employer may request.

I further understand that the employer may investigate and verify all information I have given in this application, on related documents (including, but not limited to, my résumé), and in interviews. I authorize all individuals, educational institutions, and companies named in this application to provide any information the employer may request about me, and I release them from any liability for damages for providing such information.

Applicant's signature _____   Date _____

Employment Agreement

[Designer's Letterhead]

Date _____

Mr./Ms. New Employee

_____ [address]

_____

Dear

We are pleased that you will be joining us at _____ (hereinafter referred to as the "Company"). This letter is to set forth the terms and conditions of your employment.

1. Your employment as _____ shall commence on _____, 20____.

2. Your duties shall consist of the following: _____

_____

_____

You may also perform additional duties incidental to the job description. You shall faithfully perform all duties to the best of your ability. This is a full-time position, and you shall devote your full and undivided time and best efforts to the business of the Company.

3. You will be paid annual compensation of $_____ pursuant to the Company's regular handling of payroll.

4. You will have the following benefits:

    a) Sick days _____

    b) Personal days _____

    c) Vacation _____

    d) Bonus _____

    e) Health Insurance _____

    f) Retirement Benefits _____

    g) Other _____

5. You will familiarize yourself with the Company's rules and regulations for employees and follow them during your employment.

6. This employment is terminable at will at any time by you or the Company.

7. You acknowledge that a precondition to this employment is that you negotiate and sign a restrictive covenant prior to the commencement date set forth in Paragraph 1.

8. Arbitration. All disputes arising under this Agreement shall be submitted to binding arbitration before _____ in the following location _____ and settled in accordance with the rules of the American Arbitration Association. Judgment upon the arbitration award may be entered in any court

having jurisdiction thereof. Disputes in which the amount at issue is less than $_____ shall not be subject to this arbitration provision.

9. Miscellany. This agreement shall be binding on both us and you, as well as heirs, successors, assigns, and personal representatives. This agreement constitutes the entire understanding. Its terms can be modified only by an instrument in writing signed by both parties. Notices shall be sent by certified mail or traceable overnight delivery to you or the Company at our present addresses, and notification of any change of address shall be given prior to that change of address taking effect. A waiver of a breach of any of the provisions of this agreement shall not be construed as a continuing waiver of other breaches of the same or other provisions hereof. This agreement shall be governed by the laws of the State of _____.

If this letter accurately sets forth our understanding, please sign beneath the words "Agreed to," and return one copy to us for our files.

Agreed to:

Sincerely yours,
[Company name]

_____
Employee

By _____
Name, Title

Restrictive Covenant for Employment

[Designer's Letterhead]

Date _____

Mr./Ms. New Employee

_____ [address]

_____

Dear

By a separate letter dated _____, 20__, we have set forth the terms for your employment with _____ (hereinafter referred to as the "Company").

This letter is to deal with your role regarding certain sensitive aspects of the Company's business. Our policy has always been to encourage our employees, when qualified, to deal with our clients and, when appropriate, contact our clients directly. In addition, during your employment with the Company, you may be given knowledge of proprietary information that the Company wishes to keep confidential.

To protect the Company and compensate you, we agree as follows:

1. You will not directly or indirectly compete with the business of the Company during the term of your employment and for a period of ____ months following the termination of your employment, regardless of who initiated the termination, unless you obtain the Company's prior written consent. This means that you will not be employed by, own, manage, or consult with a business that is either similar to or competes with the business of the Company. This restriction shall be limited to the geographic areas in which the Company usually conducts its business, except that it shall apply to the Company's clients regardless of their location.

2. In addition, you will not during the term of your employment or thereafter directly or indirectly disclose or use any confidential information of the Company, except in the pursuit of your employment and in the best interest of the Company. Confidential information includes, but is not limited to, client lists, client files, trade secrets, financial data, sales or marketing data, plans, designs, and the like, relating to the current or future business of the Company. All confidential information is the sole property of the Company. This provision shall not apply to information voluntarily disclosed to the public without restrictions or which has lawfully entered the public domain.

3. As consideration for your agreement to this restrictive covenant, the Company will compensate you as follows:

_____

_____

4. You acknowledge that, in the event of your breach of this restrictive covenant, money damages would not adequately compensate the Company. You, therefore, agree that, in addition to all other legal and equitable remedies available to the Company, the Company shall have the right to receive injunctive relief in the event of any breach hereunder.

5. The terms of this restrictive covenant shall survive the termination of your employment, regardless of the reason or causes, if any, for the termination, or whether the termination might constitute a breach of the agreement of employment.

6. Miscellany. This agreement shall be binding on both us and you, as well as our heirs, successors, assigns, and personal representatives. This agreement constitutes the entire understanding. Its terms can be modified only by an instrument in writing signed by both parties. Notices shall be sent by certified mail or traceable overnight delivery to you or the Company at our present addresses, and notification of any change of address shall be given prior to that change of address taking effect. A waiver of a breach of any of the provisions of this agreement shall not be construed as a continuing waiver of other breaches of the same or other provisions hereof. This agreement shall be governed by the laws of the State of _____.

If this letter accurately sets forth our understanding, please sign beneath the words "Agreed to," and return one copy to us for our files.

Agreed to: Sincerely yours,
                                               [Company name]

_____   By _____
          Employee   Name, Title

Project Employee Contract

An interior design firm may want to hire someone who falls into an intermediate position between an independent contractor (discussed with respect to form 39) and a permanent employee. If the person is to work on a project for a period of months, it is quite likely that he or she meets the legal definition of an employee. While the person may meet the IRS tests for who is an employee, the design firm may prefer not to give the person the full benefits of the typical employment contract.

The first consideration in such a situation is whether the person could be hired as an independent contractor. Since IRS reclassification from independent contractor to employee can have harsh consequences for the design firm, including payment of back employment taxes, penalties, and jeopardy to qualified pension plans, the IRS has promulgated guidelines to help an employer determine who is an employee.

Basically, an employee is someone who is under the control and direction of the employer to accomplish work. The employee is not only told what to do, but how to do it. On the other hand, an independent contractor is controlled or directed only as to the final result, not as to the means and method to accomplish that result. Some twenty factors enumerated by the IRS dictate the conclusion as to whether someone is an employee or an independent contractor, and no single factor is controlling. Factors suggesting someone is an independent contractor would include that the person supplies his or her own equipment and facilities; that the person works for more than one party (and perhaps employs others at the same time); that the person can choose the location to perform the work; that the person is not supervised during the assignment; that the person receives a fee or commission rather than an hourly or weekly wage; that the person can make a loss or a profit; and that the person can be forced to terminate the job for poor performance but cannot be dismissed like an employee. The designer should consult his or her accountant or attorney to resolve any doubts about someone's status.

Assuming that these criteria suggest that a person to be hired for a project is an employee, the design firm may choose to designate him or her as a project employee. Project employees are usually hired for a minimum of four months. They may be transferred from one assignment to another. Project employees are usually eligible for most benefits offered other regular employees, such as medical/dental benefits, life insurance, long-term disability, vacation, and so on. However, project employees would not be eligible for leaves of absence and severance pay. If a project employee moves to regular status, the length of service will usually be considered to have begun on the original hire date as a project employee.

Filling In the Form

This contract would normally take the form of a letter written on the company's letterhead. Fill in the name of the project employee in the salutation. Then specify the type of work that the project employee will be doing—i.e., interior designer, assistant, account executive, and so on. Indicate the start date for work and the anticipated project termination date. In the second paragraph give the salary on an annualized basis as well as on a biweekly basis. In the third paragraph state benefits for which the project employee will not be eligible, such as leaves of absence, tuition reimbursement, and severance pay. Insert the company name in the last paragraph and again after "Sincerely". Both parties should sign the letter.

Project Employee Contract

[Designer's Letterhead]

Dear _____

This will confirm that you have accepted a Project Job as _____ with our company. This assignment will begin on _____, and has an expected project termination date on or before _____ .

As we agreed, based on an annual salary of $_____, you will be paid $_____ on a biweekly basis, less applicable taxes and insurance. During the term of the assignment, this employment will be terminable at will either by you as Project Employee or by us as Project Employer.

As a Project Employee, you are eligible for our company's benefits except for _____
_____
_____

I cannot guarantee your employment beyond this assignment. The project employee status allows you to consider finding another job within the company. An added benefit is that if your Project Employment status changes to that of regular employee, your original Project hire date will become your start date of continuous employment.

I am very pleased to welcome you to _____ and look forward to working with you. Please let me know if you have any questions or concerns.

Sincerely,

_____
Company Name

By: _____
Project Manager

Agreed to:

_____
Project Employee

Date: _____

Copyright Application

To register an artwork (including a design incorporating an artwork), the designer must send a completed Form VA, a nonrefundable filing fee, and a nonreturnable deposit portraying the work to be registered. These three items should be sent together to the Register of Copyrights, Copyright Office, Library of Congress, Washington, DC 20559. If the designer is working with a piece that is predominantly textual (such as a corporate brochure), Form TX is used for the registration.

The instructions for filling in Form VA are provided by the Copyright Office and are reproduced here with Form VA. The Copyright Office has an information number—(202) 707-3000—and also makes available a free Copyright Information Kit. This includes copies of Form VA and other Copyright Office circulars and is worth requesting. To expedite receiving forms or circulars, the Forms and Circulars Hotline number can be used: (202) 707-9100. Request the kit for the visual arts. In addition, information can be obtained and forms downloaded from the Copyright Office Web site (*http://lcweb.loc.gov/copyright*).

Because of budget constraints, the Copyright Office will accept reproductions of Form VA such as the tear-out form in this book. If the designer wishes to make copies, however, the copies must be clear, legible, on a good grade of white paper, and printed on a single sheet of paper so that when the sheet is turned over the top of page 2 is directly behind the top of page 1.

It is wise to register any work which the designer feels may be infringed. Registration has a number of values, the most important of which is to establish proof that a particular design was created by the designer as of a certain date. Both published and unpublished designs can be registered. In fact, unpublished designs can be registered in groups for a single application fee.

For published designs, the proper deposit is usually two complete copies of the work. For unpublished designs, one complete copy would be correct. Since the purpose of registering is to protect what the designer has created, it is important that the material deposited fully show what is copyrightable.

Obviously, unique artworks or designs cannot be sent along with the application for purposes of identifying themselves, so the Copyright Office accepts other identifying materials. These are usually photographs, photostats, slides, drawings, or other two-dimensional representations of the work. The designer should provide as much identifying material as is necessary to show the copyrightable content of the design, including any copyright notice which has been used. The proper form for copyright notice, by the way, is © or Copyright or Copr., the designer's name, and the year of first publication.

The preferable size for identifying materials (other than transparencies) is 8″ × 10″, but anything from 3″ × 3″ up to 9″ × 12″ will be acceptable. Also, at least one piece of the identifying material must give an exact measurement of one or more dimensions of the design and give the title on its front, back, or mount.

For a full review of registration and its requirements, the designer can consult Copyright Office Circular 40, *Copyright Registration for Works of the Visual Arts*, and Circular 40a, *Deposit Requirements for Registration of Claims to Copyright in Visual Arts Material*.

A copyright registration is effective as of the date that the Copyright Office receives the application, fee, and deposit materials in an acceptable form, regardless of how long it takes to send back the certificate of registration. It may take 120 days before the certificate of registration is sent to the designer. To know whether the Copyright Office received the materials, they can be sent by registered or certified mail with a return receipt requested from the post office.

A designer can request information as to the status of an application. However, a fee will be charged by the Copyright Office if such a status report must be given within twenty days of the submission of the application.

For a more extensive discussion of the legal aspects of copyright, the designer can consult *Legal Guide for the Visual Artist* (Allworth Press) which offers in-depth coverage.

In addition, the designer should consider whether design patent protection (discussed under form 38) or trademark protection (see form 45) are appropriate for a design that may transcend the use of a particular client and be suitable for exploitation as an article of manufacture.

✍ Application Form VA ✍

Detach and read these instructions before completing this form.
Make sure all applicable spaces have been filled in before you return this form.

BASIC INFORMATION

When to Use This Form: Use Form VA for copyright registration of published or unpublished works of the visual arts. This category consists of "pictorial, graphic, or sculptural works," including two-dimensional and three-dimensional works of fine, graphic, and applied art, photographs, prints and art reproductions, maps, globes, charts, technical drawings, diagrams, and models.

What Does Copyright Protect? Copyright in a work of the visual arts protects those pictorial, graphic, or sculptural elements that, either alone or in combination, represent an "original work of authorship." The statute declares: "In no case does copyright protection for an original work of authorship extend to any idea, procedure, process, system, method of operation, concept, principle, or discovery, regardless of the form in which it is described, explained, illustrated, or embodied in such work."

Works of Artistic Craftsmanship and Designs: "Works of artistic craftsmanship" are registrable on Form VA, but the statute makes clear that protection extends to "their form" and not to "their mechanical or utilitarian aspects." The "design of a useful article" is considered copyrightable "only if, and only to the extent that, such design incorporates pictorial, graphic, or sculptural features that can be identified separately from, and are capable of existing independently of, the utilitarian aspects of the article."

Labels and Advertisements: Works prepared for use in connection with the sale or advertisement of goods and services are registrable if they contain "original work of authorship." Use Form VA if the copyrightable material in the work you are registering is mainly pictorial or graphic; use Form TX if it consists mainly of text. **NOTE :** Words and short phrases such as names, titles, and slogans cannot be protected by copyright, and the same is true of standard symbols, emblems, and other commonly used graphic designs that are in the public domain. When used commercially, material of that sort can sometimes be protected under state laws of unfair competition or under the federal trademark laws. For information about trademark registration, write to the Commissioner of Patents and Trademarks, Washington, D.C. 20231.

Architectural Works: Copyright protection extends to the design of buildings created for the use of human beings. Architectural works created on or after December 1, 1990, or that on December 1, 1990, were unconstructed and embodied only in unpublished plans or drawings are eligible. Request Circular 41 for more information. Architectural works and technical drawings cannot be registered on the same application.

Deposit to Accompany Application: An application for copyright registration must be accompanied by a deposit consisting of copies representing the entire work for which registration is to be made.

> **Unpublished Work:** Deposit one complete copy.
>
> **Published Work:** Deposit two complete copies of the best edition.
>
> **Work First Published Outside the United States:** Deposit one complete copy of the first foreign edition.
>
> **Contribution to a Collective Work:** Deposit one complete copy of the best edition of the collective work.

The Copyright Notice: Before March 1, 1989, the use of copyright notice was mandatory on all published works, and any work first published before that date should have carried a notice. For works first published on and after March 1, 1989, use of the copyright notice is optional. For more information about copyright notice, see Circular 3, "Copyright Notice."

For Further Information: To speak to an information specialist, call (202) 707-3000 (TTY: (202) 707-6737). Recorded information is available 24 hours a day. Order forms and other publications from the address in space 9 or call the Forms and Publications Hotline at (202) 707-9100. Most circulars (but not forms) are available via fax. Call (202) 707-2600 from a touchtone phone. Access and download circulars, forms, and other information from the Copyright Office Website at:

www.loc.gov/copyright

LINE-BY-LINE INSTRUCTIONS
Please type or print using black ink. The form is used to produce the certificate.

1 SPACE 1: Title

Title of This Work: Every work submitted for copyright registration must be given a title to identify that particular work. If the copies of the work bear a title (or an identifying phrase that could serve as a title), transcribe that wording *completely* and *exactly* on the application. Indexing of the registration and future identification of the work will depend on the information you give here. For an architectural work that has been constructed, add the date of construction after the title; if unconstructed at this time, add "not yet constructed."

Publication as a Contribution: If the work being registered is a contribution to a periodical, serial, or collection, give the title of the contribution in the "Title of This Work" space. Then, in the line headed "Publication as a Contribution," give information about the collective work in which the contribution appeared.

Nature of This Work: Briefly describe the general nature or character of the pictorial, graphic, or sculptural work being registered for copyright. Examples: "Oil Painting"; "Charcoal Drawing"; "Etching"; "Sculpture"; "Map"; "Photograph"; "Scale Model"; "Lithographic Print"; "Jewelry Design"; "Fabric Design."

Previous or Alternative Titles: Complete this space if there are any additional titles for the work under which someone searching for the registration might be likely to look, or under which a document pertaining to the work might be recorded.

2 SPACE 2: Author(s)

General Instruction: After reading these instructions, decide who are the "authors" of this work for copyright purposes. Then, unless the work is a "collective work," give the requested information about every "author" who contributed any appreciable amount of copyrightable matter to this version of the work. If you need further space, request Continuation Sheets. In the case of a collective work, such as a catalog of paintings or collection of cartoons by various authors, give information about the author of the collective work as a whole.

Name of Author: The fullest form of the author's name should be given. Unless the work was "made for hire," the individual who actually created the work is its "author." In the case of a work made for hire, the statute provides that "the employer or other person for whom the work was prepared is considered the author."

What is a "Work Made for Hire"? A "work made for hire" is defined as: (1) "a work prepared by an employee within the scope of his or her employment"; or (2) "a work specially ordered or commissioned for use as a contribution to a collective work, as a part of a motion picture or other audiovisual work, as a translation, as a supplementary work, as a compilation, as an instructional text, as a test, as answer material for a test, or as an atlas, if the parties expressly agree in a written instrument signed by them that the work shall be considered a work made for hire." If you have checked "Yes" to indicate that the work was "made for hire," you must give the full legal name of the employer (or other person for whom the work was prepared). You may also include the name of the employee along with the name of the employer (for example: "Elster Publishing Co., employer for hire of John Ferguson").

"Anonymous" or "Pseudonymous" Work: An author's contribution to a work is "anonymous" if that author is not identified on the copies or phonorecords of the work. An author's contribution to a work is "pseudonymous" if that author is identified on the copies or phonorecords under a fictitious name. If the work is "anonymous" you may: (1) leave the line blank; or (2) state "anonymous" on the line; or (3) reveal the author's identity. If the work is "pseudonymous" you may: (1) leave the line blank; or (2) give the pseudonym and identify it as such (for example: "Huntley Haverstock, pseudonym"); or (3) reveal the author's name, making clear which is the real name and which is the pseudonym (for example: "Henry Leek, whose pseudonym is Priam Farrel"). However, the citizenship or domicile of the author **must** be given in all cases.

Dates of Birth and Death: If the author is dead, the statute requires that the year of death be included in the application unless the work is anonymous or pseudonymous. The author's birth date is optional but is useful as a form of identification. Leave this space blank if the author's contribution was a "work made for hire."

Author's Nationality or Domicile: Give the country of which the author is a citizen or the country in which the author is domiciled. Nationality or domicile **must** be given in all cases.

Nature of Authorship: Catagories of pictorial, graphic, and sculptural authorship are listed below. Check the box(es) that best describe(s) each author's contribution to the work.

3-Dimensional sculptures: fine art sculptures, toys, dolls, scale models, and sculptural designs applied to useful articles.

2-Dimensional artwork: watercolor and oil paintings; pen and ink drawings; logo illustrations; greeting cards; collages; stencils; patterns; computer graphics; graphics appearing in screen displays; artwork appearing on posters, calendars, games, commercial prints and labels, and packaging, as well as 2-dimensional artwork applied to useful articles, and designs reproduced on textiles, lace, and other fabrics; on wallpaper, carpeting, floor tile, wrapping paper, and clothing.

Reproductions of works of art: reproductions of preexisting artwork made by, for example, lithography, photoengraving, or etching.

Maps: cartographic representations of an area, such as state and county maps, atlases, marine charts, relief maps, and globes.

Photographs: pictorial photographic prints and slides and holograms.

Jewelry designs: 3-dimensional designs applied to rings, pendants, earrings, necklaces, and the like.

Technical drawings: diagrams illustrating scientific or technical information in linear form, such as architectural blueprints or mechanical drawings.

Text: textual material that accompanies pictorial, graphic, or sculptural works, such as comic strips, greeting cards, games rules, commercial prints or labels, and maps.

Architectural works: designs of buildings, including the overall form as well as the arrangement and composition of spaces and elements of the design.

NOTE: Any registration for the underlying architectural plans must be applied for on a separate Form VA, checking the box "Technical drawing."

SPACE 3: Creation and Publication

General Instructions: Do not confuse "creation" with "publication." Every application for copyright registration must state "the year in which creation of the work was completed." Give the date and nation of first publication only if the work has been published.

Creation: Under the statute, a work is "created" when it is fixed in a copy or phonorecord for the first time. Where a work has been prepared over a period of time, the part of the work existing in fixed form on a particular date constitutes the created work on that date. The date you give here should be the year in which the author completed the particular version for which registration is now being sought, even if other versions exist or if further changes or additions are planned.

Publication: The statute defines "publication" as "the distribution of copies or phonorecords of a work to the public by sale or other transfer of ownership, or by rental, lease, or lending"; a work is also "published" if there has been an "offering to distribute copies or phonorecords to a group of persons for purposes of further distribution, public performance, or public display." Give the full date (month, day, year) when, and the country where, publication first occurred. If first publication took place simultaneously in the United States and other countries, it is sufficient to state "U.S.A."

SPACE 4: Claimant(s)

Name(s) and Address(es) of Copyright Claimant(s): Give the name(s) and address(es) of the copyright claimant(s) in this work even if the claimant is the same as the author. Copyright in a work belongs initially to the author of the work (including, in the case of a work made for hire, the employer or other person for whom the work was prepared). The copyright claimant is either the author of the work or a person or organization to whom the copyright initially belonging to the author has been transferred.

Transfer: The statute provides that, if the copyright claimant is not the author, the application for registration must contain "a brief statement of how the claimant obtained ownership of the copyright." If any copyright claimant named in space 4 is not an author named in space 2, give a brief statement explaining how the claimant(s) obtained ownership of the copyright. Examples: "By written contract"; "Transfer of all rights by author"; "Assignment"; "By will." Do not attach transfer documents or other attachments or riders.

SPACE 5: Previous Registration

General Instructions: The questions in space 5 are intended to find out whether an earlier registration has been made for this work and, if so, whether there is any basis for a new registration. As a rule, only one basic

copyright registration can be made for the same version of a particular work.

Same Version: If this version is substantially the same as the work covered by a previous registration, a second registration is not generally possible unless: (1) the work has been registered in unpublished form and a second registration is now being sought to cover this first published edition; or (2) someone other than the author is identified as a copyright claimant in the earlier registration, and the author is now seeking registration in his or her own name. If either of these two exceptions applies, check the appropriate box and give the earlier registration number and date. Otherwise, do not submit Form VA; instead, write the Copyright Office for information about supplementary registration or recordation of transfers of copyright ownership.

Changed Version: If the work has been changed and you are now seeking registration to cover the additions or revisions, check the last box in space 5, give the earlier registration number and date, and complete both parts of space 6 in accordance with the instruction below.

Previous Registration Number and Date: If more than one previous registration has been made for the work, give the number and date of the latest registration.

SPACE 6: Derivative Work or Compilation

General Instructions: Complete space 6 if this work is a "changed version," "compilation," or "derivative work," and if it incorporates one or more earlier works that have already been published or registered for copyright, or that have fallen into the public domain. A "compilation" is defined as "a work formed by the collection and assembling of preexisting materials or of data that are selected, coordinated, or arranged in such a way that the resulting work as a whole constitutes an original work of authorship." A "derivative work" is "a work based on one or more preexisting works." Examples of derivative works include reproductions of works of art, sculptures based on drawings, lithographs based on paintings, maps based on previously published sources, or "any other form in which a work may be recast, transformed, or adapted." Derivative works also include works "consisting of editorial revisions, annotations, or other modifications" if these changes, as a whole, represent an original work of authorship.

Preexisting Material (space 6a): Complete this space **and** space 6b for derivative works. In this space identify the preexisting work that has been recast, transformed, or adapted. Examples of preexisting material might be "Grunewald Altarpiece" or "19th century quilt design." Do not complete this space for compilations.

Material Added to This Work (space 6b): Give a brief, general statement of the **additional** new material covered by the copyright claim for which registration is sought. In the case of a derivative work, identify this new material. Examples: "Adaptation of design and additional artistic work"; "Reproduction of painting by photolithography"; "Additional cartographic material"; "Compilation of photographs." If the work is a compilation, give a brief, general statement describing both the material that has been compiled **and** the compilation itself. Example: "Compilation of 19th century political cartoons."

SPACE 7, 8, 9: Fee, Correspondence, Certification, Return Address

Deposit Account: If you maintain a Deposit Account in the Copyright Office, identify it in space 7a. Otherwise, leave the space blank and send the fee of $30 (effective through June 30, 2002) with your application and deposit.

Correspondence (space 7b): This space should contain the name, address, area code, telephone number, email address, and fax number (if available) of the person to be consulted if correspondence about this application becomes necessary.

Certification (space 8): The application cannot be accepted unless it bears the date and the **handwritten signature** of the author or other copyright claimant, or of the owner of exclusive right(s), or of the duly authorized agent of the author, claimant, or owner of exclusive right(s).

Address for Return of Certificate (space 9): The address box must be completed legibly since the certificate will be returned in a window envelope.

FORM VA
For a Work of the Visual Arts
UNITED STATES COPYRIGHT OFFICE

REGISTRATION NUMBER

_____

VA   VAU

EFFECTIVE DATE OF REGISTRATION

Month   Day   Year

DO NOT WRITE ABOVE THIS LINE. IF YOU NEED MORE SPACE, USE A SEPARATE CONTINUATION SHEET.

1

TITLE OF THIS WORK ▼

NATURE OF THIS WORK ▼ See instructions

PREVIOUS OR ALTERNATIVE TITLES ▼

Publication as a Contribution If this work was published as a contribution to a periodical, serial, or collection, give information about the collective work in which the contribution appeared.   **Title of Collective Work ▼**

If published in a periodical or serial give: **Volume ▼**   **Number ▼**   **Issue Date ▼**   **On Pages ▼**

2

a

NAME OF AUTHOR ▼

DATES OF BIRTH AND DEATH
Year Born ▼   Year Died ▼

Was this contribution to the work a "work made for hire"?
☐ Yes
☐ No

Author's Nationality or Domicile
Name of Country
OR { Citizen of ▶_____
Domiciled in ▶_____

Was This Author's Contribution to the Work
Anonymous? ☐ Yes ☐ No
Pseudonymous? ☐ Yes ☐ No
If the answer to either of these questions is "Yes," see detailed instructions.

NATURE OF AUTHORSHIP Check appropriate box(es). **See instructions**
☐ 3-Dimensional sculpture   ☐ Map   ☐ Technical drawing
☐ 2-Dimensional artwork   ☐ Photograph   ☐ Text
☐ Reproduction of work of art   ☐ Jewelry design   ☐ Architectural work

b

NAME OF AUTHOR ▼

DATES OF BIRTH AND DEATH
Year Born ▼   Year Died ▼

Was this contribution to the work a "work made for hire"?
☐ Yes
☐ No

Author's Nationality or Domicile
Name of Country
OR { Citizen of ▶_____
Domiciled in ▶_____

Was This Author's Contribution to the Work
Anonymous? ☐ Yes ☐ No
Pseudonymous? ☐ Yes ☐ No
If the answer to either of these questions is "Yes," see detailed instructions.

NATURE OF AUTHORSHIP Check appropriate box(es). **See instructions**
☐ 3-Dimensional sculpture   ☐ Map   ☐ Technical drawing
☐ 2-Dimensional artwork   ☐ Photograph   ☐ Text
☐ Reproduction of work of art   ☐ Jewelry design   ☐ Architectural work

NOTE
Under the law, the "author" of a "work made for hire" is generally the employer, not the employee (see instructions). For any part of this work that was "made for hire" check "Yes" in the space provided, give the employer (or other person for whom the work was prepared) as "Author" of that part, and leave the space for dates of birth and death blank.

3

a **Year in Which Creation of This Work Was Completed**
_____ ◀ Year   This information must be given in all cases.

b **Date and Nation of First Publication of This Particular Work**
Complete this information ONLY if this work has been published.   Month ▶_____ Day ▶_____ Year ▶_____ ◀ Nation

---

4

See instructions before completing this space.

COPYRIGHT CLAIMANT(S) Name and address must be given even if the claimant is the same as the author given in space 2. ▼

Transfer If the claimant(s) named here in space 4 is (are) different from the author(s) named in space 2, give a brief statement of how the claimant(s) obtained ownership of the copyright. ▼

DO NOT WRITE HERE
OFFICE USE ONLY

APPLICATION RECEIVED

ONE DEPOSIT RECEIVED

TWO DEPOSITS RECEIVED

FUNDS RECEIVED

MORE ON BACK ▶   • Complete all applicable spaces (numbers 5-9) on the reverse side of this page.
• See detailed instructions.   • Sign the form at line 8.

DO NOT WRITE HERE
Page 1 of _____ pages

EXAMINED BY

FORM VA

CHECKED BY

☐ CORRESPONDENCE
Yes

FOR
COPYRIGHT
OFFICE
USE
ONLY

DO NOT WRITE ABOVE THIS LINE. IF YOU NEED MORE SPACE, USE A SEPARATE CONTINUATION SHEET.

PREVIOUS REGISTRATION Has registration for this work, or for an earlier version of this work, already been made in the Copyright Office?

☐ Yes ☐ No If your answer is "Yes," why is another registration being sought? (Check appropriate box.) ▼

a. ☐ This is the first published edition of a work previously registered in unpublished form.

b. ☐ This is the first application submitted by this author as copyright claimant.

c. ☐ This is a changed version of the work, as shown by space 6 on this application.

If your answer is "Yes," give: **Previous Registration Number** ▼   **Year of Registration** ▼

5

DERIVATIVE WORK OR COMPILATION Complete both space 6a and 6b for a derivative work; complete only 6b for a compilation.
a. Preexisting Material Identify any preexisting work or works that this work is based on or incorporates. ▼

6
a
See instructions
before completing
this space.

b. Material Added to This Work Give a brief, general statement of the material that has been added to this work and in which copyright is claimed. ▼

b

DEPOSIT ACCOUNT If the registration fee is to be charged to a Deposit Account established in the Copyright Office, give name and number of Account.
Name ▼   **Account Number** ▼

7
a

CORRESPONDENCE Give name and address to which correspondence about this application should be sent.   Name/Address/Apt/City/State/ZIP ▼

b

Area code and daytime telephone number ▶ (   )   Fax number ▶ (   )

Email ▶

CERTIFICATION* I, the undersigned, hereby certify that I am the

check only one ▶ {
☐ author
☐ other copyright claimant
☐ owner of exclusive right(s)
☐ authorized agent of _____
Name of author or other copyright claimant, or owner of exclusive right(s) ▲
}

8

of the work identified in this application and that the statements made by me in this application are correct to the best of my knowledge.

Typed or printed name and date ▼ If this application gives a date of publication in space 3, do not sign and submit it before that date.

Date ▶ _____

Handwritten signature (X) ▼

X _____

Certificate
will be
mailed in
window
envelope
to this
address:

Name ▼

Number/Street/Apt ▼

City/State/ZIP ▼

YOU MUST:
• Complete all necessary spaces
• Sign your application in space 8
**SEND ALL 3 ELEMENTS
IN THE SAME PACKAGE:**
1. Application form
2. Nonrefundable filing fee in check or money order payable to *Register of Copyrights*
3. Deposit material
As of July 1, 1999, the filing fee for Form VA is $30.
MAIL TO:
Library of Congress
Copyright Office
101 Independence Avenue, S.E.
Washington, D.C. 20559-6000

9

Trademark Application

A trademark is a distinctive word, phrase, symbol, design, emblem, or combination of these that a manufacturer places on a product to identify and distinguish in the public mind that product from the products of rival manufacturers. A service mark is like a trademark except that it identifies services instead of products. Trademarks (including service marks) can be registered with the U. S. Patent and Trademark Office for federal protection and with the appropriate state office for state protection, although even an unregistered mark can have protection under the common law simply because the mark is used in commerce. An interior designer who is developing a line of products—for example, furniture, fabric designs, or art—might wish to seek trademark protection for a distinctive logo or motto.

Form 45 is the trademark (and service mark) application with the instructions issued by the U.S. Patent and Trademark Office. That office makes available not only forms, but also an excellent pamphlet titled "Basic Facts about Registering a Trademark" which can be requested from the Assistant Commissioner for Trademarks, Box New App/Fee, 2900 Crystal Drive, Arlington, VA 22202-3513 or calling (703) 308-HELP. This pamphlet, the application form, and the instructions to register a trademark (or service mark) can also be downloaded from the Web site of the U. S. Patent and Trademark Office at *www.uspto.gov.*

The designer who believes that a certain product should be trademarked will want to be certain that any chosen trademark does not infringe an already registered trademark in commercial use. This can be accomplished by conducting a trademark search prior to filling out the trademark registration application. If other names in use are too similar to that selected by the designer, a decision can be made to select a different name. To conduct a search, the designer can either go to the public search library at the U.S. Patent and Trademark Office located on the second floor of the South Tower Building, 2900 Crystal Drive, Arlington, VA, or use the CD-ROMS containing the trademark database at the patent and trademark depository libraries listed on pages 14–15 of "Basic Facts about Registering a Trademark." Even easier, the designer can go online to the Web site of the U.S. Patent and Trademark Office and use TESS, the Trademark Electronic Search System. While the trademark can be filed without such a search and without the help of an attorney or search service, the search and evaluation of the search may require such expert assistance.

An important revision of the trademark law took effect on November 16, 1989. Trademarks may now be registered before use, whereas previously they could only be registered after use. The application must include a bona fide "intent to use" statement. Every six months an "intent to use" statement must be filed again and additional fees paid, and in no event can such a preregistration period exceed three years. Trademarks can last forever if the artist keeps using the mark to identify goods or services. The federal trademark has a term of ten years, but can then be renewed for additional ten-year terms. The designer should note that to avoid having the trademark registration canceled, an affidavit must be filed between the fifth and sixth year after the initial registration. Trademarks can be licensed (see form 37), as long as the designer giving the license ensures that the quality of goods created by the licensee will be of the same quality that the public associates with the trademark. Trademarks are entitled to protection in foreign countries under treaties executed by the United States.

It is important to understand when the symbols TM, SM, and ® can and should be used. TM (for trademark) and SM (for service mark) can be used at any time, without or prior to the issuance of registration, to inform the public of the designer's claim to trademark protection for a mark. The symbol ® (for registration) should be used only when the mark has in fact been registered with the U.S. Patent and Trademark Office.

Closely related to trademarks is the area of trade dress, which has special relevance for designers and other artists who create the look of products for sale to consumers. Trade dress claims arise under section 43(a) of the Lanham Act, a federal statute. A plaintiff must prove three elements to win a trade dress claim: (1) that the features of the trade dress are primarily nonfunctional (i.e., that these features primarily identify the source of the particular goods or services); (2) that the trade dress has secondary meaning (i.e., that the public has come to identify the source of goods or services due to the associations created by the trade dress); and (3) that the competing products' respective trade dresses are confusingly similar, thus giving rise to a likelihood of confusion among consumers as to their sources.

Returning to the subject of trademark registration, the application requires the following: (1) the filled-in application form, such as Form 21, (2) a drawing of the trademark, (3) three specimens of the mark, and (4) the filing fee (currently $325) for each class of goods/services listed in the application. The U.S. Patent and Trademark Office now has online help to complete the trademark application. You can either file electronically through e-TEAS or print and mail your application. In either case, you can also use a "Form Wizard" to adapt a form to your particular needs.

With respect to the drawing of the trademark, "Basic Facts about Registering a Trademark" advises as follows:

❑ Every application must include a single drawing page . . .

The drawing must be on pure white, durable, non-shiny paper that is 8½ (21.59 cm) inches wide by 11 (27.94 cm) inches long. There must be at least a one-inch (2.54 cm) margin on the sides, top, and bottom of the page, and at least one inch between the heading and the display of the mark.

At the top of the drawing there must be a heading, listing on separate lines, the applicant's complete name, address, the goods and services specified in the application, and, in applications based on use in commerce, the date of first use of the mark and the date of first use of the mark in commerce. This heading should be typewritten. If the drawing is in special form, the heading should include a description of the essential elements of the mark.

❑ The drawing of the mark should appear at the center of the page . . .

If the mark includes words, numbers, or letters, the applicant can usually elect to submit either a typewritten or a special-form drawing. To register a mark consisting of only words, letters, or numbers, without indicating any particular style or design, provide a typewritten drawing. In a typewritten drawing, the mark must be typed entirely in CAPITAL LETTERS, even if the mark, as used, includes lower-case letters. Use a standard typewriter or type of the same size and style as that on a standard typewriter.

To indicate color, use the color linings shown below. . . . A plain black-and-white drawing is acceptable even if the mark is used in color. Most drawings do not indicate specific colors.

Be careful in preparing the drawing. While it may be possible to make some minor changes, the rules prohibit any material change to the drawing of the mark after filing.

To register a word mark in the form in which it is actually used or intended to be used in commerce, or any mark including a design, submit a special-form drawing. In a special-form drawing, the mark must not be larger than 4" × 4" (10.16 cm by 10.16 cm). If the drawing of the mark is larger than 4" × 4", the application will be denied a filing date and returned to the applicant. In addition, the drawing must appear only in black and white, with every line and letter black and clear. No color or gray is allowed. Do not combine typed matter and special form in the same drawing.

The drawing in special form must be a substantially exact representation of the mark as it appears on the specimens. . . . Do not include nontrademark matter in the drawing, such as informational matter which may appear on a label. In the end, the applicant must decide exactly what to register and in what form. The PTO considers the drawing controlling in determining exactly what mark the application covers.

While it is not mandatory to fill in the class of goods/services, some classes that would be especially relevant to designs in commerce are:

Class 14. Precious metals and their alloys and goods in precious metals or coated therewith, not included in other classes; jewelry, precious stones; horological and chronometric instruments. . . .

Class 16. Paper, cardboard, and goods made from these materials, not included in other classes; printed matter; bookbinding material; photographs; stationery; adhesives for stationery or household purposes; . . .

Class 20. Furniture, mirrors, picture frames; goods (not included in other classes) of wood, cork, reed, cane, wicker, horn, bone, ivory, whalebone, shell, amber, mother-of-pearl, meerschaum, and substitutes for all these materials, or of plastics.

Class 21. Household or kitchen utensils and containers (not of precious metal or coated therewith); . . . glassware, porcelain and earthenware not included in other classes.

Class 24. Textiles and textile goods, not included in other classes; bed and table covers.

Class 25. Clothing, footwear, headgear.

Class 26. Lace and embroidery, ribbons and braid; buttons, hooks and eyes, pins and needles; artificial flowers.

Class 27. Carpets, rugs, mats and matting; linoleums and other materials for covering existing floors; wall hangings (nontextile).

Class 28. Games and playthings; gymnastic and sporting articles not included in other classes; decorations for Christmas trees.

TRADEMARK/SERVICE MARK APPLICATION, PRINCIPAL REGISTER, WITH DECLARATION	MARK (Word(s) and/or Design)	CLASS NO. (If known)

TO THE ASSISTANT COMMISSIONER FOR TRADEMARKS:

APPLICANT'S NAME:

APPLICANT'S MAILING ADDRESS:

(Display address exactly as it should appear on registration)

APPLICANT'S ENTITY TYPE: (Check one and supply requested information)

	Individual - Citizen of (Country):
	Partnership - State where organized (Country, if appropriate): _____ Names and Citizenship (Country) of General Partners: _____
	Corporation - State (Country, if appropriate) of Incorporation:
	Other (Specify Nature of Entity and Domicile):

GOODS AND/OR SERVICES:

Applicant requests registration of the trademark/service mark shown in the accompanying drawing in the United States Patent and Trademark Office on the Principal Register established by the Act of July 5, 1946 (15 U.S.C. 1051 et. seq., as amended) for the following goods/services **(SPECIFIC GOODS AND/OR SERVICES MUST BE INSERTED HERE):**

BASIS FOR APPLICATION: (Check boxes which apply, **but never both the first AND second boxes,** and supply requested information related to each box checked.)

[ ]	Applicant is using the mark in commerce on or in connection with the above identified goods/services. (15 U.S.C. 1051(a), as amended.) Three specimens showing the mark as used in commerce are submitted with this application. • Date of first use of the mark in commerce which the U.S. Congress may regulate (for example, interstate or between the U.S. and a foreign country): _____ • Specify the type of commerce: _____ (for example, interstate or between the U.S. and a specified foreign country) • Date of first use anywhere (the same as or before use in commerce date): _____ • Specify intended manner or mode of use of mark on or in connection with the goods/services: _____ (for example, trademark is applied to labels, service mark is used in advertisements)
[ ]	Applicant has a bona fide intention to use the mark in commerce on or in connection with the above identified goods/services. (15 U.S.C. 1051(b), as amended.) • Specify manner or mode of use of mark on or in connection with the goods/services: _____ (for example, trademark will be applied to labels, service mark will be used in advertisements)
[ ]	Applicant has a bona fide intention to use the mark in commerce on or in connection with the above identified goods/services, and asserts a claim of priority based upon a foreign application in accordance with 15 U.S.C. 1126(d), as amended. • Country of foreign filing: _____ • Date of foreign filing: _____
[ ]	Applicant has a bona fide intention to use the mark in commerce on or in connection with the above identified goods/services and, accompanying this application, submits a certification or certified copy of a foreign registration in accordance with 15 U.S.C 1126(e), as amended. • Country of registration: _____ • Registration number: _____

NOTE: Declaration, on Reverse Side, MUST be Signed

PTO Form 1478 (REV 6/96)
OMB No. 0651-0009 (Exp. 06/30/98) There is no requirement to respond to this collection of information unless a currently valid OMB Number is displayed.

U.S. DEPARTMENT OF COMMERCE/Patent and Trademark Office

DECLARATION

The undersigned being hereby warned that willful false statements and the like so made are punishable by fine or imprisonment, or both, under 18 U.S.C. 1001, and that such willful false statements may jeopardize the validity of the application or any resulting registration, declares that he/she is properly authorized to execute this application on behalf of the applicant; he/she believes the applicant to be the owner of the trademark/service mark sought to be registered, or if the application is being filed under 15 U.S.C. 1051(b), he/she believes the applicant to be entitled to use such mark in commerce; to the best of his/her knowledge and belief no other person, firm, corporation, or association has the right to use the above identified mark in commerce, either in the identical form thereof or in such near resemblance thereto as to be likely, when used on or in connection with the goods/services of such other person, to cause confusion, or to cause mistake, or to deceive; and that all statements made of his/her own knowledge are true and that all statements made on information and belief are believed to be true.

_____

DATE

_____

SIGNATURE

_____

TELEPHONE NUMBER

_____

PRINT OR TYPE NAME AND POSITION

INSTRUCTIONS AND INFORMATION FOR APPLICANT

TO RECEIVE A FILING DATE, THE APPLICATION <u>MUST</u> BE COMPLETED AND SIGNED BY THE APPLICANT AND SUBMITTED ALONG WITH:

1. The prescribed **FEE ($325.00)** for each class of goods/services listed in the application;
2. A **DRAWING PAGE** displaying the mark in conformance with 37 CFR 2.52;
3. If the application is based on use of the mark in commerce, **THREE (3) SPECIMENS** (evidence) of the mark as used in commerce for each class of goods/services listed in the application. All three specimens may be the same. Examples of good specimens include: (a) labels showing the mark which are placed on the goods; (b) photographs of the mark as it appears on the goods, (c) brochures or advertisements showing the mark as used in connection with the services.
4. An **APPLICATION WITH DECLARATION** (this form) - The application must be signed in order for the application to receive a filing date. Only the following persons may sign the declaration, depending on the applicant's legal entity: (a) the individual applicant; (b) an officer of the corporate applicant; (c) one general partner of a partnership applicant; (d) all joint applicants.

SEND APPLICATION FORM, DRAWING PAGE, FEE, AND SPECIMENS (IF APPROPRIATE) TO:

Assistant Commissioner for Trademarks
Box New App/Fee
2900 Crystal Drive
Arlington, VA 22202-3513

Additional information concerning the requirements for filing an application is available in a booklet entitled **Basic Facts About Registering a Trademark,** which may be obtained by writing to the above address or by calling: (703) 308-HELP.

This form is estimated to take an average of 1 hour to complete, including time required for reading and understanding instructions, gathering necessary information, recordkeeping, and actually providing the information. Any comments on this form, including the amount of time required to complete this form, should be sent to the Office of Management and Organization, U.S. Patent and Trademark Office, U.S. Department of Commerce, Washington, D.C. 20231. Do NOT send completed forms to this address.

Selected Bibliography

Alderman, Robert L. *How to Prosper as an Interior Designer.* New York: John Wiley & Sons, 1997.

Battle, Carl W. *The Patent Guide.* New York: Allworth Press, 1997

Berger, C. Jaye. *Interior Design Law and Business Practices.* New York: John Wiley & Sons, 1994.

DeWalt, Suzanne. *How to Start a Home-Based Interior Design Business.* Guilford, Connecticut: The Globe Pequot Press, 2000.

Epstein, Lee. *Legal Forms for the Designer.* New York: N. & E. Hellman, 1977.

Knackstedt, Mary V., and Haney, Laura J. *The Interior Design Business Handbook.* New York: John Wiley & Sons, 1992.

Leland, Caryn. *Licensing Art & Design.* New York: Allworth Press, 1995.

Loebelson, Andrew. *How to Profit in Contract Design.* New York: Interior Design Books, 1983.

Piotrowski, Christine. *Interior Design Management.* New York: Van Nostrand Reinhold, 1992.

Sack, Steven Mitchell. *The Complete Collection of Legal Forms for Employers.* Merrick, New York: Legal Strategies Publications, 1996.

Sack, Steven Mitchell. *From Hiring to Firing.* Merrick, New York: Legal Strategies Publications, 1995.

Sampson, Carol A. *Estimating for Interior Designers.* New York: Whitney Library of Design, 1991.

Siegel, Harry. *Business Guide for Interior Designers.* New York: Whitney Library of Design, 1976.

Siegel, Harry, with Siegel, Alan M. *A Guide to Business Principles and Practices for Interior Designers.* New York: Whitney Library of Design, 1982.

Siegfried, Steven M. *Introduction to Construction Law.* Philadelphia: The American Law Institute, 1986.

Thompson, Jo Ann Asher. *ASID Professional Practice Manual.* New York: Whitney Library of Design, 1992.

Wilson, Lee. *The Copyright Guide.* New York: Allworth Press, 2000.

Wilson, Lee. *The Trademark Guide.* New York: Allworth Press, 1998.

Index

Books from Allworth Press

Business and Legal Forms for Graphic Designers, Revised Edition
by Tad Crawford and Eva Doman Bruck (paperback, includes CD-ROM, 8½ × 11, 240 pages, $24.95)

Legal Guide for the Visual Artist, Fourth Edition
by Tad Crawford

Licensing Art and Design, Revised Edition
by Caryn R. Leland (paperback, 6 × 9, 128 pages, $16.95)

The New Business of Design
by The International Design Conference in Aspen (paperback, 6 ¾ × 10, 256 pages, $19.95)

An Artist's Guide: Making it in New York City
by Daniel Grant (paperback, 6 × 9, 224 pages, $18.95)

Careers by Design:
A Headhunters Secrets for Success and Survival in Graphic Design, Revised Edition
by Roz Goldfarb (paperback, 6¾ × 10, 224 pages, $18.95)

AIGA Professional Practices in Graphic Design
The American Institute of Graphic Arts, edited by Tad Crawford
(paperback, 6¾ × 10, 320 pages, $24.95)

The Trademark Guide: A Friendly Guide for Protecting and Profiting from Trademarks
by Lee Wilson (paperback, 6 × 9, 192 pages, $18.95)

The Copyright Guide: A Friendly Guide for Protecting and Profiting from Copyrights
by Lee Wilson (paperback, 6 × 9, 192 pages, $18.95)

Business and Legal Forms for Fine Artists, Revised Edition
by Tad Crawford (paperback, includes CD-ROM, 8½ × 11, 144 pages, $19.95)

Business and Legal Forms for Illustrators, Revised Edition
by Tad Crawford (paperback, includes CD-ROM, 8½ × 11, 192 pages, $24.95)

Business and Legal Forms for Photographers, Revised Edition
by Tad Crawford (paperback, includes CD-ROM, 8½ × 11, 224 pages, $24.95)